# Preventing Child Sexual Abuse

# Preventing
# Child
# Sexual Abuse

*Sharing the Responsibility*

■

Sandy K. Wurtele and
Cindy L. Miller-Perrin

University of Nebraska Press
Lincoln and London

First paperback printing: 1993
Most recent printing indicated
by the last digit below:
10 9 8 7 6 5 4 3 2 1

Library of Congress Catalog-
ing-in-Publication Data
Wurtele, Sandy K.
(Sandy Kay), 1955–
Preventing child sexual abuse:
sharing the responsibility/
Sandy K. Wurtele and
Cindy L. Miller-Perrin.
P.    cm.
Includes bibliographical
references (p.    ) and index.
ISBN 0-8032-9750-5 (pa)
ISBN 0-8032-4753-2 (cl)
1. Child molesting – United
States.
2. Child molesting – Preven-
tion – United States.
I. Miller-Perrin, Cindy L.
(Cindy Lou), 1962–    II. Title.
HQ72.U53W87    1992
362.7'6–DC20    92-3600
CIP
Second cloth printing: 1993

∞

# Contents

# TABLES

# Foreword

*The Board urges each citizen to recognize that a serious emergency related to the maltreatment of children exists within American society and to join with all other citizens in resolving that its continued existence is intolerable.* —U.S. ADVISORY BOARD ON CHILD ABUSE AND NEGLECT (1990, RECOMMENDATION 1)

In its first report, the U.S. Advisory Board on Child Abuse and Neglect (ABCAN, 1990), of which I am a member, surveyed the state of child protection in the United States and declared it to be in a state of emergency. ABCAN rested its declaration on three broad findings. First, the stunning magnitude of the problem—now more than 2.5 million reports of suspected cases per year in the United States—is sufficient in itself to warrant a declaration of national emergency. More than doubling in the 1980s, the number of reports has risen at a breathtaking rate. Second, the child protection system has been unable to cope with the increasing number and complexity of cases. Regardless of the component of the system that is assessed, it is *"overwhelmed, . . . it is on the verge of collapse,* and . . . if and when it does [collapse], children will be even more seriously at risk than they are now, thus causing countless additional American children to suffer irreparable harm" (ABCAN, 1990, p.43, emphasis in the original). Third, the costs resulting from the problem of child maltreatment are enormous. Billions of dollars are being spent on a failing child protection system, and probably billions more are being spent in an attempt to respond to the consequences of child maltreatment.

Although the emergency is not specific to any one form of maltreatment, the crisis became particularly acute because of the "discovery" of sexual abuse in the mid-1980s. Not only did that social phenomenon result in an enormous increase in reports of maltreatment, but it also intensified the child protection system's seemingly purposeless preoccupation with investigation, because (a) sexual abuse, unlike all other nonfatal forms of maltreatment, has been perceived as a matter at least in part for criminal prosecution, and (b) the proof problems for sexual abuse are greater than commonly is the case for other forms of child maltreatment. The discovery of sexual abuse also multiplied the already growing complexity of identified child protection cases, because (a) sexual abuse is less linked to any particular constellation of social and psychological factors than are other forms of maltreatment, (b) the demands of the criminal justice system increase the problems of coordination and prevention of harm within the child protection system itself, and (c) there is little public consensus about either the proper conceptualization of the problem or the appropriate response to it.

Taken together, these factors have resulted, as ABCAN noted, in a situation in which "it has become far easier to pick up the telephone to report one's neighbor for child abuse than it is for that neighbor to request and receive help before the abuse happens" (p.80). Expedient, low-cost single-shot solutions to the national crisis in child protection have been the norm, instead of a planned, comprehensive response.

In regard specifically to the problem of sexual abuse, the policy response commonly has taken two forms, both of questionable efficacy. First, despite the fact that few abused children ever testify, legislatures have adopted a myriad of special trial procedures designed to minimize the purported harm of the children's involvement in the legal process. Second, schools have been encouraged or mandated to adopt sexual abuse education programs—most of them of the "yell and tell" variety.

As Wurtele and Miller-Perrin note, I (Melton, 1992) have argued that neither evaluation research nor knowledge about cognitive and social development gives any reason to believe that sexual abuse education programs are effective in preventing abuse. More-over, on the basis of research on the epidemiology and process of sexual abuse, I have expressed doubt that prevention of sexual abuse is possible, and, if it is possible, whether prevention can be achieved without substantial negative side effects.

Amid this controversy, I welcome the publication of this volume in the Child, Youth, and Family Services series. I do so for two reasons. First, Wurtele and Miller-Perrin take a scholarly approach to a topic that, unfortunately, seldom has been subjected to such analysis. Accordingly, their conclusions are much more circumspect than those of most advocates of sexual abuse education programs, and their analysis is better informed by knowledge of child development. They acknowledge the lack of clear evidence for efficacy of sexual abuse education programs in prevention of sexual abuse (although they suggest other positive effects of such programs, at least for older children and adolescents), and they propose discontinuing the label of such programs as *sexual abuse prevention*. Indeed, Wurtele and Miller-Perrin reframe the problem of prevention of sexual abuse. Acknowledging the difficulty of prevention of sexual abuse altogether, they focus to a large extent on detection of ongoing abuse (what they term *secondary prevention*) so that offenders can be incapacitated or deterred from further victimizing children.

Second, although the approach that Wurtele and Miller-Perrin take is still largely educational, they differ from more conventional advocates of sexual abuse prevention programs in the range of audiences that they view as important. Accordingly, they admirably avoid the trap into which others have fallen of implicitly placing the primary responsibility for prevention of abuse on children themselves. Child-focused abuse prevention programs not only are unlikely to be effective; such programs also are unfair. In that regard, Wurtele and Miller-Perrin adopt an approach consistent with ABCAN's insistence on the moral responsibility of every adult to protect children from harm and to safeguard their dignity as persons.

In short, Wurtele and Miller-Perrin present perhaps the most comprehensive analysis thus far of the nature and efficacy of prevention of sexual abuse. They do so in a manner that is respectful of children and based on systematic study of empirical assumptions underlying existing programs. I admire their thoughtfulness, and I am certain that this volume will be viewed as an important contribution by both educators and policymakers.

GARY B. MELTON
*Series Editor*

# Preface

The past decade has seen a dramatic increase in the attention paid to the problem of child sexual abuse (CSA) from professionals in the fields of social work, mental health, medicine, education, and law. Research into the prevalence, etiology, and consequences of CSA has burgeoned. A multitude of interventions for victims of CSA and their families and for offenders have been described. Perhaps the most rapidly expanding efforts at confronting the problem have focused on preventing CSA, particularly through classroom-based child assault prevention programs. In this book, we critique this approach and review recent efforts directed toward other groups of individuals playing pivotal roles in the prevention of CSA (i.e., parents, professionals, policymakers, researchers, and the general public).

We begin the book by reviewing current knowledge about the definition, scope, correlates, and consequences of CSA. We also trace the development of the CSA prevention movement and critically analyze its progress. Various etiological models of CSA are then synthesized in an attempt to provide a heuristic framework for organizing prevention efforts. CSA is conceptualized as being multiply determined by forces at work in the individual (victim and offender) and the family, as well as in the community and the society in which both the individual and family are embedded. We propose an expansion of prevention efforts consistent with this multidimensional model of abuse. In the following chapters, we review efforts aimed at children (chapter 2), parents (chapter 3), and professionals (chapter 4). In chapter 5 we suggest possible roles that various groups contained within society might take to combat CSA, including policymakers, researchers, and the general public. Finally, in our concluding remarks, we briefly summarize what needs to happen at each point on the prevention continuum.

Throughout the book, we have sought to keep our commitment to responsible scholarship. It is our hope that those not accustomed to empirical data and scientific writing will be able to sift through the information presented and glean the messages appropriate to them. The book was written to benefit policymakers, practitioners, researchers, program developers and providers, and parents. It is our intention to provide useful information to these diverse groups, in order to delineate the specific roles and responsibilities each of us must share in eliminating the sexual exploitation of children. We also offer recommendations and suggestions to stimulate program development and guide research advances.

Our goal is to encourage divergent thinking regarding the appropriate scope and nature of prevention approaches. We advocate an expansion from a primary focus on classroom-based approaches toward broader and more system-wide reforms. Our thesis is that child-centered approaches can be most effective when augmented by school-, family-, and community-based efforts, each of which should be viewed as contributing toward the prevention of CSA. We must all share the responsibility for preventing this widespread social problem.

It gives us particular pleasure to acknowledge the help we have received from research participants, colleagues, funding agencies, and our families. We would like to acknowledge all the parents who gave of their time and energy to share their beliefs and attitudes about CSA and its prevention. We also thank the hundreds of children who participated in our studies and who taught us a great deal about how children view sexual abuse and learn the material contained in personal safety programs. We are also appreciative of all the school administrators, teachers, and day-care professionals who were willing and concerned enough to allow our research teams to disrupt their typical routines in order to advance our knowledge about prevention. We also acknowledge the financial support provided by private and federal agencies. Our classroom-based prevention research has been supported by grants from the Northwest Area Foundation (St. Paul, MN) and from the National Institute of Mental Health (Grant #MH42795).

We are also pleased to pay tribute to the many individuals in the field who have made important contributions to our understanding of CSA. There are also colleagues who read chapters of this book at crucial points in its development and offered suggestions and encouragement. They include David Finkelhor, Deborah Daro, William Friedrich, Lisa Currier, and Elizabeth Gillispie. We wish to express our gratitude to the University of Nebraska Press and particularly to Camille North for her commitment to the book and her belief in our ability to produce it. We also thank Heather Moxley for her assistance in manuscript preparation.

Finally, our biggest thanks go to our families, without whose continual support this project would not have been possible. Special thanks go to Glenn, who challenged Sandy to keep a healthy balance between work and play. Special thanks also go to Robin and Jacob, who provided Cindy with the perfect amount of both distraction and solitude and were a constant reminder of life's most important priority. We would also like to thank our parents, who assured our right to enjoy an abuse-free, healthy, and nurturing childhood, and hope that this book will in some way assure the same for other children.

# Understanding Child Sexual Abuse:
## Implications for Prevention

*Once we perceive, question and challenge the existence of the sexual abuse of children, we have taken the first crucial step toward the elimination of the degradation, humiliation and corrosion of our most valuable human resource—our young.* —FLORENCE RUSH, 1980

Ideally, the development and implementation of prevention approaches should be based on a comprehensive understanding of the targeted problem. Child sexual abuse (CSA) is a multifaceted problem, extraordinarily complex in its characteristics, dynamics, causes, and consequences. In this chapter we will review the literature addressing these issues in order to provide basic information about the CSA problem. In addition, we will briefly outline initial responses to the CSA problem and present a rationale for an expanded prevention response.

## Acknowledging the Problem of Child Sexual Abuse

Although the sexual abuse of children has been documented throughout history, what has varied considerably has been society's willingness to recognize it as a problem. In ancient times, using children as sex objects was not only accepted but often encouraged by adults (see Benjamin & Masters, 1964; Mrazek, 1981a; Rush, 1980; Schetky, 1988a; L. G. Schultz, 1982). Participating in sexual activities with adults was not seen as wrong or harmful but as appropriate and even healthy for children (e.g.,

Aristotle believed that masturbating boys would hasten their manhood; DeMause, 1974).

In the prevailing morality of 19th-century Vienna, children's claims of sexual abuse would likely have been dismissed. This reluctance to acknowledge behavior that today would be called CSA was given scientific credence, perhaps inadvertently, by Freud. Although Freud originally proposed that a child's premature sexual experience was an etiological factor in hysteria, he later abandoned the seduction theory and proposed instead that these experiences were most often fantasies that expressed a child's Oedipal conflicts (Masson, 1984). Although the Oedipal conflict was a step forward in the development of psychodynamic theory, Freud's reluctance to acknowledge actual childhood sexual experience or its relationship to adult problems proved to be an unfortunate step backward in society's willingness to acknowledge the problem of CSA (Schetky, 1988a).

Although charity and social workers in the United States in the late 19th century were familiar with CSA and knew that its most common form was intrafamilial, their view of child sexual assault changed significantly during the early 20th century. By the 1920s, a three-part transformation in attitude had occurred: the problem was perceived to be in the streets, rather than in the home, the perpetrator was perceived as a perverted stranger rather than a male family member, and the victim was perceived as a temptress rather than an innocent child (L. Gordon, 1990). Influenced by Freudian thought, social workers explained away the claims of children who maintained they had been seduced by their fathers. Not only did social workers de-emphasize incest, but academicians dismissed it as being extremely rare, occurring in only one in a million cases (Weinberg, 1955). Kinsey's studies in the middle of the 20th century established that childhood sexual experiences were far from rare, but he did not view them as problematic. Kinsey noted, "It is difficult to understand why a child, except for its cultural conditioning, should be disturbed at having its genitals touched, or disturbed at seeing the genitalia of other persons" (Kinsey, Pomeroy, Martin, & Gebhard, 1953, p.121). The CSA problem was acknowledged but its consequences minimized.

Only in recent times have prohibitions about sexual matters abated enough to enable discussion of sexual anomalies. The sexual revolution of the 1960s and 1970s created an atmosphere in which adults who had been sexually victimized as children were encouraged to discuss their experiences, and gradually, public awareness of the problem increased. As official reports of sexual abuse began to mushroom and child sexual abuse began to receive unprecedented media coverage, the public quickly realized that CSA was a serious social problem. In the span of a few years, we have seen a national revolution in our awareness of CSA and in the mobilization of professionals from many different disciplines to combat the problem.

## Defining Child Sexual Abuse: A Multidisciplinary Overview

Any attempt to define CSA is fraught with difficulties, as all definitions are time- and culture-bound as well as direct reflections of the values and orientations of communities and societies at large. Definitions of CSA also depend on the perception of the observer, including biases of an individual's culture, personal values, and professional training and experience. In this section, we will review how professionals (from medicine, law, mental health, and social work), researchers, members of the general public, developers of prevention programs, and children all define CSA.

Within a medical frame of reference, the sexual abuse itself may become confused with the consequences of abuse and be defined according to the presence or absence of genital injuries or venereal disease. The legal perspective focuses on the documentation and proof of the existence of abusive acts by a perpetrator. Prohibited acts vary according to the activity, use of force or coercion, victim-perpetrator relationship, victim's age, and victim-perpetrator age discrepancy. Mental health professionals endorse a broader definition of abuse than do legal professionals and often consider a wider range of situations abusive, for example, parents being nude in front of their children or parents and children sleeping in the same bed (Atteberry-Bennett & Reppucci, 1986). Social service workers within child welfare departments define sexual abuse in terms of physical evidence or corroborating reports (i.e., a substantiated report), which is a practical though inadequate solution because substantiation decisions differ by state, county, and even worker and may be influenced by case-worker time constraints, agency resources, and service capabilities (Faller, 1985; Hechler, 1988).

Researchers have defined sexual abuse according to the type of act, the victim's perceptions, and victim-perpetrator age discrepancy. The restrictiveness of the criteria for type of act has varied between researchers: some include both contact abuse (fondling of breasts and genitals, oral or anal sex, intercourse) and noncontact abuse (solicitation or exhibitionism), and others use a more restrictive definition (contact abuse only). Some researchers have considered the victim's perspective in defining abuse and have included in their definition experiences considered by the victim to be abusive (Finkelhor, 1984), unwanted (D. E. H. Russell, 1983), or coercive (Wyatt, 1985). Some investigators have defined sexual abuse as experiences that occurred exclusively with adults (Kinsey et al., 1953) or at least with older partners (Finkelhor, 1979, 1984), whereas others have considered sexually aggressive acts by peers in their definitions (Dimock, 1988; D. E. H. Russell, 1983; Wyatt, 1985).

The two most important variables in a layperson's determination of sexual abuse appear to be the age of the perpetrator and the type of sex act committed (Finkelhor & Redfield, 1984). Members of the general public are most apt to define a situation as sexual abuse if the perpetrator is an adult and if the act involves intercourse or attempted intercourse. To help young children understand sexual abuse, prevention programmers often talk about different kinds of touches and the resultant feelings to define sexual abuse (e.g., touches that feel bad or cause confusion). In many programs, children are taught to "trust their feelings" as a way of determining the appropriateness of a touch. Thus, it is left up to the children to define sexual abuse.

Investigations into how children define sexual abuse are limited. Recently, we asked abused and nonabused children for their definitions of sexual abuse and found that abused children more often defined it as "sexual touching" than did nonabused children, who were "unsure" (Miller-Perrin, Wurtele, & Kondrick, 1990). Only half of the abused sample offered a correct definition, however, suggesting this is a difficult task even for children who have experienced abuse.

It is apparent that consensus regarding the appropriate definition for CSA has not been reached. Such variation is a result of each group's viewing the problem through a different cognitive lens, resulting from varying orientations, perspectives, objectives, and goals for addressing the problem. The commonality is that all groups share the goals of confronting the problem and protecting children from sexual abuse.

Given the complex nature of CSA, different definitions are needed for different purposes: legal definitions guide legal decision making that specifies what acts or conditions justify state intervention into family life; case management definitions guide clinical decision making about victims, perpetrators, and families; and research definitions provide the scientific basis for studying causal relationships among abuse-related variables (Aber & Zigler, 1981). The definition of CSA used for this book is broad and in accordance with the definition originally formulated by the National Center on Child Abuse and Neglect (NCCAN) in 1978:

> Contacts or interactions between a child and an adult when the child is being used for the sexual stimulation of the perpetrator or another person. Sexual abuse may also be committed by a person under the age of 18 when that person is either significantly older than the victim or when the perpetrator is in a position of power or control over another child. (p.2)

Thus, CSA perpetrated by adults involves the exploitation of adult authority and power for sexual ends. This definition also includes children and adolescents as perpetrators if a situation involves the exploitation of a child by virtue of the perpetrator's size, age, sex, or status. It also includes experiences of physical contact between perpetrator and victim and those where contact may be limited or absent (e.g., child pornography). Whether perpetrated by adults or more powerful children, sexual abuse involves the exploitation of children's ignorance, trust, and obedience.

## The Extent of the Child Sexual Abuse Problem

Although problems of definition exist, they have not hampered efforts to determine the scope of the problem. Two methods of study have been employed to evaluate the extent of CSA in the United States: incidence studies (i.e., the number of new cases occurring within a specific time period, usually a year) and prevalence studies (i.e., the proportion of a population that reports having been sexually victimized during childhood).

INCIDENCE STUDIES
The first National Incidence Study (Department of Health & Human Services [DHHS], 1981) counted cases of CSA that came to the attention of community professionals and child protection agencies in a national probability sample of 26 counties in ten U.S. states. This study arrived at an annual rate of abuse of 0.7 cases per 1,000 children (based on 1980 census data, this represents 42,900 children under the age of 18). The second National Incidence Study (DHHS, 1988; see amendment to study by Sedlack, 1990), using a probability sample of 29 counties, estimated that 119,200 children nationwide had been sexually abused in 1986, an increase of 178% over the 1980 figure. In this study, sexually abusive acts included penile penetration, genital contact, and unspecified behaviors (e.g., fondling and exposure) perpetrated by parents or parent substitutes. The use of a revised, broader definition of sexual abuse (including teenagers as perpetrators and situations where the child's health or safety was endangered) resulted in an incidence rate of 133,600 children nationwide in 1986. From official reports documented by child protective service agencies nationwide, the American Association for Protecting Children (1988) estimated that there were 132,000 children sexually abused in 1986. More recently, the National Committee for the Prevention of Child Abuse (NCPCA, 1990), basing their findings on their annual 50-state survey of child abuse reports, estimated that there

were between 360,000 and 408,000 reports of sexual abuse filed in 1989.

Deriving accurate incidence figures from the number of new cases reported is difficult because sexual abuse (like all types of abuse) tends to be underreported by court and police agencies (Luther & Price, 1980); hospitals and social agencies (DHHS, 1988; Finkelhor, Gomes-Schwartz, & Horowitz, 1984; James, Womack, & Strauss, 1978); professionals (Kalichman, Craig, & Follingstad, 1988, 1989); and the victims and families themselves (Finkelhor, 1979; D. E. H. Russell, 1983). The discrepancy between reported cases and actual incidence was highlighted when the second National Incidence Study revealed that only half of the maltreatment cases identified by a sample of professionals across the country were formally reported (Sedlak, 1990).

The definition of sexual abuse also greatly affects reporting statistics. That 14,400 children would be defined as *abused* by one definition but not another in the second National Incidence Study exemplifies the effect of differing definitions on incidence rates. In addition, inconsistencies in court and police records can result from a lack of standardization of statutes; hospitals may fail to report if there is no physical or laboratory evidence of sexual contact; social service agencies may define cases as substantiated only if they are serious enough to warrant state intervention and if there are available resources to manage cases; professionals may be reluctant to report cases if the statutory definitions are vague; the family may fail to report if the activity does not meet their definition of sexual abuse; and victims may fail to disclose abuse because of ignorance regarding what constitutes abuse. Most professionals consider incidence figures to underestimate the scope of the problem, and a comparison of incidence figures with prevalence figures supports this proposition.

PREVALENCE STUDIES
*General Population.* Although subject to the problem of the selective recall of participants, extant prevalence studies indicate that an important fraction of men and women report having experienced sexual abuse as children. As indicated in Table 1, sexual

abuse rates in retrospective studies range from 7% to 62% for females (with an average of 22% for contact abuse) and 3% to 16% for males (with an overall average of 7%). Such wide variations in reported prevalence reflect differences in the definitions of CSA used in various studies (e.g., whether abuse is limited to contact with the genitals or whether only unwanted experiences are considered), the ceiling age of abuse used, the types of samples employed, and the methods for gathering data (e.g., via telephone, anonymously completed questionnaire, or direct interview).

*Clinical Populations.* The prevalence of abuse is even higher among clinical or select populations. The highest rates of childhood sexual abuse (between 73% and 90%) have been found among patients with multiple personality disorder (Bliss, 1984; Coons, Bowman, Pellow, & Schneider, 1989; Coons & Milstein, 1986; Dell & Eisenhower, 1990; Putnam, Guroff, Silberman, Barban, & Post, 1986; Ross, Miller, Reagor, Bjornson, Fraser, & Anderson, 1990; R. Schultz, Braun, & Kluft, 1989). Among female patients with borderline personality disorder, rates vary from 52% to 86% (Bryer, Nelson, Miller, & Krol, 1987; Herman, Perry, & van der Kolk, 1989; Ogata et al., 1990; Westen, Ludolph, Misle, Ruffins, & Block, 1990). Females with posttraumatic stress disorder also report high levels of childhood sexual abuse (57% in Coons et al., 1989). Among psychiatric inpatients, Jacobson and Herald (1990) found the prevalence of childhood sexual abuse to be 26% for males and 54% for females. Briere and Zaidi (1989) reported a sexual abuse rate of 70% in women who presented at a psychiatric emergency room.

A history of childhood sexual abuse has also been found among female chronic pain patients (39% in Wurtele, Kaplan, & Keairnes, 1990), females with gastrointestinal disorders (30% in Drossman et al., 1990), and females presenting with symptoms of premenstrual syndrome (22% in Paddison et al., 1990). High rates among female inpatient substance abusers (77% in Rohsenow, Corbett, & Devine, 1988) and female patients diagnosed with anorexia or bulimia (50% in R. C. W. Hall, Tice, Beresford, Wooley, & Hall, 1989), have also been documented. In addition, a history of child-

# Table 1: Large-Scale U.S. Prevalence Studies

| | | | Prevalence | |
| --- | --- | --- | --- | --- |
| | Sample & Method | Definition | Females (%) | Males (%) |
| **University Samples** | | | | |
| Finkelhor (1979) | 530 undergraduate women and 266 men from six New England universities; anonymous questionnaire survey | All types of contact and noncontact abuse; age discrepancy of 5 yrs up to age 12, of 10 yrs between ages 13–16 (before age 17) | 19 | 9 |
| Fritz, Stoll, & Wagner (1981) | 540 undergraduate women and 412 men from Seattle, WA; anonymous questionnaire survey | Contact abuse; prepuberty victim and postadolescent perpetrator | 8 | 5 |
| Fromuth (1986) | 482 undergraduate women from Auburn, AL; anonymous questionnaire survey | Same as Finkelhor (1979) | 22 | |
| Risin & Koss (1987) | National sample of 2,972 undergraduate men; anonymous questionnaire survey | All types of contact and noncontact abuse; age discrepancy of 5 yrs up to age 12; of 8 yrs for boys 13 or older, if coercion involved, or perp was caregiver (before age 14) | | 7 |
| Haugaard & Emery (1989) | 664 undergraduate women and 425 men from a mid-Atlantic university; anonymous questionnaire survey | Both a narrow (contact abuse and unwanted) and broad definition (contact or noncontact, wanted or unwanted); age discrepancy of 5 years (before age 17) | 10*<br>12† | |
| **Community Samples** | | | | |
| D. E. H. Russell (1983) | Probability sample of 930 women from San Francisco; standardized personal interview | Both a narrow (contact abuse only) and broad definition (contact and noncontact) and sexual experience was unwanted (extrafamilial) or exploitative (intrafamilial) (before age 18) | 38*<br>54† | |
| Finkelhor (1984) | Random sample of 334 mothers and 187 fathers from Boston, MA; standardized personal interview | All types of contact and noncontact abuse; age discrepancy of 5 yrs and respondent considered the experience to have been sexual abuse (before age 17) | 15 | 6 |
| Kercher & McShane (1984b) | Random sample of 593 females and 461 males from Texas; anonymous questionnaire survey | Contact and noncontact abuse by adult or person in power (before age 18) | 11 | 3 |
| Wyatt (1985) | Probability sample of 248 women from Los Angeles county; standardized personal interview | All types of contact and noncontact abuse; age discrepancy of 5 yrs or sexual experience was unwanted and involved some degree of coercion (before age 18) | 45*<br>62† | |
| Siegel, Sorenson, Golding, Burnam, & Stein (1987) | Probability sample of 1,645 women and 1,480 men in Los Angeles; standardized personal interview | Forced or pressured sexual contact (before age 16) | 7 | 4 |
| Finkelhor, Hotaling, Lewis, & Smith (1990) | National random sample of 1,481 women and 1,145 men; standardized telephone interview | All types of contact and noncontact abuse and respondent considered it to be sexual abuse (before age 19) | 27 | 16 |

* = contact
† = contact + noncontact

hood sexual abuse has been reported by 52% to 73% of prostitutes (Bagley & Young, 1987; James & Meyerding, 1977; Ross, Anderson, Heber, & Norton, 1990; Silbert & Pines, 1981) and by 21% to 55% of runaway youths (Janus, Burgess, & McCormack, 1987; Powers, Eckenrode, & Jaklitsch, 1990; Reich & Gutierres, 1979).

Although consensus is lacking about the exact scope of the problem, the data clearly imply that a significant number of women and men remember having been sexually victimized during the course of their development. (Prevalence rates based on adult samples likely underestimate the actual extent of the problem, as there may be many more men and women who were victimized as children but do not remember their experiences.) Much of the current interest in identifying and treating abuse victims, in addition to preventing CSA, can be attributed to this research, which confirms that sexual victimization during childhood is not a rare event.

## Epidemiological Characteristics of Child Sexual Abuse

Epidemiological studies provide the research base for prevention efforts (Schwab & Schwab, 1978). Causes and patterns can be identified from tracing the distribution of CSA in a population, and prevention activities can then be designed and implemented.

### CHARACTERISTICS OF VICTIMS

A disproportionate number of female victims (77–85%) exists among the majority of sexual abuse reports (American Association for Protecting Children, 1988; DHHS, 1988; A. B. Russell & Trainor, 1984), although it is believed that the abuse of male children is underreported (Nasjleti, 1980; Peake, 1989; Rew & Esparza, 1990). Suggested reasons for the underreporting of males include: (a) societal expectations for boys to be dominant and self-reliant; (b) societal notions that early sexual experiences are a normal part of boys' lives; (c) boys' fears of being considered homosexual, since most boys are abused by men; and (d) societal pressures on males not to express helplessness or vulnerability. New evidence suggests that a higher proportion of males are being abused than previously thought. Reports from treatment programs reveal that a substantial proportion of referrals involve boys (e.g., 24% in Gale, Thompson, Moran, & Sack, 1988; 40% in Krugman, 1986). Some have suggested that boys may be at higher, possibly equal risk for sexual victimization, as males are the preferred targets of child sex-ring organizers (Lanning & Burgess, 1984). Further evidence suggesting that boys may be equally at risk comes from studies of adult offenders. For example, Abel and associates found that nonincarcerated sex offenders sexually molested young boys with an incidence that was five times greater than that of molesting young girls (Abel et al., 1987).

Ages of victims may range from early infancy to 18 years. Cases of CSA have been medically documented with victims as young as 3.5 months (Ellerstein & Canavan, 1980), 6 months (DeJong, Emmett, & Hervada, 1982), 9 months (P. J. Mrazek, Lynch, & Bentovim, 1983), and 1 year (DeJong, Hervada, & Emmett, 1983). Many clinical studies indicate that the mean age of children reporting abuse falls within the prepubescent range of 9 to 11 years (DeJong et al., 1982; Gomes-Schwartz, Horowitz, & Cardarelli, 1990; Kercher & McShane, 1984a; Rimsza & Niggemann, 1982; Shah, Holloway, & Valkill, 1982; Tilelli, Turek, & Jaffe, 1980). These figures may be misleading, however, because they reflect the average age of reporting rather than the age of onset of CSA. It is also possible that young children are less likely and older children more likely to reveal abuse, both factors biasing the ages of reporting in such studies (Tilelli et al., 1980). Nevertheless, retrospective studies of adults abused as children also indicate that children are more vulnerable to sexual abuse during the prepubescent period: between ages 8 and 12 (Finkelhor & Baron, 1986). For example, in their samples of adult women, D. E. H. Russell (1983) and Wyatt (1985) found the median age of the onset of abuse to be 11.2 years. Finkelhor (1984) found median ages of 10.2 for girls and 11.2 for boys, and in Finkelhor et al., (1990) the median ages of onset for girls and boys were 9.6 and 9.9 years, respectively.

The true distribution of risk cannot be obtained from mean or median figures, as they do not reflect the relative vulnerability at different ages. In response to this problem, Finkelhor and Baron (1986) constructed proportions of risk for several age groups from a select group of retrospective studies and concluded that vulnerability is increased at ages 6 to 7 and 10 to 12 and decreased for children under the age of 6. However, there are reasons to doubt the proposed decreased vulnerability for children younger than 6. Retrospective survey respondents may not accurately recall onset of abuse that occurred when they were very young. It is easy for such memories to be distorted, especially when they occur to children without a cognitive framework for interpreting such experiences (Waterman, 1986). Many children are unaware of the start of the abuse and are unable to recognize the abusive nature of the activity.

The belief that young children are rarely the victims of sexual abuse has also been challenged by recent research showing a distinct bimodal age distribution (peaking at ages 4 and 14–15) of sexual abuse reports (American Association for Protecting Children, 1986; DeJong et al., 1983; Eckenrode, Munsch, Powers, & Doris, 1988; Tilelli et al., 1980). Findings from clinical samples also indicate that sexual abuse is a problem for young children. Several reports indicate that one-third to one-half of sexual abuse victims are children under the age of 7 (Berliner & Stevens, 1982; Cupoli & Sewell, 1988; Faller, 1988; Jaudes & Morris, 1990; Jenny, Sutherland, & Sandahl, 1986; Lang, Rouget, & van Santen, 1988; Mannarino & Cohen, 1986; Mian, Wehrspann, Klajner-Diamond, LeBaron, & Winder, 1986). Such findings challenge the assumption that young children are rarely abused. Indeed, Lang et al.'s (1988) finding that child victims of sexual abuse are more likely to be sexually and physically immature compared with non-abused matched children suggests that the young child's sexually immature body shape may hold a unique attraction for men who prefer sex with a child. It is apparent that children of all ages are at risk for sexual abuse, with age-risk differences influenced by memory recall, type of perpetrator (e.g., pedophile vs. nonpedophile), and underreporting.

Some researchers have compared victims and nonvictims to determine if certain groups of children are at higher risk for victimization than others (see Finkelhor & Baron, 1986, for a review). Finkelhor (1980) found several social variables to be associated with increased risk of CSA for females: living in a family with a stepfather, having a family income of less than $10,000 a year, having lived at certain times without a mother, being emotionally distant from one's mother, having a mother who had never finished high school and who was particularly punitive about sexual matters, receiving no physical affection from one's father, and having few close friends.

Using a small sample of delinquent females, Gruber and Jones (1983) found three background variables significantly discriminated youths who had been sexually victimized from those who had not. Victims' parents were more likely to have poor marital relations. In addition, victims were more likely to have been living with a step- or foster father, and contrary to Finkelhor's research, to have had a close relationship with their mothers. In their community survey of adults, Finkelhor ct al. (1990) found that men and women were more likely to have been sexually victimized as children if they reported that their family life had been unhappy or if they had lived without one of their natural parents. Women were at higher risk if they reported receiving an inadequate sex education. Certainly, more needs to be learned about what child and family characteristics increase and decrease vulnerability to sexual victimization.

VICTIM-PERPETRATOR RELATIONSHIP
Using figures derived from large-scale community surveys of women reporting childhood histories of abuse (i.e., Finkelhor et al., 1990; D. E. H. Russell, 1983; Siegel et al., 1987; Wyatt, 1985), approximately 25% of victimized respondents report being abused by strangers, close to half (46%) report being abused by acquaintances (e.g., authority figures, baby-sitters, neighbors, friends of the family), about 8% report abuse by a father or father substitute, and 18% report being abused by other relatives (e.g., uncles, grandfathers, cousins, siblings). For males, victim-perpetra-

tor relationship percentages (calculated from Finkelhor et al., 1990, and Siegel et al., 1987) were strangers (34%), acquaintances (46%), relatives (12%), and fathers (0%). Thus, in the majority of cases, male and female children are sexually victimized by people they know and trust. These findings suggest that most CSA victims have to deal not only with the trauma of the molestation but also the violation of trust. Furthermore, these data confirm that "stranger danger" warnings, for all their media appeal, are of little relevance in preventing a significant number of CSA cases.

## TYPE OF SEXUAL ACTIVITY

Sgroi, Blick, and Porter (1982) explain that sexual activity can range from exhibitionism to intercourse, often progressing through nudity, observing the child undressing or bathing, kissing, fondling, mutual masturbation, fellatio, cunnilingus, digital and penile penetration of the anus, and digital and penile penetration of the vagina. The typical scenario is a progression over multiple encounters from less intimate types of activities (e.g., exposure) to actual body contact (e.g., fondling, masturbation, oral or genital contact), and then to some type of penetration. Most sexual be- havior consists of exhibitionism, fondling, masturbation, or oral or genital contact; fewer victims report experiencing intercourse as part of their molestation (Haugaard & Reppucci, 1988). When intercourse does occur, it is likely to be with older, more sexually mature children (Lang et al., 1988).

CSA also encompasses the exploitation of children for sexual stimulation and commercial gain in the form of pornography, prostitution, or sex rings. Sexual activities in child sex rings can include oral, vaginal, and anal sex; bondage; sadomasochism; and bestiality. These activities may be photographed or videotaped (Hunt & Baird, 1990; Wild, 1989).

## THE DYNAMICS OF ABUSE

Although there has been minimal systematic study of the process whereby perpetrators identify and recruit child victims, prelimi- nary reports (Budin & Johnson, 1989; Conte, Wolf, & Smith, 1989; Lang & Frenzel, 1988) suggest that they prefer passive, quiet, trusting, unhappy children from divorced homes. Once identified, they often desensitize the children to sexual activity by *grooming* them, that is, by progressing from nonsexual to sexual touch within the context of a gradually developing relationship. Strategies used to engage and maintain children in sexual activity include offering material enticements (e.g., money; purchases of special toys or other articles), misrepresenting standards (e.g., assuring the child that the sexual contact is normal and accepted behavior), using verbal threats (e.g., to harm the child or a significant other), or overt aggression (e.g., physically overpowering the child).

Secrecy is an essential element of sexual abuse (Summit, 1983). Studies of adults victimized as children indicate that only a small percentage revealed their abuse during childhood. For example, in D. E. H. Russell's (1983) community survey, only 2% of women who had experienced intrafamilial and 6% who had experienced extrafamilial sexual abuse had ever reported the assault to an authority. Somewhat higher rates of disclosure have been obtained in studies of sexually victimized children, although the majority do not disclose immediately. In Conte and Berliner (1981), 15% of the 274 children sexually abused by family members reported the victimization within 48 hours of the last incident, and 24% of the victims studied by Sauzier (1989) told within a week after being abused.

Several factors may contribute to the secrecy. For example, the victim may fear the repercussions of telling (e.g., he or she will not be believed, parents may react adversely, the family will break up). The child may keep the secret because the offender has offered positive inducements for doing so (e.g., attention, gifts). A strong emotional bond between the victim and perpetrator might make disclosure difficult, as the child may want to protect the assailant or fear losing the perpetrator's affection if disclosure occurs. Threats (e.g., to harm or kill the child, a significant other, or a pet; to send the victim to a frightening place; to show pictures of the child involved in sexual acts to the parents) may be used to reinforce secrecy (Budin & Johnson, 1989; Conte et al., 1989; Lang & Frenzel, 1988).

Developmental variables also contribute to delayed disclosure. Because of their naïveté, young children may not know that the activity is wrong or they may lack the verbal ability to report an incident; older children may be too embarrassed to report. Young children's tendency to accommodate to the demands of adults (Summit, 1983) makes it likely that they will participate in the activity and keep the secret. Guilt may also serve as a deterrent to disclosure, as child victims may feel responsible for the abuse because they participated in the activity or because perpetrators have convinced them that they are to blame. Communication barriers may also contribute to the victim's silence. Young children may lack the appropriate vocabulary (e.g., names of body parts) to describe what has happened. Their reports may go unnoticed if presented in a cryptic manner (e.g., "I don't like my babysitter"). Finally, children may have been given the message that sexual issues are not to be discussed.

## CHARACTERISTICS OF PERPETRATORS

Although there are an increasing number of studies appearing in the literature that focus on the perpetrators of CSA, our knowledge regarding these individuals is still limited. Except for the fact that they engage children in sexual activities for their own gratification, child sexual abusers are indistinguishable from other people (Crewdson, 1988). Race, religion, intelligence, education, occupation, or socioeconomic status do not distinguish perpetrators from nonperpetrators (Groth, Hobson, & Gary, 1982). Furthermore, a psychological profile of the typical child molester has yet to be developed; they constitute a markedly heterogeneous group (Becker & Coleman, 1988; Knight, Rosenberg, & Schneider, 1985).

One area of consensus regards the preponderance of male perpetrators. Most studies indicate that among reported perpetrators, 90% or more are male (Finkelhor, 1984; Kercher & McShane, 1984a; D. E. H. Russell, 1983; Siegel et al., 1987). Not only are reported perpetrators primarily male, but there is recent evidence suggesting that a significant minority of the normal male population has committed this type of sexual offense. In their nationwide random-sample survey, Finkelhor and Lewis (1988) found that between 4 and 17% of the male population acknowledged having molested a child.

Similarly, Briere and Runtz (1989) found that 21% of male undergraduate students reported having experienced sexual attraction to children and 7% indicated some likelihood of having sex with a child if they could avoid detection and punishment.

There are female offenders; most have been accomplices of males (Adams-Tucker, 1982; Faller, 1989a; Finkelhor, Williams, & Burns, 1988; McCarty, 1986). Some argue, however, that males are overrepresented because female offenders simply go undetected. Because of culturally prescribed physical intimacy during routine infant and child care, females have more opportunities to sexually stimulate children that may go unnoticed (Crewdson, 1988; Schetky & Green, 1988). Other research indicates that the prevalence of female offenders may be obscured by issues of definition. For example, Haugaard and Reppucci (1988) found that when the experiences of their sample of college undergraduates were classified as "unwanted," 38% of males reported that they had been abused by females, compared with 60% when "wanted" experiences were included. Others have suggested that a culturally based unwillingness to believe that women commit such acts exists, resulting in an underestimation of the actual extent to which females are sexual offenders (Banning, 1989). Nevertheless, at this point the preponderance of research has failed to demonstrate that a large quantity of abusive experiences are perpetrated by women, despite the ample opportunities they have for sexually abusing children. Future research may reveal that female perpetrators are not atypical. Such evidence would require a shift from viewing child sexual exploitation as a gender issue to viewing it as a human issue.

A prominent stereotype of molesters has been that they are "dirty old men." To the contrary, most offenders are in their mid- to late thirties (Abel, Becker, Cunningham-Rathner, Mittelman, & Rouleau, 1988; Kaplan, 1989; Groth, Burgess, Birnbaum, & Gary, 1978; Mohr, 1981). In 1981, Groth and Loredo argued that the extent to which adolescents commit sexual assault was not fully recognized nor its significance appreciated. Such behavior was being dismissed as sexual curiosity ("boys will be boys"), situational in nature, or a result of the normal aggressiveness of a sexually maturing adolescent.

The literature has seen an increasing focus on the juvenile sexual offender, confirming earlier suspicions. This focus is a result not only of the high proportion of adolescents who commit sexual offenses (Ageton, 1983; G. E. Davis & Leitenberg, 1987; Knopp, 1982; Otey & Ryan, 1985) but also of results of studies suggesting that the majority of sexual offenders develop deviant sexual interests before age 18 (Abel & Rouleau, 1990). Furthermore, many researchers are reporting that a substantial proportion of their offenders are adolescents (Gomes-Schwartz et al., 1990; Khan & Sexton, 1983; Krugman, 1986; Rogers & Thomas, 1984) and that the largest percentage of their victims are children (Awad & Saunders, 1989; Deisher, Wenet, Paperny, Clark, & Fehrenbach, 1982; Fehrenbach, Smith, Monastersky, & Deisher, 1986). Adolescent perpetrators appear to commit more severe sexual abuse (involving intercourse and physical assault) compared with older perpetrators (Margolin & Craft, 1989, 1990). Reports of children victimizing children younger than themselves are also appearing (T. C. Johnson, 1988, 1989), as are reports indicating that coercive child-child sexual experiences are not rare and can have negative effects on the victims (Haugaard & Tilly, 1988). It is becoming clear that sexual abuse does not always begin with the onset of the adulthood of the offender.

Recognizing the heterogeneity of sexual offenders, typological systems have been developed in order to provide more homogeneous subgroups for study. The hope is that information on *who* abuses children will elucidate the reasons *why* they abuse. The traditional classification of incestuous versus nonincestuous perpetrators is becoming obsolete as a useful distinction, because many men who molest within their family also molest children outside of it and often have other sexually deviant behaviors as well (Abel et al., 1987, 1988; Rogers & Thomas, 1984).

Other classification systems have been proposed, including Karpman's (1954) original distinction between perpetrators who have a stable erotic "preference" for children and those who use children as "surrogates" for adult sexual partners. More recently, Groth and his colleagues used a similar conceptualization dividing molesters into "fixated" and "regressed" offenders (Groth et al., 1982). Fixated (also referred to as "preference": Howells, 1981) offenders have a primary sexual preference for children, whereas regressed (sometimes referred to as "situational") offenders have normal adult sexual orientations but regress to sexual activities with children in stressful situations. Fixated molesters commonly fit the criteria for pedophilia established in the *Diagnostic and Statistical Manual of Mental Disorders* (DSM-III-R: American Psychiatric Association, 1987). People with pedophilia (a disorder characterized by "recurrent, intense, sexual urges and sexually arousing fantasies, of at least six months' duration, involving sexual activity with a prepubescent child," DSM-III-R, p. 284) are further divided into either the exclusive type (attracted only to children) or nonexclusive type (also attracted to adults) and are classified as to whether they are attracted to same sex, opposite sex, or same and opposite sex children. Other researchers have likewise divided perpetrators according to their gender (e.g., Earls & Quinsey, 1985; Groth & Birnbaum, 1978) and age preferences (e.g., Barbaree & Marshall, 1989).

Knight, Carter, and Prentky (1989) divide offenders into groups of socially competent and incompetent, based on their success in employment, adult relationships, and social responsibilities, and also distinguish between offenders who spend a substantial amount of time in close proximity to children (high contact) and those who spend little or no time with children outside of sexual assaults (low contact). There have been attempts to classify perpetrators based on their motivations for molesting (e.g., for sexual gratification or to hurt the child; Knight et al., 1985), or whether their sexually aggressive acts toward children are addictive or compulsive behaviors, similar to alcoholism, drug abuse, smoking, or compulsive gambling (Carnes, 1983; Pithers, Kashima, Cumming, & Beal, 1988). Others have classified perpetrators based on the type of engagement strategy they use to get the child to participate in the sexual activity (e.g., force, threats, bribery; Avery-Clark &

Laws, 1984; Groth et al., 1982). Finally, perpetrator profiles have been created from their responses to psychological tests, such as the Minnesota Multiphasic Personality Inventory, or MMPI (Duthie & McIvor, 1990).

Given that the vast majority of typological studies are conducted with samples of offenders who are convicted, hospitalized, or receiving psychotherapy, the obtained findings may be seriously affected by reporting and judicial biases (Howells, 1981). Discovery and conviction rates are most likely related to a host of confounding factors, including social class, race, intelligence, psychopathology, and severity of the offense (Tierney & Corwin, 1983). Undoubtedly, there are many different types of child sexual offenders, and present classification systems do not adequately characterize all of them. The common denominators appear to be an offender's lack of sensitivity to the child's wishes and needs, along with a willingness to exploit the child's trust for the abuser's own gratification, profit, or selfish purposes.

IMPLICATIONS FOR PREVENTION
In this section we have highlighted the epidemiological characteristics of the CSA problem. As this review indicates, the characteristics of sexual abuse are multiple, varied, and complex. There is no one kind of sexual abuse nor one type of perpetrator or victim. Although our knowledge about the characteristics of victims and perpetrators has dramatically increased over the last decade, there are many areas where definitive answers are still lacking. Despite these limitations, available information provides a number of prevention implications.

Given that CSA is not restricted to a certain gender or age, broad-based prevention efforts are needed to target both males and females of all ages, including preschool-aged children. Children need to be taught a repertoire of self-protective responses and should be encouraged to report abusive experiences in order to reduce the secrecy surrounding CSA. Children, as well as parents and professionals, must be given accurate portrayals of potential perpetrators and informed about what types of activities might be involved, along with the tactics offenders use to entice or groom child targets. That the sexual abusers of children are rarely strangers but more typically relatives or acquaintances must be stressed. That offenders often begin abusing at young ages suggests that CSA prevention could be accomplished if effective treatment were provided early in the offender's career. Because our knowledge regarding perpetrators is scant, programs aimed at preventing individuals from becoming child sexual offenders have not been developed, although they have been called for (Cohn, 1986; Cohn, Finkelhor, & Holmes, 1985; Swift, 1979).

## Consequences of Child Sexual Abuse

CSA constitutes a major social problem, not only because of the high frequency of occurrence but also because of its initial and long-term effects on victims. Although some authors have concluded from limited samples that childhood sexual experiences are not damaging (Bender & Blau, 1937; Gagnon, 1965; Landis, 1956; Yorukoglu & Kemph, 1966) or may even be beneficial (Guyon, 1941; J. Henderson, 1983; Westermeyer, 1978; Yates, 1978), the majority of studies provide evidence that such maltreatment often has deleterious effects (see reviews by Alter-Reid, Gibbs, Lachenmeyer, Sigal, & Massoth, 1986; Browne & Finkelhor, 1986; Conte, 1985; Hanson, 1990; Lusk & Waterman, 1986; Miller-Perrin & Wurtele, 1990; Walker, Bonner, & Kaufman, 1988; V. V. Wolfe & Wolfe, 1988; Wyatt & Powell, 1988).

Initial effects of CSA documented in the empirical literature include affective disturbances (e.g., anxiety, depression, shame and guilt, low self-esteem, hostility, anger), physical problems (e.g., genital injury; urinary tract infections), psychosomatic reactions (e.g., enuresis; disturbed sleep patterns, abdominal pain), cognitive disturbances (e.g., low school achievement, poor concentration, preoccupation, inattentiveness, dissociation), and sociobehavioral disturbances (e.g., aggression, withdrawal, disturbed peer relations, strong dependency needs). The symptom most commonly identified in sexually abused children is oversexualized behavior (e.g., overt sexual acting-out toward adults or other children, com-

pulsive masturbation, excessive sexual curiosity, sexua
ity, precocious sexual play and knowledge).

The emotional consequences of childhood sexual vi............
can extend into the adult years. Over the long term, the experience
can affect emotional reactions (e.g., depression, suicidality, anxiety, low self-esteem, guilt), interpersonal relationships (e.g., difficulty trusting others, feelings of isolation, alienation, and insecur-
ity), cognitive reactions (e.g., reexperiencing traumatic events
through intrusive thoughts, flashbacks, nightmares; dissociation),
sexual adjustment (e.g., anorgasmia, arousal and desire dysfunction, sexual phobia or aversion), and behavioral functioning (e.g.,
substance abuse, eating disorders, delinquency, sexual revictimization). These long-lasting mental health consequences are not just
found among clinical samples. Researchers assessing psychological
reactions associated with childhood sexual assault among random
samples of adults have found that survivors of CSA report high
levels of anxiety, depression, drug abuse, and revictimization (Bagley & Ramsey, 1985; Burnam et al., 1988; Kilpatrick et al., 1985;
Sedney & Brooks, 1984; Siegel et al., 1987).

In addition to the myriad of symptoms documented in sexual
abuse victims, CSA has been associated with a wide range of psychopathology. For example, Mannarino and Cohen (1986) found
that of 45 sexually abused children studied, 69% had clinically
significant psychological symptoms on a symptom checklist,
whereas 31% had minor or no symptoms. Friedrich, Urquiza, and
Beilke (1986) used the Child Behavior Checklist (Achenbach &
Edelbrock, 1983) to assess the effects of sexual abuse on 61 females and found that 46% had significantly elevated scores on the
Internalizing Scale (e.g., depression, withdrawn behavior) and 39%
had elevated scores on the Externalizing Scale (e.g., acting-out behaviors). Similar levels of dysfunction would be expected in only
2% of the general population of children. Almost 40% of the
sexually abused children studied by Sirles, Smith, and Kusama
(1989) were diagnosed with clinical disorders. Of the victimized
children studied by Gomes-Schwartz et al. (1990), 17% of the
preschool group (4–6 years) evidenced "clinically significant pathology," 40% of the school-aged group (7–13 years) scored in

the seriously disturbed range, and 8% of the adolescent victims (14–18 years) exhibited severe psychopathology.

Retrospective studies also indicate that many adults who survived childhood sexual abuse report that the experience was harmful. In a community sample of adult females, Herman, Russell, and Trocki (1986) found that 55% remembered their sexual abuse by relatives as being very or extremely upsetting. In terms of self-assessment, 53% of the survivors of incest in D. E. H. Russell's (1986) community survey reported that the experience resulted in "some" or "great" long-term effects on their lives. In Baker and Duncan (1985), 37% of the male and 64% of the female survivors reported that the abuse had had a damaging effect on their lives.

Thus, evidence accumulated to date strongly suggests that childhood sexual abuse results in disturbing psychological sequelae in a significant portion of victims. In their review of the literature, Browne and Finkelhor (1986) concluded that from 20% to 40% of abused children seen by clinicians manifest pathological disturbance, and 20% of adults who were sexually abused as children evidence serious psychopathology. It is also apparent from these figures that some CSA victims survive relatively unscathed. Future studies need to focus on these seemingly resilient children. Do these children have special "protective factors" (Rutter, 1985) such as biological predispositions, personal competencies, coping strategies, family resources, external relationships, or environmental circumstances that act to mitigate against their traumatic experiences?

Finally, it is important to recognize that CSA harms not only victims but also the family system, offenders, schools, and society. For example, when the perpetrator is a parent, the nonoffending spouse and the victim's siblings can also suffer, as they may be torn between supporting and blaming the victim. The sexual abuse can lead to marital dissolution, subsequent financial stressors, and alteration in familial roles (Hubbard, 1989). When the perpetrator is a nonparent relative, every family member can experience divided loyalty (child vs. perpetrator), along with guilt resulting from this difficult decision. Even when the perpetrator is a stranger or unrelated adult, the victim's parents and siblings can also share in the pain and suffering. In extrafamilial abuse, parents often feel guilty about their inability to prevent the abuse, feel angry at the offender (and sometimes the child), and are stressed by their child's involvement in the court process (Burgess, Hartman, Kelley, Grant, & Gray, 1990; Regehr, 1990). Parents of CSA victims have been found to report high levels of stress and multiple behavioral, somatic, and psychological reactions, suggesting that they, too, are victimized by the abuse (DeJong, 1988; Finkelhor, 1984; Winton, 1990). Siblings may feel stigmatized by the abuse and worry that they will be ostracized by their peers.

The offender is also impacted, most obviously by criminal prosecution or removal from the home. His or her arrest, imprisonment, probation, or mandated separation from the family presents emotional (e.g., suicide; Morrison, 1988), relational, financial, and employment problems (Rencken, 1989). This is not to discount an offender's responsibility but to acknowledge the wide range of effects of CSA. Schools are also impacted by the problem, as they must contend with victimized children who experience the cognitive, emotional, and behavioral effects of the abuse. Economic costs are also incurred to taxpayers, which include direct (protection, prosecution, punishment) and indirect costs (loss of productivity, welfare support, medical and mental health services). Thus, everyone is victimized by the CSA problem, suggesting that we all need to be involved in efforts to solve *our* problem.

### Initial Responses to the Child Sexual Abuse Problem

After centuries of condoning and even encouraging the sexual abuse of children, our present society has largely developed a decreased tolerance for the sexual exploitation of children, along with an increased willingness to tackle the CSA problem. In this section, we will briefly review the initial steps taken to combat this problem.

TREATMENT

An early response to the CSA problem was to provide therapeutic services to victims, their families, and offenders. Several incest treatment programs originated in the early 1970s, and in 1977 four programs received funding from the National Center on Child Abuse and Neglect (NCCAN). Although the development of treatment centers resulted in victim identification and therapeutic assistance, the restricted number of programs across the country and their focus on intrafamilial abuse meant that many victims were left without assistance. The scarcity of treatment programs for child victims still remains a problem today. Less than 10% of the community service agencies surveyed by Daro, Abrahams, and Robson (1988) reported operating groups for sexually abused children. Even when programs are available, few victims are referred for treatment following identification (Krugman, 1990; Pierce & Pierce, 1985). Furthermore, although major advances have been made in the treatment of offenders and adult victims of sexual abuse (e.g., Abel, Becker, Cunningham-Rathner, Rouleau et al., 1984; P. C. Alexander, Neimeyer, Follette, Moore, & Harter, 1989; Barnard, Fuller, Robbins, & Shaw, 1989; Briere, 1989; Courtois, 1988; Jehu, 1989a; Kelly, 1982; Marshall & Barbaree, 1988; Meiselman, 1990; Salter, 1988), progress in empirically validating treatment programs for children has lagged behind (see Friedrich, 1990, for guidelines). Concerns about the iatrogenic effects of therapy for child victims have also been raised (Haugaard & Reppucci, 1988; Kolko, 1987; Wakefield & Underwager, 1988). In response to the common and traumatic nature of CSA, and because of a humanitarian desire to help children avoid the suffering associated with sexual victimization, a movement developed to prevent its occurrence.

PREVENTION
The impetus behind CSA prevention can be traced to several movements beginning in the 1970s and continuing into the 1990s. In the late 1960s and early 1970s, the women's movement helped to increase society's awareness of the CSA problem. In groups across the country, participants discussed not only the problems of being female in modern society but also shared the common trauma of sexual exploitation in adulthood and similar experiences during childhood. Several courageous women wrote about

their histories of sexual abuse as children, sharing not only their abusive experiences but also others' failure to believe them and to intervene (Allen, 1980; Armstrong, 1978; Butler, 1978). Researchers became more willing to listen to these victims, systematically study the problem, and express their concerns publicly (Finkelhor, 1979). Their work confirmed what had long been suspected—that a substantial proportion of adults had been sexually abused as children—and thus provided a scientific data base supporting the reality of CSA. With scientific backing for their cause, the focus of the women's antirape movement broadened into a movement against CSA.

As early as 1975, several rape crisis centers had designed prevention talks for adolescents, focusing mainly on rape by strangers or dates (Plummer, 1986). By 1977, several were providing classroom-based instruction for children of all ages. Programs designed to prevent CSA began springing up across the country. The grassroots prevention movement received a boost when federal dollars were designated in 1980 for the study of such programs. Federal endorsement for prevention programs served to emphasize the enormity of the problem and to inspire other communities to develop and use prevention programs. In regards to CSA, "an ounce of prevention" has had a powerful appeal, specifically for classroom-based instruction.

The late 1970s also marked a time of national interest in the prevention of psychological disorders. The prevention movement stemmed from the Community Mental Health Center (CMHC) Construction Act of 1963, which called for the prevention of psychological disorders to have a significant role in CMHCs. In response to the President's Commission on Mental Health, appointed by President Carter (Report to the President, 1978), the National Institute of Mental Health (NIMH) established a Center for Studies of Prevention to encourage, fund, and coordinate research and prevention activities in mental health. At the state level, Children's Trust Funds were developed in the late 1970s as a way of providing financial support for child abuse prevention programs in communities, and these funds currently operate in 49 states (NCPCA, 1990). Throughout the 1980s, the prevention movement flourished and saw the emergence of professional journals devoted to prevention in mental health (e.g., *The Journal of Primary Prevention*), several books and chapters of books (e.g., Felner, Jason, Moritsugu, & Farber, 1983; Roberts & Peterson, 1984), conferences (e.g., the Vermont Conferences on the Primary Prevention of Psychopathology), and organizations (e.g., National Prevention Coalition; National Committee for the Prevention of Child Abuse) supporting the prevention philosophy. Thus, a large body of knowledge exists to potentially guide CSA prevention efforts.

The child advocacy movement also flourished during this time, as physical child abuse quickly rose to prominence as a social problem in the 1970s. The passage of the federal Child Abuse Prevention and Treatment Act (PL 93-247) in 1974 served as a significant catalyst for federal and state efforts to recognize and address the problem of child maltreatment (including CSA) and also stimulated research on the prevention of abuse and neglect. To implement the objectives of the act, the National Center on Child Abuse and Neglect (NCCAN) was established. NCCAN's definition of child abuse and neglect (presented earlier in this chapter under the heading "Defining the Child Sexual Abuse Problem") moved beyond a specific focus on physical abuse and neglect and into the more controversial areas of emotional maltreatment and CSA.

As part of the victim's rights movement, concern about victims of sexual and nonsexual abuse also grew during the 1970s and into the 1980s. Along with concerns about the welfare of adult victims of sexual and nonsexual abuse came concerns about the way the criminal justice system was handling these cases; ultimately this focus expanded to include how the same system treats child victims of sex crimes.

The confluence of these movements in the 1980s resulted in concern about CSA on a national level. During this decade, the general public has been exposed to a vast amount of publicity regarding CSA, including news coverage of highly publicized cases (e.g., the McMartin Preschool trial in Los Angeles), cover stories (e.g., *Newsweek, Life*), TV news programs (e.g., *60 Minutes*, 20-

*20, Nightline*), and movies (e.g., *Something About Amelia*). This exposure has served to make people aware of a social problem that previously was not talked about and has led to the adoption of CSA prevention programs for children across the nation.

Some individuals, however, are beginning to question the efficacy of child-focused sexual abuse prevention programs and are raising the question of whether they may do more harm than good (Bales, 1988). Some researchers have even advocated the phasing out of educational programs for young children (e.g., Gilbert, Berrick, Le Prohn, & Nyman, 1989). By and large, these prevention programs have been adopted without undergoing systematic evaluation. Such programs, as well as CSA prevention efforts in general, have also been criticized because they are based on anecdotal information rather than empirical study. Prevention efforts have also flourished in the absence of a theoretical foundation. This state of affairs has come about, in part, because of our limited understanding of the etiology of CSA.

## Etiology of Child Sexual Abuse

Major steps toward more effective prevention cannot take place without a firm understanding of why children are sexually abused. In this section, we haved compiled numerous conceptualizations about the presumed causes of the CSA problem. CSA has been conceptualized as an individual phenomenon with roots in the vulnerability of children or the psychodynamics of abusers, as a symptom of a dysfunctional family, and as a sociocultural phenomenon in which social and cultural forces play a role in precipitating abuse.

INDIVIDUAL LEVEL:
THE CHARACTERISTICS OF THE CHILD
Several researchers have proposed that certain characteristics of children might make them vulnerable to CSA. Child victims have been described as isolated (Finkelhor, 1979) and having strong needs for attention, affection, and approval (Berliner & Conte, 1990; Erickson, Egeland, & Pianta, 1989; Finkelhor et al., 1990;

Peters, 1976). Their few social ties, coupled with strong needs for affection and attention, are seen as increasing their vulnerability to the attention and affection of a potential molester. Other characteristics of children that may make them vulnerable to abuse include their limited decision making or problem solving skills, natural passivity and submission to authority, and limited knowledge about sexuality and sexual abuse.

INDIVIDUAL LEVEL:
THE CHARACTERISTICS OF THE PERPETRATOR
Offender dysfunction theories view sexual abuse as resulting from the perpetrator's pathology. Early attempts at explaining CSA relied upon the psychiatric model, which assumed that the causes of abuse were to be found in the aberrant personality characteristics of the perpetrator. (The reader should note that the following information is based on research with male perpetrators.)

*Psychopathology.* For example, early offender dysfunction theories viewed abusers as psychotic, brain damaged, senile, or mentally retarded (Ellis, 1933; von Krafft-Ebing, 1935; Weinberg, 1955). Recent research, however, has not supported the etiological role of psychiatric, intellectual, or neurological problems (Langevin, Wortzman, Wright, & Handy, 1989). A variety of less severe forms of psychopathology have been described in connection with sexual abusers, including disregard for the concerns of others (psychopathy; e.g., Scott & Stone, 1986) or inadequate control of impulses (Bresee, Stearns, Bess, & Packer, 1986; Groth et al., 1982; Summit & Kryso, 1978). There is evidence that some molesters are shy, unassertive, overly sensitive about their performance with women, and deficient in heterosocial skills (Abel, Mittelman, & Becker, 1985; Howells, 1981; Katz, 1990; Langevin, 1983; Overholser & Beck, 1986; Segal & Marshall, 1985). Others have described them as having deep-seated feelings of vulnerability, dependency, inadequacy, immaturity, and emotional loneliness (Groth, 1982; Groth et al., 1982; Marshall, 1989). Their inappropriate relationships with children may be attempts to have some of these needs met.

*Sexual Arousal and History of Sexual Victimization.* Perpetrators seek out sexual encounters with children primarily because they are sexually attracted to children (Abel, Becker, & Cunningham-Rathner, 1984; Finkelhor, 1984; Langevin, 1983; Marshall, Barbaree, & Butt, 1988). The origins or causes of their sexual attraction are less well understood. Many have suggested that childhood sexual victimization contributes to perpetrating sexual abuse as an adult (see review by Hanson & Slater, 1988). For example, Overholser and Beck (1989) note that 58% of their child molesters report being molested as children, compared with 25% of their rapists and only 5% of matched controls. Previous sexual victimization has also been reported in 25% to 61% of male and 100% of female adolescent sexual offenders (Becker, Kaplan, Cunningham-Rathner, & Kavoussi, 1986; T. C. Johnson, 1988, 1989; T. J. Kahn & Lafond, 1988; Katz, 1990; W. Smith, 1988).

There have been many attempts to explain how previous victimization might lead to the later abuse of children. For example, Groth (1979b) has noted:

> The offender's adult crimes may be in part the repetitious actings out of sex offenses he was subjected to as a child and as such may represent a maladaptive effort to solve an unresolved early sexual trauma or series of traumas. It can be observed, especially with reference to the child molester, that his later offenses appear to duplicate his own molestation. (p. 15)

From an information-processing perspective, subsequent abuse is viewed as an effort to assimilate and master the anxiety resulting from the previous abuse (Hartman & Burgess, 1988). Perhaps lacking a nurturing parental relationship, being betrayed as a child, or repeatedly having one's needs subordinated to those of the perpetrator stifles the development of empathy or sensitivity to others (Ginsburg, Wright, Harrell, & Hill, 1989; Rohner, 1975). (Deficits in offenders' ability to empathize with their children have frequently been found in the incest literature; L. M. Williams & Finkelhor, 1990.) Repeatedly having one's needs subordinated to those of a perpetrator and having one's body invaded or manipulated may also result in unmet dependency needs, thus contributing to feelings of powerlessness and a later need to exploit others to regain personal power and control. Sexual abuse may lower a child's self-esteem, and the subsequent sexual offense involving control over a child's body and will may be a way of restoring self-worth. Still another possibility is that by identifying with the aggressor, the child victim develops a sense of entitlement to exploit others, including sexually. Perhaps by experiencing victimization (either directly or indirectly by witnessing the sexual abuse of siblings or other children), the offender learns through modeling that children can be used for sexual gratification (Laws & Marshall, 1990).

Although research on the intergenerational transmission of sexual abuse can be questioned on methodological grounds (e.g., reliance on retrospective designs, self-report data, and correlational studies; lack of appropriate comparison groups; perpetrators reporting histories of abuse as rationalizations for their behaviors), it is likely that some association exists. Fortunately, most children who are sexually abused do not grow up to abuse other children. This is particularly true for women. (Given that most child molesters are males, identifying with the aggressor may be easier for boys than for girls.) Instead, many females seem to respond to childhood sexual abuse by internalizing the experience of victimization. Some become victims of additional abuse (from their own acts as in self-abusive or self-destructive behaviors) or they become victims of rape (P. C. Alexander & Lupfer, 1987; Koss & Dinero, 1989; D. E. H. Russell, 1984a; Sedney & Brooks, 1984). Perhaps female victims learn to sacrifice their own needs, leaving them devoid of self-protective mechanisms and more vulnerable to subsequent abuse and exploitation (Carmen & Rieker, 1989).

As with physical abuse (see J. Kaufman & Zigler, 1987), being sexually abused as a child may put one at risk for becoming abusive, but the association is far from complete. There is no simple causal relationship between early sexual victimization and subsequent status as an adult molester; previous victimization must interact with other personal, situational, or sociocultural factors to increase the risk of abusing. Research is needed into what mediates the effects of CSA to allow victims to break the cycle. Why do some people who were victimized as children grow up to victimize other children, whereas others escape the cyclical pattern? Some evidence in the physical abuse literature suggests that having social supports (e.g., via personal or therapeutic relationships), fewer life stresses, and coming to terms with one's history of abuse can help to break its intergenerational transmission (Egeland, Jacobvitz, & Papatola, 1987; Egeland, Jacobvitz, & Sroufe, 1988).

*Disinhibitors.* Not all individuals who are sexually aroused by children act on their feelings. There have been many attempts to explain how inhibitions about adult-child sex might be overcome (see also Finkelhor's (1984) Four Preconditions Model). For example, some have speculated that perpetrators misattribute certain feelings (e.g., anger; anxiety; feelings evoked by children; arousing effects of alcohol) as "sexual" emotions (Howells, 1981; Marshall & Christie, 1981). Alcoholism and substance abuse have also been proposed as disinhibiting factors (Abel et al., 1985; Finkelhor, 184; Peters, 1976; Rada, 1976). Others may develop elaborate cognitive distortions to rationalize and defend their behavior (e.g., "Having sex with children is a good way to teach them about sex," "No one is injured by it," "It is better to abuse a daughter than to have an affair or to seek out a prostitute," "Children need to be liberated from the sexually repressive bonds of society"; see Abel, Becker, & Cunningham-Rathner, 1984; Abel et al., 1989; de Young, 1988; Segal & Stermac, 1990; T. A. Smith, 1987; Stermac & Segal, 1989). (Whether such cognitions develop as rationalizations for perpetrators' sexual misbehavior or play an etiological role in the development of their sexual interest in children has yet to be determined.) Another powerful disinhibitor may be the child's initial acceptance of the activity or willingness to participate.

*Deviant Fantasies.* Sexual arousal and disinhibitions serve to initiate the abuse; the basic urge for sexual contact with children can be maintained or strengthened through fantasies of sexual activity with children and masturbating to those fantasies (Laws & Marshall, 1990). Clinicians working with offenders note that most sex offenders have a long history of masturbating to deviant fantasies of sexual activity with children (Salter, 1988). The pleasure derived from masturbation and/or the sexual assault reinforces and strengthens sexual impulses toward children and increases the likelihood that perpetrators will continue to exploit children.

*Situational Factors.* Situational factors have also been proposed to account for child molesting, such as when perpetrators commit sexual abuse during periods of personal stress (e.g., unemployment, loss of a sexual partner). These factors are viewed as increasing the likelihood that someone who is sexually interested in children might act on those feelings. The processes through which stressors trigger sexual abuse are likely varied. Unemployment, for example, can result in frustration over lack of monetary resources. Its resulting sense of powerlessness might promote sexual exploitation of children if status is regained by manipulating defenseless children. The psychological and health effects of unemployment have been shown to be substantial, often resulting in major depression, alcohol abuse, and family (including father-child) disturbances (Liem & Ramsay, 1982; McLoyd, 1989). In addition to its role of inducing stress, unemployment can also leave a father at home alone with his children and provide opportunities for sexual exploitation. No evidence exists, however, to support a causal relationship between unemployment and CSA. Instead of a direct cause, unemployment could be a symptom of interpersonal ineffectiveness or other psychological problems that, in turn, may be more directly related to the abuse.

Having financial problems in general may function as a disinhibitor of sexual impulses. Low income has been implicated as a risk factor in CSA, although results regarding socioeconomic status have been inconsistent (Finkelhor, 1984; D. E. H. Russell, 1986; Wyatt, 1985). The second National Incidence Study (DHHS, 1988) found sexual abuse to be five times more frequent among children from lower-income (i.e., those whose annual income was less than $15,000) homes than among those from families with higher incomes. Of course, it is important to recognize that reporting rates may vary across socioeconomic groups. Furthermore, if poverty had a direct effect on CSA, we would expect many more women, particularly single mothers, to be perpetrators. (In 1987, mother-only families received an average annual income of $9,838, only 28% of the $35,423 average for two-parent families; Bianchi, 1990.) There is some support, however, for the hypothesis that poverty, when linked with family disruption, may play a role in CSA (Gomes-Schwartz et al., 1990). A survey of a nationally representative sample of economically diverse parents asking about a history of sexual abuse among their children would help to examine potential socioeconomic differences. Controlled studies are also needed to determine whether CSA rates in an area change when socioeconomic stress levels increase or decrease.

It is also important to consider the context in which the abuse occurs. Potential perpetrators must have access to potential victims. Situations in which offenders are alone with children, especially if they are in positions of authority, increase the likelihood of abuse.

FAMILY LEVEL

Moving beyond a single-factor model, family dysfunction models view incest as a symptom of a dysfunctional family system. These theories hold that the family in general and mother in particular play central roles in creating the environment that permits and possibly encourages the sexual victimization of children. It is believed that the incest develops as a way of maintaining the behavior and interaction patterns of the family. Because these theories have been proposed primarily to account for intrafamilial abuse where females are the victims, their heuristic value in explaining extrafamilial CSA or cases where males are the victims remains limited. We will note where findings have supported the role of family factors in extrafamilial CSA.

*Marital Conflict.* Marital conflict has been frequently related to both intrafamilial (M. Gordon, 1989; Lustig, Dresser, Spellman, & Murray, 1966; Molnar & Cameron, 1975; Paveza, 1988; Weinberg, 1955) and extrafamilial CSA (Finkelhor, 1979; Gruber

& Jones, 1983). Several explanations for how poor parental relations might be related to CSA have been proposed. For example, to reduce the tension that exists within the marital relationship, a father might distance himself from his wife by turning his sexual and emotional attention to his daughter. This distancing stabilizes the marital conflict and reduces the likelihood of a breakup. Marital conflict may leave children insecure and anxious about being abandoned, which in turn may lead to sex between family members in an effort to prevent family disintegration (Lustig et al., 1966). To explain how marital conflict might be related to extrafamilial abuse, Gruber and Jones (1983) suggest that victims living in an unstable home may seek some sense of emotional stability (i.e., through compensatory personal relationships) outside of the home. Additionally, marital discord may lower children's self-esteem, which in turn increases their vulnerability to offers of affection. Further, parents who are preoccupied with their marital conflicts may not adequately supervise their children, and children are more vulnerable to sexual abuse when they are poorly supervised (DeFrancis, 1969; Sgroi, 1982a).

*Isolation.* Incestuous families have also been characterized by a high degree of social (Bagley, 1969; Finkelhor, 1979; Weinberg, 1955; L. M. Williams & Finkelhor, 1990) and geographic isolation (D. Henderson, 1972). In fact, all forms of abuse have been associated with families that are isolated and lack social support through community ties, friendships, or organizational affiliations (Garbarino, 1977; Gelles, 1974; Straus, Gelles, & Steinmetz, 1980). Given the important role social support plays in reducing the psychological impact of stress (Liem & Liem, 1978; Mitchell, Billings, & Moos, 1982), an absence or inadequacy of support may leave family members more vulnerable. Being isolated from the scrutiny of outside parties is also thought to create a climate in which sex between family members is allowed to occur. Family members turn toward each other for support and stimulation (including sexual gratification), instead of toward people outside the family. Social and geographic isolation also render discovery by outside parties less likely, thus allowing the abuse to continue. An isolated environment may also make the child more susceptible to offers of attention and affection. Alternatively, abuse-prone families may gravitate toward isolated areas to avoid detection, or both abuse and isolation may reflect personal or interpersonal deficits.

*Sexual Milieu.* Some researchers have suggested that incestuous families are oversexualized, where children are sexually stimulated by their own parents in homes characterized by a "loose sex culture" (de Young, 1982). Here, obscenities, nudity, overt sexual behavior, and pornography may be pervasive. Children in these homes may become prematurely sexually stimulated; in combination with limited supervision, this stimulation can lead to sexual imitation (de Young, 1981).

In contrast, others have described homes in which CSA is present as sexually punitive and lacking in information about sex (Finkelhor, 1984). Children who grow up in families where sexual information is absent, limited, or inaccurate may be more vulnerable to offenders' assurances about the appropriateness of the sexual behavior. In addition, parents who prohibit or punish normal sexual behaviors in their children (e.g., masturbation) could create a climate whereby children feel guilty about their sexual feelings or perceive their genitals negatively. When these natural tendencies are suppressed or punished, the child's sexual development is negatively affected, which might increase the risk of being victimized or of becoming a victimizer.

*Family Stability.* The composition of the family has also been given an etiological role in CSA. Living without a natural parent has been identified as a major risk factor in a number of studies (Finkelhor et al., 1990; Goldman & Goldman, 1988; Gomes-Schwartz et al., 1990; D. E. H. Russell, 1986). Boys living with their mothers alone or with two nonnatural parents were found to be at risk in Finkelhor et al. (1990). Girls with stepfathers and father substitutes (e.g., mother's boyfriend) appear to be more vulnerable to sexual victimization, both by the father substitute and by outside friends and family members (Finkelhor, 1979; M. Gordon, 1989; M. Gordon & Creighton, 1988; Gruber & Jones,

1983; Margolin & Craft, 1989; Parker & Parker, 1986; D. E. H. Russell, 1984b).

A number of explanations have been proposed to account for the increased vulnerability in reconstituted families. The dramatic changes to which a reconstituted family must accommodate may result in disorganization and stress, leaving the entire family more vulnerable. Stepfathers and paramours may also bring family members and friends into the home who may not be as protective of the children as they would be of the natural children of a friend (Finkelhor, 1979). There may be less of a commitment to a father role on the part of the stepfather (M. Gordon & Creighton, 1988), and if his friends and acquaintances sense a lack of protective feelings, they may assume the same posture toward the children. A stepfather's lack of involvement in early child care and nurturance may also be a risk factor for subsequent CSA (Parker & Parker, 1986), as it is theorized that intimacy early in life serves to neutralize sexual desire (R. Fox, 1980). Finally, the taboos against stepfather-stepdaughter sexual contact may be weaker and therefore have less of a deterrent effect (de Young, 1982; D. E. H. Russell, 1984b).

*Family Dynamics.* Those who focus on family dynamics view incestuous families as socializing some members into the role of perpetrator, others into silent partners, and others into victims. One line of inquiry has been on how power is distributed in the marital dyad, with some characterizing the families as strongly male dominated, where the father is an aggressive and dominant individual who turns to his daughter to fulfill his emotional and sexual needs because his wife is insecure and immature (Browning & Boatman, 1977; Finkelhor, 1979; Herman, 1981; Summit & Kryso, 1978). In the other type of incestuous family, the mother is described as hostile and dominant and the father as a dependent and passive individual who turns to his daughter as a substitute wife and mother (Groth, 1982; Peters, 1976). Common to both types of families are power imbalances.

There is some empirical support for the power imbalance theory. For example, P. C. Alexander and Lupfer (1987) found that female university students who had experienced incest rated their family structure as having greater power differences in male-female relationships than those who either had been victims of extrafamilial sexual abuse or had not been abused. The finding that incestuous fathers are likely to physically abuse their wives at the same time they are sexually abusing their children (Paveza, 1988; Sirles & Franke, 1989; Truesdell, McNeil, & Deschner, 1986) also provides support for the power imbalance theory.

Another characteristic of families thought to predispose children to sexual abuse is the blurring of boundaries between parents and children, a characteristic of "enmeshed" families. By definition, an adult's use of a child for his or her own gratification constitutes role confusion. Numerous writers have also commented on parent-child role reversal, in which an incapacitated or absent mother assigns maternal role to the child, so that the daughter assumes many of the household and child care responsibilities, and by natural extension, the sexual responsibilities (Browning & Boatman, 1977; Jehu, 1989b; Justice & Justice, 1979; Lustig et al., 1966; P. B. Mrazek, 1981b; Summit & Kryso, 1978). Although there are exceptions (Carson, Gertz, Donaldson, & Wonderlich, 1990), some research has supported a theory of boundary problems in incestuous families (Hoagwood & Stewart, 1989). For example, P. C. Alexander (1985) describes a lower middle-class incestuous family in which the whole family used the same toothbrush, the teen-age girls shared the same bra, and the four girls shared two twin beds. In addition, Sgroi (1982a) argues that other examples of blurred boundaries (e.g., inappropriate genital exposure, lack of privacy with respect to bathroom and sleeping arrangements, and permitting children to witness or participate in physically intimate behaviors) may predispose to CSA.

*Characteristics of Mothers.* A number of theories focus on how mothers contribute in direct or indirect ways to their children's victimization. (See K. McIntyre, 1981, and Wattenberg, 1985, for feminist analyses of "mother-blaming" in the incest literature.) Unfortunately, research on mothers has often relied on clinical impressions or retrospective data. It must be noted that many of the so-called contributing characteristics ascribed to mothers could be the result of living with a perpetrator.

I. Kaufman, Peck, and Tagiuri (1954) believed mothers unconsciously gave their daughters permission for the incestuous behavior "by setting up a situation where this could occur" (p.276). They provided the example of a mother who placed her daughter in bed with her husband while she went to another room to escape his snoring. Others have asserted that mothers are aware of or even collude in the sexual abuse of their daughters (Bagley, 1969; Brant & Tisza, 1977; D. Henderson, 1972; Justice & Justice, 1979; Zuelzer & Reposa, 1983). Mothers have also been held responsible for the abuse by "denying" sexual relations to their husbands, thereby increasing their husbands' sexual frustration (D. Henderson, 1972; Justice & Justice, 1979; Lustig et al., 1966; Maisch, 1972; Weiner, 1962). Yet, in his work with incarcerated offenders, Groth (1979a) did not find evidence to support the etiological factor of sexual frustration:

> In fact, the sexual encounters with children coexisted with sexual contacts with adults. For example, in incest cases, we found that the men were having sexual relations with their daughters or sons *in addition to*, rather than instead of, sexual relations with their wives. (Groth, 1979a, p.146; emphasis ours)

A perpetrator's report that the sexual activity with a child stemmed from sexual frustration may be self-serving. Indeed, Salter (1988) notes that many sex offenders will blame their sexual deviancy on either the wife's or victim's behavior. Accepting such rationalizations is naïve and can only lead to error and unfair mother- and victim-blaming.

Mothers of incest victims have been described as dependent, inadequate, and infantile (Herman & Hirschman, 1977; Justice & Justice, 1979; Lustig et al., 1966; Rist, 1979), physically and/or emotionally incapacitated (Browning & Boatman, 1977; Herman & Hirschman, 1981; Maisch, 1972), or absent because of divorce, sickness, or even full-time employment (Herman & Hirschman, 1981; I. Kaufman et al., 1954; Maisch, 1972). A poor mother-daughter relationship has also been proposed as an etiological factor (Finkelhor, 1979; Forward & Buck, 1978; Herman & Hirschman, 1977), as it is thought to increase the daughter's need for affection and decrease the likelihood that she would turn toward her mother for support and protection. Some support for a conflicted relationship between incest mothers and their daughters exists (P. M. Cole & Woolger, 1989; Levang, 1989), although a poor relationship could be the result, not cause, of the abuse.

An increased risk of abuse (both intrafamilial and extrafamilial) among the children of women who were themselves sexually victimized during childhood has also been noted (Faller, 1989b; Gomes-Schwartz et al., 1990; Goodwin, McCarthy, & DiVasto, 1981; Rosenfeld, Nadelson, & Krieger, 1979). For example, Goodwin et al. (1981) found a significantly higher prevalence of a history of incest in mothers of abused children (24%) compared with a roughly matched group of control women (3%). (Note that the majority of mothers did not have a history of abuse.) Several hypotheses have been proposed to explain why their children may be at higher risk. Lacking an adequate representation of a secure mother-child relationship, previously victimized mothers may contribute to their children's abuse through emotional and physical distance from their children (Friedrich, 1990; Goodwin et al., 1981). Faller (1988; 1989b) suggests that these women may gravitate toward men who are similar to their own abusers or who will not make sexual demands upon them because they are sexually attracted to children. These mothers may also have a difficult time discussing the topic of sexual abuse with their own children, as raising these issues may bring back painful memories (Finkelhor, 1984).

SOCIOCULTURAL LEVEL
Moving into the larger context of the community and society, the sociocultural model identifies the cultural and social forces that may play a role in socializing individuals into sexually abusive behavior. Many of the models implicate societal attitudes and beliefs regarding children, male-female relationships, sexuality, and adult-child sexual relationships.

*Attitudes Toward Children.* Rush (1980) points out that traditionally both women and children have shared the same minority status and have been viewed as helpless, dependent, and powerless, and consequently both have been sexually used and abused by men. She has extensively documented how sexual relationships between adult males and children have been sanctioned by religion and law throughout history. As noted by Walters (1975), "The . . . sexual abuse of children does not occur in a cultural vacuum. Rather, America has a long history of treating children as inferiors, as little more than chattel to be done with as the adult caretaker pleases" (p.9). Pogrebin (1983) observes: "America is a nation fundamentally ambivalent about its children, often afraid of its children, and frequently punitive toward its children" (p.42). These attitudes provide support for the maltreatment of children and suggest that children are not highly valued. A low value placed on children is also reflected in the number of children who live in economically impoverished environments and who lack adequate health and substitute child care.

*Male Socialization.* One area of consensus about CSA is that it is committed mostly by men. This preponderance exists despite the fact that men spend far less time with children and are less often the primary caregivers for children. From a sociological perspective, it is important to speculate whether there are aspects of male socialization that play contributory roles. For example, instead of identifying specific personality disorders that might "cause" perpetrating behavior, Rothblum, Solomon, and Albee (1986) encourage researchers to seek the "cause of the causes," by looking "for the larger cause in the sexist nature of our society with its emphasis on male domination of females, with the focus in the mass media on male violence and female passivity, and with a pervasive and subtle sexism that is everywhere present" (p.169).

In attempting to answer the question of why CSA is a predominantly male behavior, Finkelhor and Lewis (1988) turn to the problem of masculine sexualization and consider several hypotheses, including: (a) given that sex is one of the few acceptable vehicles through which most men can have their emotional needs met, sexual abuse may result from an oversexualization of the normal emotional needs evoked by children; (b) men are socialized to be attracted to sexual partners who are younger, smaller, and more vulnerable than themselves, whereas women are socialized to be attracted to sexual partners who are older, larger, and more powerful; and (c) through their socialization, the development of empathy toward children is blocked in a number of ways (e.g., child care acquires a negative connotation for boys; masculinization results in a disdain for such childlike emotional characteristics as neediness or immaturity).

Gilgun (1988) suggests that the socialization of males for stoicism may be a factor in the overrepresentation of males among child sexual abusers. Not being in touch with their own feelings results in self-centeredness, which she believes is a part of a causal chain leading to exploitative behaviors. Others have implicated both gender and generational power inequalities to explain CSA (Breines & Gordon, 1983; Gross, 1978; Herman, 1981; Hite, 1981; D. E. H. Russell, 1984a). Thus, males and adults are viewed as having greater power than females and children, and CSA results from an abuse of this power.

Feminist writers have claimed that socialization processes for men emphasize gratification as an end in itself and promote an orientation in which they see the other person as an object, to be used for their sexual gratification (DeBeauvoir, 1953). Louise Armstrong, author of *Kiss Daddy Goodnight: A Speakout on Incest*, asserts that an incestuous father must have "a sense of paternalistic prerogative in order to even begin to rationalize what he's doing. . . . He must have a perception of his children as possessions, as objects" (1978, pp.234–235). In their work with male perpetrators, Gilgun and Connor (1989) found that they perceived the children not as persons, but as objects, during the sexual act. When children are regarded as possessions, unusual and undetected liberties can be taken with them. The possession of children by their parents has been given legal and religious sanction throughout history and the legacy of the patriarchal family system remains with us today (Rush, 1980).

If the male socialization model is carried to its logical extension, all men would be rapists or child molesters. Obviously (and thankfully) they are not. Furthermore, patriarchal norms regarding masculine socialization are changing. There is increasing societal concern about women's and children's rights along with a decreasing acceptance of male dominance. Even with these changes, we have not seen a reduction in the incidence of sexual abuse. It is simplistic and incorrect to assume that male socialization factors are the sole cause of CSA. For certain individuals, however, these factors might provide a context that promotes or condones the sexual exploitation of children.

*Mass Media and Pornography.* Erotic portrayals of children in advertising and in the mass media may stimulate adult sexual interest in children. Child pornography is another cultural factor that may stimulate sexual interest in children (Rush, 1980; D. E. H. Russell, 1988). Child pornography is defined as photographs, films, videotapes, magazines, and books that depict male or female children (up to ages 16–18, depending upon the state) in sexually explicit acts. The exact contribution of pornography to the commission of sexual crimes against children remains uncertain (see review by Murrin & Laws, 1990). Some researchers have found no support for the hypothesized relationship between pornography use and child sexual offending (Langevin et al., 1988; Malamuth & Briere, 1986), whereas others have found that child molesters do use pornography, even more than rapists (Carter, Prentky, Knight, Vanderveer, & Boucher, 1987).

It has also been suggested that pornography serves as a releaser of sexual violence only among those people who have had early sexual activity and interest (Donnerstein, 1984; Koss & Dinero, 1988). Child pornography can harm children both directly (e.g., physically and psychologically) and indirectly, by helping to maintain male dominance, objectifying children, and supporting interpersonal violence (Knudsen, 1988; Malamuth & Briere, 1986; Wheeler, 1985). Exposure to child pornography may teach potential offenders to become aroused by children, or masturbating to this material may maintain an arousal to children. Such material also increases the legitimacy and removes the inhibitions about having sex with children (Finkelhor, 1984), creates a market for children to be victimized, and is used by offenders to educate and stimulate victims (Langevin et al., 1988). It is also used as blackmail, to reinforce children's sense of responsibility for the abuse and thus ensure their silence (Burgess & Hartman, 1987; Hunt & Baird, 1990).

*Attitudes Toward Sexuality.* Beliefs and values regarding sexuality must also be considered, such as widespread social support for sexually coercive behavior (Burt, 1980). Repressive sexual norms about masturbation could serve to block alternative sexual outlets for perpetrators. Society's repressive attitudes toward sexuality in general and childhood sexuality in particular make it difficult for children to obtain information about appropriate and inappropriate sexual behavior. Even researchers have been reluctant to explore the subject of childhood sexuality, which "lies mostly in that territory at the edges of our psychological maps bearing only the legend, 'Here there be dragons' " (Constantine & Martinson, 1981, p.3). Thus, we know very little about how normal or deviant sexual behaviors develop. In addition, schools are reluctant to educate children about the topic, and few parents discuss sexuality with their children. Consequently, there is a general neglect of children's sexual development both at home and at school, and children and adolescents are left on their own with regard to knowledge or concerns about sexuality. Unfortunately, by trying to keep children innocent, we keep them ignorant and thus vulnerable to sexual exploitation.

*Prosecution of Perpetrators.* Finally, Armstrong (1983) proposes that the reluctance of contemporary legal systems to prosecute and punish offenders makes it easier for potential molesters. Such leniency may reflect society's condoning of adult-child sexual activities. In contrast, a strong possibility of being caught, apprehended, and punished would likely serve as an inhibitor for potential offenders, as well as an educational function for the general population.

CRITIQUE OF ETIOLOGICAL THEORIES

A review of the various theories makes it clear that a consensus regarding the etiology of CSA is lacking. Some have argued that certain characteristics of children make them more vulnerable to abuse, whereas others contend that disturbances in the offender's psychological makeup, characteristics of the family in general or mother in particular, situational stressors, or cultural beliefs and values are primarily responsible for CSA. Current knowledge about etiology is fragmented because different professionals have addressed the problem from different perspectives, each emphasizing one dimension of a problem that is, in fact, multidimensional. Placing responsibility for CSA with only one party, whether it be the perpetrator, the victim, or the mother, and neglecting to consider other factors limits the explanatory power of any one theory.

Another limitation of these "unitary" (C. M. Newberger & Newberger, 1982) models of causality is that many of the proposed causes could instead be the results of the abuse (e.g., marital conflict) or symptoms of other underlying causes more directly related to the abuse (e.g., social isolation as a symptom of family disorganization; Finkelhor, 1979). Furthermore, many of the individual factors that supposedly differentiate offenders from non-offenders (e.g., history of maltreatment) or incestuous families from nonincestuous ones (e.g., marital conflict) characterize many persons and families who do not exploit children. In studying this complex problem it is extremely difficult to separate out the antecedent conditions, correlates, and effects of sexual exploitation (Tierney & Corwin, 1983). No causes have yet been identified, only factors that are related to the abuse.

## From Theory to Policy: A Comprehensive Prevention Response

We approach the sexual victimization of children as a behavior that is influenced by factors inherent at several different levels: the individual, family, and sociocultural. Characteristics of offenders most likely interact with child characteristics, as well as familial and sociocultural factors, in fostering the sexual exploitation of children (see Figure 1). Considering the person-environment inter-

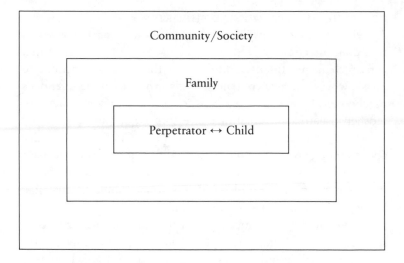

Figure 1. An ecological model of CSA

action is the hallmark of the ecological model (Bronfenbrenner, 1977, 1979), a term that highlights the interaction between and among various elements in each system. Using the language of Bronfenbrenner, the child's and offender's individual risk factors (the Ontogenic system) are embedded in the characteristics of the child's family (or other Microsystems such as school, day care), which are nested within the context of the community/society (the Macrosystem).

According to this multifactor model, CSA is seen as occurring in a context consisting of a person predisposed to viewing children as sexual objects, who has access to children who are vulnerable to exploitation (related to inadequate supervision and/or the child's lack of knowledge or need for attention), and who functions in an environment that promotes (or condones) the sexual activity. These individual, familial, and environmental factors interact to lower the threshold for perpetrating CSA. Undoubtedly, diverse interactions of variables can form multiple pathways to abuse. Research is needed to determine what combination of variables heighten the risk of sexual maltreatment. Given its lack of empirical validity, this multifactor causation model is intended to be descriptive and to facilitate prevention planning.

### TARGETING CHILD SEXUAL ABUSE RISK AND COMPENSATORY FACTORS

Clearly there is no simple answer to the question, "Why would someone sexually abuse a child?". CSA is a complex phenomenon: there is neither a single kind of act committed against children, nor a single cause that gives rise to the exploitation. There are many possible causes. Perhaps we are asking the wrong question. Instead of looking for the "why," which implies causation, a more heuristic approach for directing prevention efforts may be to focus on the "how." Asking, "How did the abuse happen?" directs our attention to the individual, familial, situational, and societal dynamics that increase the probability that a child would be sexually exploited. It is clear that we need a model for understanding the process by which abuse might occur. From the research on etiology reviewed previously, we have compiled a list of risk factors thought to increase the likelihood of abuse occurring (see Table 2).

First, there are factors in the potential offender that predispose some individuals toward using children sexually. These factors are mentioned first because a perpetrator's interest in involving a child in sexual activities is a prerequisite for sexual abuse. The perpetrator has some sexual attraction toward children and is willing to act upon those sexual feelings. The willingness to act may be a function of certain personality factors, disinhibiting factors (Finkelhor, 1984), situational stresses, beliefs that support sexual offending, or a childhood history that provided exploitative models and/or lacked nurturing ones.

Second, factors within a child, such as lack of knowledge regarding sexual behavior, hunger for attention, or low self-esteem, may make certain children more vulnerable than others. Characteristics of children make sense as elicitors of abuse *only* when considered vis-à-vis the offender's attributes (Belsky, 1980). Characteristics of the child's family may also contribute to an exploitative situation. Children who are emotionally needy, insecure

## Table 2: Possible Risk and Protective Factors Associated With Child Sexual Abuse

| Components of CSA | Risk Factors | Protective Factors |
|---|---|---|
| Offender | Male<br>Sexual attraction toward children<br>Lack of empathic concern for children<br>Cognitions or fantasies supporting sexual contact with children<br>Poor impulse control<br>Narcissistic identification with children<br>Use of alcohol/drugs to lower inhibitions<br>History of abuse or betrayal<br>Feelings of inadequacy, loneliness, vulnerability, dependency<br>Poor interpersonal (especially heterosocial) skills<br>High stress (e.g., unemployment, financial problems)<br>Need for power and control (possibly related to early life experience that resulted in feelings of helplessness) | If past history of abuse, has awareness of CSA<br>History of a positive relationship with a good parental role model<br>Good interpersonal skills<br>Respect for children<br>Empathy for, sensitivity to others<br>Good decision-making skills<br>High self-esteem<br>Social support<br>Good coping abilities |
| Child | Lack of knowledge of appropriate and inappropriate sexual behavior<br>High need for attention or affection<br>Overly trusting<br>Low self-esteem, self-confidence<br>Isolated<br>Emotionally neglected<br>Passive, unassertive<br>Taught to be obedient<br>Poor decision-making or problem-solving skills | Knowledgeable about appropriate and inappropriate sexual behavior<br>Assertive<br>High self-esteem, self-competence<br>Have support persons<br>Good problem-solving, decision-making skills |
| Child's Family | Emotional neglect of children<br>Inappropriate expectations regarding child's responsibilities (e.g., role reversal)<br>Inefficient or sporadic supervision<br>Marital discord<br>Family characterized by secretiveness, poor communication<br>Over- or under-sexualized home<br>Lack of privacy; household crowding<br>Situations in which offenders have access to victims<br>Power imbalance in marital dyad<br>Self-protective behavior not modeled by parents<br>Inappropriately close or distant parent-child boundaries<br>Stressors in family (unemployment; poverty)<br>Socially or geographically isolated home<br>Father substitute present<br>History of abuse in either parent<br>Exploitation of children to meet the needs of adults<br>Absence of natural parent | Low stress<br>Good social supports<br>Economic security<br>Supportive parents<br>Age-appropriate sexual knowledge<br>Efficient supervision<br>Open climate; good communication patterns<br>Child's sexual development promoted<br>Child's self-esteem promoted<br>Importance of personal safety stressed in home<br>Respect for each other's privacy by adults and children<br>Affectionate parent-child relationship<br>Positive male/female relationships (mutual, symmetrical)<br>Effective problem solving modeled by adults<br>Positive sense of self modeled by adults<br>Appropriate boundaries between adults and children |

## Table 2, continued

| Components of CSA | Risk Factors | Protective Factors |
|---|---|---|
| Community/ Society | View of children as possessions<br>Cultural acceptance for deriving sexual satisfaction from children<br>Easy access to victims<br>Easy access to child pornography<br>Portrayal of children as sexual beings in media and advertising<br>Reluctance of legal system to prosecute and punish offenders<br>Sexually restrictive culture<br>Lack of community support for families<br>Strong masculine sexualization (dominance, power in sexual relationships)<br>Patriarchal-authoritarian subcultures<br>Belief that children should always obey adults<br>Few opportunities for male/child nurturant interchanges that contain no sexual component<br>Lack of sexuality education in educational system<br>Devaluation of children<br>Community denial of the CSA problem | Culture opposed to deriving sexual satisfaction from children<br>Quick prosecution and consistent punishment of offenders by legal system<br>Cultural emphasis on equality between males and females<br>Provision of sexuality education for children<br>Community support for families<br>Children highly valued<br>Low tolerance for sexually coercive behaviors<br>Community awareness of the CSA problem and efforts devoted to its prevention<br>Research programs designed to further our understanding of CSA and how to prevent it |

because of conflicts in the marital dyad, lack supervision, are emotionally estranged from their parents, or live in a home that is either over- or undersexualized may be at higher risk. Other features may increase the opportunities for illicit sexual contact to occur within the home (e.g., geographic and social isolation).

The situational context can also increase the likelihood of abuse. Inefficient or sporadic adult supervision, or situations in which offenders have easy access to potential victims (e.g., in supervisory roles), may increase the possibility of abuse. Finally, perpetrators' propensities to abuse may be enhanced by certain characteristics of the community or society in which they live. Subcultures vary in terms of male cultural expectations and themes in masculine sexualization that make children what Finkelhor (1984) calls "emotionally congruent objects for sexual interest" (p. 39). Other societal risk factors may include low value placed on children, cultural supports for sexually coercive behavior, availability of child pornography, or low apprehension and conviction rates for molesters, among others.

We have also included in Table 2 possible protective factors, factors thought to reduce the risk of abuse. The inclusion of protective factors within each system directs our attention to the individual, familial, and environmental dynamics that decrease the probability that a child would become a victim. Although research investigating these factors is limited, we theorize that the presence, in some degree, of protective factors within each level would reduce the potential for sexually abusive behavior.

## IMPLICATIONS FOR PREVENTION STRATEGIES

This multifactor conceptualization suggests that a reduction in the incidence of CSA will only be achieved by developing a comprehensive, multifaceted approach, whereby prevention programs in each system are part of a coordinated service continuum. Prevention approaches need to target the personal, familial, and environmental conditions that both increase and decrease the likelihood of abuse occurring. Although no one factor is a perfect predictor of CSA, sufficient evidence exists to assume that the more risk factors that are involved across all systems, the higher the likelihood for abuse to occur, and thus the greater need for preventive efforts. Conversely, the more protective factors that are involved across all systems, the lower the likelihood for abuse to occur, suggesting that increasing these factors should be a goal of prevention efforts.

Identifying factors that may increase and decrease the likelihood of abuse also provides researchers with a set of intermediary variables to use in evaluating prevention programs. Although a program evaluation may not document a reduction in the incidence of sexual abuse, it may report a change in those factors believed to contribute to the likelihood of sexual exploitation (e.g., children's lack of knowledge regarding inappropriate touching), and the program can be viewed (albeit cautiously) as successful if it alters such factors. A prevention program that is able to change a factor associated with CSA may indeed succeed in reducing the incidence of sexual exploitation, but we cannot be certain of this reduction without direct evidence. This strong cautionary note is based on the fact that our knowledge about risk and protective factors is limited and is based on correlational data. Clearly, more research is needed on the conditions or factors that encourage and inhibit sexually abusive behavior. Prospective studies need to be conducted to determine the sensitivity, specificity, and predictive value of these factors.

## ORGANIZATION OF PREVENTION STRATEGIES

We have organized strategies for preventing CSA along two dimensions: the target for preventive interventions and the level of prevention.

*Targets.* Prevention efforts can be targeted toward groups of children, parents, professionals, policymakers, researchers, and the general public. Noticeably absent in our list of targets are offenders. The emphasis placed on offenders in our multifactor model clearly implies that offender-focused prevention efforts must be developed and evaluated. Progress in this area is contingent upon methodologically sound research with offenders. Particularly needed are studies on the characteristics of molesters, both detected and undetected; their modus operandi; how sexually deviant behaviors develop; and on the conditions or factors that both encourage and inhibit sexually abusive behavior. Although perpetrators will not be included as a target group in this book, we will offer some suggestions for reducing the likelihood of sexually exploitative behavior in chapters 2 and 5.

Organizing the book according to targets suggests that prevention efforts have orthogonal effects: that changes in one target group can occur independently of changes in another. It is important to realize, however, that prevention programs operating on one level can and do affect other systems. For example, teaching children to be assertive regarding their personal rights may cause problems if the family system is unresponsive to or critical of such changes. Instructing children in a classroom to disclose their abuse is being irresponsible if school personnel have not been helped to feel competent responding to such disclosures and/or if reporting agencies are not equipped to handle the increase in the number of reports. Clearly, prevention efforts do not operate in a vacuum.

And in reality, many communities have mounted prevention efforts aimed at multiple targets. For example, most programs that target children also include components for parents and teachers. Nonetheless, for ease of understanding, we have organized the book according to targets.

*Levels of Prevention.* Within each target group, we have organized CSA prevention efforts according to different levels of prevention. Models of prevention have largely adopted biomedical sciences theory (Bloom, 1981) and have defined prevention in terms of primary, secondary, and tertiary levels (Caplan, 1964). With its emphasis on treating and ameliorating the consequences of abuse, we will not be covering tertiary prevention, although efforts to treat both sexual offenders, to prevent their reoffending, and victims, to prevent a "victim to victimizer" cycle (Ryan, 1989) are crucial for eradicating the problem. Instead, we will emphasize primary and secondary prevention efforts.

Primary prevention efforts aim at preventing children from ever being abused. Thus, primary prevention seeks to reduce the number of new cases (incidence) in the population (Bloom, 1984). This is largely a population-focused intervention (as opposed to individual-oriented) that occurs with essentially well people, not those already affected. Stemming from the public health model, primary prevention models incorporate two basic strategies: (a) to eliminate or change the environmental stressor, or (b) to strengthen an individual's resources to avoid the stressor and to defend against it. Most CSA prevention programs are of the second type.

Secondary sexual abuse prevention seeks to identify prodromal signs of abuse early, so that prompt, effective steps can be taken to terminate the abuse and reduce dire psychological consequences resulting from sexual victimization. This approach aims at reducing the duration of a disorder by developing early case finding and providing prompt early treatment (Bloom, 1979, 1984). Our focus in secondary prevention of CSA will be on encouraging victims' disclosures of past and ongoing sexual abuse and on improving adults' responses to these disclosures, so that children can receive early intervention and protection to reduce the negative consequences of sexual exploitation.

## Summary

The first chapter is an overview of the CSA problem. As noted, it has taken several centuries for professionals and the general public to recognize the existence of CSA and to view sexual activities with children as abusive. The extent of the problem, as reflected in incidence and prevalence studies, indicates that CSA is a widespread social problem. That CSA is not restricted to a certain gender or age group suggests that broad-based prevention efforts are needed. Evidence of harmful effects (to children, families, and society) also supports the need for prevention efforts. From our review of various etiological models of CSA, we suggest that this phenomenon is best conceptualized as being multiply determined by forces at work in the individual (victim and offender), the family, as well as the community and society in which both the individual and family are embedded. Consistent with this multidimensional model of CSA, we propose an expansion of prevention strategies, to be more thoroughly explored in the remaining chapters.

# Child-Focused Prevention Programs:
# A Partial Solution

*Children are the most vulnerable members of our society, yet they are the last to be given any information about how to protect themselves.*
—FLORA COLAO & TAMAR HOSANSKY, 1987

As reviewed in chapter 1, an initial response to the CSA problem was to present sexual abuse information to children. In this chapter, we will address the importance and efficacy of prevention efforts targeting children.

## Rationale

The rationale for child-focused prevention programs rests on a number of realities about CSA. Information presented in chapter 1 suggests that an important percentage of children suffer such abuse and that this trauma can result in psychological sequelae in a significant portion of victims. Because of the secretive nature of CSA, most abused children do not reveal their victimization and are thus unlikely to be helped, emphasizing the importance of reaching children before victimization occurs. That perpetrators often misrepresent the sexual activity as normal suggests the need to educate children regarding appropriate and inappropriate body contact. Finally, classroom-based prevention programs have appeal because of their ability to reach large numbers of children of every race, creed, ethnic, and socioeconomic group in a relatively cost-efficient fashion.

## Objectives

Prevention information has been presented in a number of ways; books, structured curricula, coloring books, theatrical presentations, lectures, television and videotape programs, puppet shows, films, and behavioral skills training programs have all been employed. Programs are delivered to groups of children in a classroom, either by staff from outside agencies, or by school personnel (e.g., teachers, family-life educators, school counselors). Their length varies from half-hour sessions to multiday presentations. Programs also vary according to how children interact with the materials (e.g., child reads a book, watches a film, listens to an instructor, observes a model, role plays safety skills). Although there is considerable variability in how prevention information is presented, there is more consistency in program objectives.

### DEFINE AND DESCRIBE SEXUAL ABUSE

The first major objective of prevention programs is to help children recognize potentially abusive situations. The importance of achieving this first objective cannot be underestimated: warnings can only be effective if children have a clear idea of what it is they are being warned about. Given the differing definitions of CSA covered in chapter 1, it comes as no surprise that programs define sexual abuse in a variety of ways. Some programs teach children that sexual abuse is when children get forced or tricked into sexual contact. Others include more abstract information about a perpetrator's motivation or intentionality (e.g., "when touch is done for one's pleasure but the other person doesn't want it"; or "sexual abuse is the use of a child for the sexual gratification of an adult").

Most programs attempt to teach children about sexual abuse without discussing sexuality or even recognizing that children are sexual beings. Even though the implicit goal of these programs is to prevent *sexual* exploitation, the explicit goal is usually to teach personal safety, not sex education. The shift in emphasis is often devised to enhance community acceptance and avoid conflict with schools and parents. As one example of this compromise, the majority of prevention programs use the concepts of "touches" and "feelings" to explain sexual abuse (Tharinger et al., 1988). Stemming from C. Anderson's (1979) "touch continuum," children are taught about good, bad, and confusing touches, and the feelings resulting from these touches. In these programs, children are taught to use their feelings to decide whether a touch is appropriate or inappropriate (e.g., children are taught to say "no" to any touch that makes them feel uneasy or uncomfortable).

As another example of this compromise, very few programs teach children anatomically correct terms for the genitals but instead refer to sexual organs as "private parts," "private zones" (Dayee, 1982), or "the parts of your body covered by a bathing suit." Some have argued that separating sexual abuse prevention from sexuality education can become a problem when prevention programs, with their vague references to "private parts" and an emphasis on "saying no," constitute the first and possibly only classroom reference to sexuality (Trudell & Whatley, 1988). The concern is whether children are learning that sexuality is bad, secretive, or even dangerous. Furthermore, if children are not taught anatomically correct terminology and given practice using sexual words and phrases, then they may be hindered in disclosing inappropriate sexual activity. Results from recent surveys of parents (Conte & Fogarty, 1989; Wurtele, Kvaternick, & Franklin, in press) suggest that parents may be receptive to having this information included in personal safety programs. We strongly encourage teaching children the names of all of their body parts, including the genitals. For ease of discussion, these parts can then be referred to collectively as "private parts."

The situations described and terminology used in prevention programs also reflect caution on the part of programmers who are sensitive to the controversial nature of the topic. For example, the types of abusive situations presented to children pale in comparison to some reports of actual abuse (e.g., Strasser & Bailey, 1984). Many programs avoid discussing sexual activities; instead, they describe getting bullied by bigger children or getting pinched on the cheek by a relative. Among programs that do describe sexual activity, the most frequently depicted abusive actions are exhibitionism, voyeurism, and touching of the genitals. Oral-genital contact and vaginal or anal penetration are rarely, if ever, described in detail, which may be a product of our specific sociocultural framework (Mulhern, 1990).

## DESCRIBE OFFENDERS

Although early efforts to protect children concentrated on teaching them to be wary of strangers, the evidence suggesting that strangers represent but a small portion of offenders led to a movement away from "stranger-danger" to an awareness that a family member or other trusted person may be the perpetrator. Some programs refer to these known offenders as "someone you know and like"; a definition that for young children may not translate into a specific person (e.g., father or baby-sitter). Programs generally portray offenders as young adult males; few include parents, children, or adolescents as potential perpetrators (Tharinger et al., 1988). Prevention programmers face a dilemma, for in order to help children recognize potential abusers, it is essential that the most common types of perpetrators be described. Yet, what are the effects of telling children that they may be at risk from their fathers or father substitutes, particularly young children, for whom attachment to and trust of significant caregivers is so important for healthy development? Furthermore, although Swan, Press, and Briggs (1985) found that a prevention program helped children to acknowledge that a family member could be a perpetrator, findings from some unpublished research suggest that this is a difficult concept for children to grasp (see Finkelhor & Strapko, 1992).

## STRESS EMPOWERMENT

According to Tharinger et al. (1988), the implicit conceptual framework underlying the majority of prevention programs is that of "empowerment." The belief underlying this concept is that if children are given adequate information, a sense of personal power, and a list of community resources, then they will be enabled to assist in their own self-protection (Plummer, 1986). Thus, the majority of prevention materials emphasize the rights of children (e.g., the right to be "safe, strong, and free" as in Child Assault Prevention Project, 1983; the power to refuse adult requests; the right to refuse unwanted sexual contact). There is no evidence that children, especially young ones, can understand such abstract concepts, nor is there evidence that they are able to discriminate between those situations where they can assert their rights and those where adults' rights supersede. Rarely addressed is whether the right to say "no" implies that a child also has the right to say "yes" to wanted touches, or that rights are also associated with responsibilities (e.g., to be responsible for one's own safety; to not sexually exploit younger children).

Consistent with the themes of empowerment and primary prevention, all programs teach children some type of personal safety skills to repel sexual advances. Some programs (e.g., Child Assault Prevention Project, 1983) teach children such strategies as a self-defense yell or physical self-defense skill (e.g., kicking the perpetrator's shin or stomping on the instep). We have concerns about children's abilities to physically defend themselves and whether this strategy might endanger them further. In addition, some research suggests that children may use these skills in inappropriate circumstances (Nibert, Cooper, Ford, Fitch, & Robinson, 1989).

In an effort to avoid or resist abuse (a primary prevention goal), the majority of programs teach children that they should say "no" and remove themselves from the perpetrator. A few programs teach children that they can say "no" to a sexual touch even if they said "yes" to a nonsexual one. Concerns about whether young children would be realistically able to say "no" and escape has resulted in more prevention programs encouraging children "to tell" after an abusive encounter.

PROMOTE DISCLOSURE

In recognition of the secrecy inherent in the sexual abuse of children, program participants are taught not to keep such activities secret. Many programs attempt to define secrets, and some try (oftentimes in vain) to help children distinguish secrets from surprises, or "good" secrets from "bad" (e.g., Child Assault Prevention Project, 1983). Others teach children to use the request to keep the activity a secret as a clue to its inappropriateness. Toward the secondary prevention goal of early identification of victims, most programs encourage children to report previous or ongoing abuse to an authority figure immediately. Children are often taught to tell "someone they trust," an abstract concept that needs to be operationalized for young children. Encouraging disclosure early in the abuse experience is an important objective, as children are more seriously affected by long-lasting abuse (e.g., Friedrich et al., 1986). Furthermore, telling or threatening to tell have been suggested as effective deterrents by both victims and offenders (Berliner & Conte, 1990; Conte et al., 1989).

## The Development of Sexual Abuse Prevention Research

Whether or not CSA prevention programs are effective is a matter of widespread debate. In his chapter entitled "The Improbability of Prevention of Sexual Abuse," Melton (1992) concludes that such programs are unlikely to result in a substantial preventive effect, whereas Finkelhor and Strapko (1992) in the same volume conclude that "children do indeed learn the concepts they are being taught." Others have concluded that CSA prevention programs are ineffective and thus inappropriate for preschoolers (Gilbert et al., 1989; Krivacska, 1990). In this section, we will review 26 extant evaluations of classroom-based prevention programs in order to examine past attempts at prevention education and provide guidance for the future development of the field. (In the following chapter we will review studies of home-based prevention programs.) Program descriptions lacking a formal evaluation will not be included, nor will unpublished evaluations.

The limited number of evaluations relative to the large number of prevention programs in existence demonstrates that program development and distribution have been substantially ahead of program evaluation (see also Roberts, Alexander, & Fanurik, 1990). Why has wide-scale introduction of these programs occurred in the absence of evaluation and validation? Many grass-roots prevention programs have been caught in a Catch-22 situation where they lack the resources or expertise to undertake quality evaluations, yet without data to demonstrate their effectiveness they have difficulty obtaining financial support for their programs. In addition, program directors may be confident that their programs are valuable, based on children's and parents' claims of satisfaction. Thus, the expenditure of time and money to "prove what's proven" does not seem worthwhile.

To determine the effectiveness of the prevention programs, researchers have used their own unique outcome measures. This pervasive idiosyncrasy has made it extremely difficult to compare findings and make overall generalizations about effectiveness. The tendency to design new instruments for each new program has also hampered efforts to improve instruments or build a body of normative data. Furthermore, few researchers report the necessary data for determining effect-size statistics (i.e., means and standard deviations for dependent variables). Consequently, to describe the various outcomes, we will report results from statistical analyses (when available) and the extent to which children learned the concepts and skills taught in the program (reported as the percentage of the total possible score for each measure).

## FIRST STAGE OF PREVENTION STUDIES

The first stage of research focused on whether school- and preschool-aged children would demonstrate significant increases in personal safety knowledge and skills after participating in a prevention program. Stage-one studies most often used a design in which children were pretested, exposed to a prevention program, and then posttested.

*School-Aged Children.* Sixty-three children in Swan et al. (1985) were pretested and then watched a 30-minute play that focused on positive, negative, and forced sexual touches. Afterwards, they were asked to discriminate among these types of touches portrayed in videotaped vignettes and to identify self-protective responses. After seeing the play, significantly more children reported they would "tell someone" about the sexual molestation (i.e., from 57% to 82% at posttesting), and 88% agreed that a family member could be a perpetrator of sexual assault (up from 39% at pretesting). There were no differences between pre- and posttest scores on children's abilities to identify different types of touches (most children were able to identify the forced sexual touching scene at pretest).

In Sigurdson, Strang, and Doig (1987), 137 students were pretested, participated in the nine-hour *Feeling Yes, Feeling No* (National Film Board of Canada, 1985) program, which included videos and group discussion, and were then posttested. Significant improvements in knowledge from pre- to posttesting were found on only 7 of the 29 questions. Girls showed more significant changes in knowledge than boys did.

Garbarino (1987) studied 73 children's responses to a special issue of *Spiderman* comic dealing with sexual abuse. Participants were asked 10 multiple-choice questions about the comic; 6 of them dealt with sexual abuse. Results indicated that children answered the majority of these questions correctly (on average, 89%). In contrast to Sigurdson et al.'s (1987) findings, boys scored higher than girls (possibly because of the male-oriented nature of the comic).

Binder and McNiel (1987) administered a 13-item knowledge scale to 88 children before and after they participated in the Child Assault Prevention Project (a two-hour workshop using role play and guided group discussion). Although children showed statistically significant increases in their knowledge about strategies for coping with potentially abusive situations (e.g., to tell an adult), their high pretest mean suggests the children were already familiar with most of the concepts taught in the program.

*Preschoolers.* The 83 preschoolers in Borkin and Frank (1986) watched a puppet show about good and confusing touches and then participated in a coloring period. During this time, puppeteers interacted with the children and reinforced the messages taught during the puppet show. When asked at follow-up, "What should you do if someone tries to touch you in a way that doesn't feel good?" (a confusing question for preschoolers), only 4% of the 3-year-olds and 43% of the 4 and 5-year-olds correctly recalled any of the safety rules taught in the show.

Hill and Jason (1987) interviewed 23 preschoolers before and after they participated in a prevention curriculum that included short stories and discussion questions. Experimental children's responses were compared to those obtained from 20 children who had been randomly assigned to a control group. Parents of children in both groups attended a two-hour workshop on CSA. Results indicated that children who had participated in the program gave more assertive answers at posttesting compared with controls (71% vs. 44% of maximum) and also increased significantly from pre- to posttesting on an information measure (from 49% to 92% of maximum), on a measure of whom they could report "touching problems" to (from 32% to 34% of maximum), and on a skills measure (from 41% to 57% of the maximum). The control group's information score also increased significantly from pre- to posttesting (from 26% to 68% of maximum), most likely because of the parent education component. Problematic statistical analyses, the lack of a true control group, and the absence of information about the psychometric properties of the dependent measures limit the contribution of this study.

Christian, Dwyer, Schumm, and Coulson (1988) asked parents to interview their preschool children before and after they participated in a program that emphasized feelings and good versus bad touches. Pre- and posttest data were available on only 10% of the children. Obvious limitations include significant loss of subjects over time and unstandardized (possibly biased) interviews. These researchers concluded that the influence of the program on the children was unclear and suggested focusing more on interventions with parents rather than preschoolers.

A similar conclusion was reached by the Berkeley Family Welfare Research Group (Gilbert et al., 1989), who evaluated 118 preschoolers' responses to seven different prevention programs operating in California.[1] To assess program effects, children were

1. The effects of each prevention program were not determined; instead, the children were combined into one group and pre- and posttested. Consequently, the format, content, and length of the programs varied considerably, as did the presenters. For example, the programs ranged from a single 20-minute presentation by an outside consultant to a 27-day presentation by a teacher.

asked how a rabbit figure would feel and act in certain situations, and how a "little bunny" would respond when asked by a "big rabbit it doesn't know" to get into a car (in an attempt to measure children's level of stranger wariness[2]). After the programs, children showed some increase, although small, in their ability to explain how feelings might be associated with certain touches and had particular difficulty understanding the concept of "confusing" touches. The proportion of children indicating that the bunny should reveal a secret that has made it feel "mixed-up" increased from 45% to 56%. When asked who the bunny might turn to for assistance if it was sad, the proportion identifying an adult increased after the program, but only by 10%. Although their level of stranger wariness significantly increased from pre- to posttesting, overall it remained low (60% would still have the little bunny go with the big one). The researchers concluded that preschool prevention programs yield very limited gains in knowledge and recommended phasing out preschool training, focusing instead on older children and teachers.

Nibert et al. (1989) pretested 33 preschoolers, presented the Child Assault Prevention (CAP) Project Preschool Model and then posttested the children. Children were asked to: (a) verbally describe what a same-sex child should do in several threatening situations, (b) point to a picture that represented the best thing for the child to do, and (c) verbally describe what they would do in the same situation. Significant increases in the percentage of children giving a correct response were found on only 4 of the 11 situations, and many children were capable of giving correct responses at pretest. In the same report, the CAP program was presented at another preschool site, where children were assigned (not randomly) to either an intervention group (*n* = 41) or a control group (*n* = 42) and pre- and posttested. Comparisons between groups

---

2. In addition to focusing on abduction rather than sexual abuse, the choice of dependent measures is problematic given that the programs varied considerably on their relative emphases on feelings and "stranger danger," with at least one program relying less on feelings as a primary source of information about safety (i.e., *Talking About Touching*) and one program not discussing strangers at all (i.e., *Project SAAFE*).

indicated no statistically significant differences, and again, pretest scores were high. Although the researchers suggested that their findings indicate a high capacity for young children to acquire basic and concrete prevention strategies, their data do not support this conclusion. From their findings, it also appeared that the preschoolers overgeneralized their learning of the physical self-defense skills and applied them in inappropriate circumstances.

*Summary.* Findings from these stage-one studies are fairly consistent. Preschoolers did not appear to benefit from participating in these programs. In contrast, elementary school–aged children learned some information from prevention programs, but not much. There was some support that these programs might be effective in teaching older children to report sexual assault (which is, of course, an important outcome). In several of these studies, however, participants' pretest scores were often high, suggesting that children knew many of the concepts and skills before the program. Furthermore, the absolute increase in scores from pre- to posttest was minimal. Without a control group, it cannot be assumed that the programs were responsible for this improvement, however minimal. Children may have been exposed to sexual abuse information at home during the time of the program, or they may have learned something on the first test that helped them on the second. The methodological and measurement problems of these studies preclude us from making any definitive conclusions about the effectiveness of CSA prevention programs. It is unfortunate that some of these authors did not use such caution before concluding that prevention resources should be shifted away from preschoolers. Such a conclusion is inaccurate at worst and premature at best.

## SECOND STAGE OF PREVENTION STUDIES

During the second stage of research, we find more methodologically sound studies. Researchers included random assignment of subjects and control groups (except where noted) and examined the effectiveness of various types of programs and presenters with children who varied on several dimensions (e.g., age, sex, race, or academic achievement). Program format has varied along a continuum from those employing a didactic approach (e.g., film or group discussion) and emphasizing children's understanding of the concepts to those employing an action-oriented approach (e.g., learning and rehearsing self-protection skills) and focusing on the acquisition of certain behavioral skills.

*Didactic Approaches.* In Conte, Rosen, Saperstein, and Shermack (1985), 20 school- and preschool-aged children were exposed to three one-hour presentations given by deputy sheriffs. The changes in the children's scores from pre- to posttesting were compared with changes obtained from children in a wait-list control group. Relative to controls, experimental children increased their knowledge about prevention concepts. Older children learned more than younger children, and both groups had difficulty with abstract concepts. Overall, the authors questioned the absolute amount of learning obtained by all children, as after training they knew only slightly more than 50% of the concepts (compared with 28% at pretest). This relatively small knowledge gain may have been limited because the presenters did not adhere to their program materials but instead placed more emphasis on stranger abduction, assertiveness, and "horror" stories than the original model specified.

In Saslawsky and Wurtele (1986), 67 children from four grades (kindergarten, first, fifth, and sixth) either watched a film about sexual abuse (*Touch*; Illusion Theater, 1984) and discussed its contents, or participated in a discussion of self-concept and personal values. Compared with controls, children who viewed the film demonstrated significantly greater knowledge about sexual abuse (86% vs. 75% correct for Film vs. Controls) and enhanced personal safety skills (90% vs. 83%). Older children achieved higher scores on both measures than younger children. These gains were maintained at the three-month follow-up assessment. Although the differences between experimental and control group scores were statistically significant, the high percentage of correct answers from control children limits what we can say about the effectiveness of this film.

The 290 fourth- and fifth-grade children in D. A. Wolfe, MacPherson, Blount, and Wolfe (1986) either watched skits and participated in classroom discussions about physical and sexual abuse, or served as wait-list control subjects. On a seven-item true-false test administered at posttest only, experimental children answered 75% of the items correctly, compared with control children who correctly answered 67%. Although statistically significant, the absolute difference is small, suggesting that children already knew many of the concepts taught in the program. Unfortunately, few of the items were specific to sexual abuse and several involved debatable propositions (e.g., "If children tell someone they trust that an adult is hurting them, probably no one will believe them").

In two studies involving a total of 587 third and fourth graders, Kolko and associates (Kolko, Moser, & Hughes, 1989; Kolko, Moser, Litz, & Hughes, 1987) evaluated the effectiveness of a prevention program that featured the *Red Flag, Green Flag People* coloring book (J. Williams, 1980), a film (*Better Safe Than Sorry II*; Film Fair Communications, 1979), and a discussion of inappropriate touching. Children from schools that participated in the program were compared with children from a wait-list control school (neither children, nor schools were randomly assigned to treatment). Relative to controls, children in the experimental group rated themselves as being more likely to report being victimized to an adult (94% vs. 82%, found only in Kolko et al., 1987), learned more about concepts taught in the program (81% vs. 74%, found in Kolko et al., 1989), and were more likely to say they would use the prevention skills if an adult made a sexual advance (24% of experimental vs. 12% of controls recommended all three preventive responses in Kolko et al., 1989). Once again, the magnitude of change for the experimental group was small, as was the absolute difference between experimental and control group scores, and in several cases the experimental children's scores decreased over time. The percentage of children saying they would use the prevention skills taught in the program, although significantly greater than the percentage of control group children who said they would, was still low. Furthermore, the lack of random assignment presents the possibility of selection factors operating, thus limiting the contributions of these two studies. Kolko and associates, however, are to be commended for obtaining information from children, school personnel, and parents regarding reports of inappropriate touching.

*Action-Oriented Approaches.* Several researchers have explored whether children learn from programs that incorporate a more active mode of training. For example, in Stilwell, Lutzker, and Greene (1988), preschoolers improved in their ability to demonstrate appropriate examples of a good touch, say "no" to an offender, and tell about a confusing touch incident, as a function of participating in a six-lesson prevention program. Acquisition of the saying "no" and telling skills was more variable and limited, perhaps because of a reduction in the number of program lessons (from 23 to 6) or the complicated behavioral responses required of the children (the criteria for the saying "no" response was to say "no" in a firm voice, shake the head from side to side, stand straight, make direct eye contact, and then move away from the offender).

Using a much larger sample, Harvey, Forehand, Brown, and Holmes (1988) randomly assigned 71 kindergarten children to either a sexual abuse prevention program or an attention-control program. Children in the prevention program were taught how to differentiate among good, bad, and sexually abusive touches and how to respond in potentially abusive situations (i.e., say "no," get away, and tell). Although the authors indicated that instructions, modeling, rehearsal, and social reinforcement were used as teaching procedures, the actual description of the three-day program suggested that only instruction and modeling using dolls were employed. Relative to the control group, treatment children demonstrated a better ability to distinguish between types of touches (70% vs. 57% correct), enhanced knowledge about safety rules concerning sexual abuse (70% vs. 41%), and higher levels of personal safety skills in response to novel simulated scenes involving sexual abuse (66% vs. 54%). Although statistically significant, the magnitude of the difference between the two groups on the measure of personal safety skills was limited, possibly because of minimal skill rehearsal. Differences between treatment and control groups were maintained seven weeks after treatment.

Similar findings were reported by Ratto and Bogat (1990). They evaluated the effectiveness of a five-day program (the Grossmont College Child Sexual Abuse Prevention Program) with 39 preschoolers. Children were randomly assigned to either a control or experimental group and participated in the program at their daycare centers. Information was taught through the use of a picture book, a puppet show, discussion, activities, and role play. Children's knowledge, skill, and fear levels were assessed before and directly after the curriculum was taught, as well as three months later. Results indicated that children in the experimental group had higher knowledge scores than control children at both posttesting and follow-up. Participation in the program did not affect their skill scores, perhaps because of the limited use of role-playing situations. No significant increase in fear was noted among program participants. Several methodological problems limit the potential contribution of this study, including the select nature of the subjects (only 3 day-care centers out of 102 agreed to participate) and the fact that not all interviewers were blind to the treatment conditions and experimental hypotheses.

To determine if a personal safety program incorporating active rehearsal would be effective with a group of 4-year-old children, Wurtele (1990b) randomly assigned 24 preschoolers to either the Behavioral Skills Training program (BST: Wurtele, 1986) or an attention-control program. The BST program includes discrimination training of appropriate and inappropriate genital touches and uses modeling, behavioral rehearsal, and feedback to train self-protective responses. Knowledge and skill scores for all children were low at pretest, reflecting young children's naïveté and suggesting their possible vulnerability to abuse. At posttesting, BST participants demonstrated a better ability to identify inappropriate touches in novel situations (97% vs. 50% correct for BST vs. Control), greater knowledge about sexual abuse (78% vs. 63% correct), and higher levels of personal safety skills (68% vs. 34%). Supplemental analyses indicated that BST subjects were more likely to say they would escape from a potential perpetrator and inform a resource person about the incident. In contrast, few controls indicated they would tell someone about the inappropriate situations. BST children's knowledge and skill gains were maintained at the one-month follow-up.

Kraizer, Witte, and Fryer (1989) evaluated the five-part *Safe Child Program* (Kraizer, 1988) with 670 children, ages 3 to 10, from schools in three states. The program includes teacher-directed role playing, discussion, and activities to enhance mastery of prevention skills. It emphasizes prevention of sexual, emotional, and physical abuse and abduction and teaches safety for children in self-care. Children are instructed to say "no" to any touch that makes them feel uneasy or uncomfortable. Treatment and control children were pre- and posttested (random assignment was not indicated) using a role-play assessment to measure behavioral change. In this technique, a confederate put his or her arm around the child and tried various techniques to persuade the child to allow such touching. Scoring was based on the child's verbal response (e.g., saying "no") and body language (e.g., standing up, moving the confederate's hand). Treatment children improved in their verbal and nonverbal skills related to refusing uncomfortable touches (59% of maximum), whereas control children's scores remained stable and low (at 35% of maximum).

Hazzard, Webb, Kleemeier, Angert, and Pohl (1991) compared 286 third and fourth graders' responses to an adaptation of the *Feeling Yes, Feeling No* program (including videotapes, group discussion, behavioral rehearsal, and a comic book on sexual abuse) to those obtained from 113 control children (schools, not children, were randomly assigned to conditions). Treatment children exhibited significantly greater knowledge compared with controls (82% vs. 62% correct at posttesting), along with a somewhat better ability to discriminate safe from unsafe situations (79% vs. 74% correct at posttesting). Treatment and control children did not differ signficantly in how they would respond in potentially abusive situations portrayed on videotape (and averaged 74% of maximum skill scores). Fourth graders had higher knowledge scores than third graders, and girls had higher scores than boys. There were no differences in knowledge according to subject race or achievement level. Gains in knowledge and skills were maintained at the one-year follow-up.

*Comparing Approaches.* Other studies have compared didactic and action-oriented approaches. For example, Woods and Dean (1986) randomly assigned approximately 4,500 third- through fifth-grade students to either participate in the action-oriented *Talking About Touching* curriculum (Committee for Children, 1983), read the *Spiderman* comic, or serve as controls. The authors reported that a statistically significant pre- to posttest increase in knowledge occurred for students who participated in the personal safety curriculum (actual scores were not provided). In contrast, children who were given only the comic book to read did not exhibit a significant increase in overall personal safety knowledge. The authors suggested that the dynamic process of classroom learning may have accounted for the superiority of the personal safety curriculum.

Wurtele, Saslawsky, Miller, Marrs, and Britcher (1986) randomly assigned 71 children (from kindergarten and grades 1, 5, and 6) to: (a) participate in the Behavioral Skills Training (BST) program; (b) observe a film about sexual abuse (*Touch*; Illusion Theater, 1984); (c) participate in a combination of *a* and *b*; or (d) participate in an attention-control program. The BST program, alone or in combination with the film, significantly enhanced knowledge gain over that resulting from a control presentation (percentages correct were 95%, 88%, 84%, and 75% for BST, BST + Film, Film, and Control, respectively). Findings on a skill measure approached significance, with BST children scoring higher than controls (93% vs. 82%). Older children performed better than younger ones, but the programs did not have differential effectiveness depending on the age of the children. The BST and film programs differed not only in their content but also in their format. The BST program used an action-oriented approach, in contrast to the film program, which used a passive, didactic approach to impart information to the children. Two subsequent studies varied first the format, then the content, to identify the critical ingredients.

In an examination of format differences, Wurtele, Marrs, and Miller-Perrin (1987) compared a program that included participant modeling (PM, self-protective skills were taught through modeling and active rehearsal) with a similar program using symbolic modeling (SM, children observed as skills were modeled by an experimenter). Twenty-six kindergarten children were randomly assigned to one of the two programs. The findings provided evidence for the greater efficacy of PM than SM for the teaching of personal safety skills (skill scores were 93% vs. 70% correct for PM vs. SM).

To determine whether content differences affect preschoolers' abilities to learn from the programs, Wurtele, Kast, Miller-Perrin, and Kondrick (1989) randomly assigned 100 preschoolers to either the Behavioral Skills Training (BST) program, a feelings-based program, or an attention-control program. The format for presenting the information was held constant (i.e., both the BST and the feelings-based programs used instructions, modeling, rehearsal, and feedback), but the content varied between the two programs. In the feelings-based program, children were instructed to use their feelings to distinguish between "OK" touches (i.e., those that feel good) and "Not-OK" touches (i.e., those that feel bad or confusing). In contrast, the BST program provided children with a concrete rule to protect their genitals and encouraged children to use this rule to discriminate between "OK" and "Not-OK" touches. Compared with a control presentation, both training programs were effective in enhancing children's sexual abuse knowledge and in teaching them *how* to respond effectively to those inappropriate-touch situations common to the two programs (skill scores averaged 67%, 60%, and 42% for BST, Feelings, and Controls, respectively). The two training programs differed, however, in their relative abilities to teach children *when* to use their personal safety skills. Children taught to "trust their feelings" when making safety decisions were confused when asked to identify the appropriateness of two incongruous situations (i.e., when an appropriate touch feels bad and when an inappropriate touch feels good). It appears that the feelings-based approach, which is used in the majority of prevention programs, may impede, rather than enhance, preschoolers' abilities to discriminate between appropriate and inappropriate touching of the genitals.

Blumberg, Chadwick, Fogarty, Speth, and Chadwick (1991) recently compared two programs that varied in both format and content to determine children's abilities to discriminate between appropriate and inappropriate types of touching. Two hundred sixty-four kindergarten through third grade children were randomly assigned by classroom to either: (a) a role-play (RP) program that used role-play, modeling, rehearsal, and discussion to teach sexual abuse prevention concepts; (b) a multimedia (MM) program that used stuffed animals, puppets, films, and discussion to teach children about sexual, physical, and emotional abuse; or (c) a control program about fire prevention. Results indicated greater pre- to posttest improvement for the RP group than for the control group on total correct touch discriminations (percentages correct were 81% and 68% for RP and control, respectively). There was no significant difference in learning between the MM and control groups (70% vs. 68%). Unfortunately, the two treatment programs varied considerably in their content (i.e., sexual abuse prevention in RP vs. sexual, physical, and emotional abuse prevention in MM), their format (action-oriented in RP vs. didactic in MM), and in their definitions of sexual abuse ("When an older person touches you in a private place when you don't need help" in RP vs. "When touches mix us up or confuse us" in MM). Thus, it is impossible to determine what variable, or set of variables, accounted for the superiority of the RP program. However, the RP program's teaching of a concrete rule to protect private parts and its action-oriented approach both have support from previous research and likely contributed to its effectiveness.

*Type of Trainer.* Finally, one study has investigated whether program effectiveness varies according to type of trainer. Hazzard, Kleemeier, and Webb (1990) compared the relative effectiveness of teachers versus outside consultants in implementing the *Feeling Yes, Feeling No* prevention curriculum with 558 third- and fourth-grade children. No significant differences in the impact of the prevention program were found between children taught by the two types of presenters, as children demonstrated equivalent knowledge gains (i.e., all children increased their correct responses from 72% at pretest to 88% at posttest) and skill scores at posttesting (i.e., 78% of maximum). The authors caution, however, that their findings may be limited to teachers who receive extensive preparation before program presentation and who feel comfortable presenting such information.

*Summary.* Programs incorporating more active modes of training have resulted in greater gains in knowledge and skills than those employing a didactic approach. In the studies of elementary school–aged children, researchers found that program participants exhibited greater knowledge and skills, along with better ability to discriminate between appropriate and inappropriate touch situations, compared with controls. In contrast to stage-one studies, these program were found to enhance preschoolers' knowledge about sexual abuse, along with their ability to discriminate between safe and unsafe situations and to respond in hypothetical abusive situations, whereas same-aged controls exhibited a low level of knowledge and skills. Such results suggest that without training, preschoolers are deficient in their abilities to recognize and respond to potential molesters, and that they can benefit from participating in these action-oriented programs. Findings from stage-two studies with preschoolers do not support Krivacska's (1990) claim that "below the age of 7 instruction in CSA concepts is contraindicated" (p.67) and also suggest that stage-one researchers were confusing preschoolers' performance with their potential. When the mode of information transmission is compatible with the children's capacities, children are able to assimilate complex information at early ages. It must be noted, however, that on measures of personal safety skills, young children did not achieve 100% accuracy in recognizing and responding in potentially abusive situations, even though their performances were significantly better than those of control children in most studies. This moderate skill gain is not surprising given the programs' limited duration (the modal duration was only 1.5 hours). Research is needed to determine how children who achieve criterion performance differ from those who do not. That some children fail to master certain concepts or skills also demands that researchers correct any inaccuracies or misunderstandings after posttesting.

From this sample of stage-two studies we can conclude: (a) program participants increase in knowledge about sexual abuse prevention concepts and their ability to recognize inappropriate sexual touching, although their skill gains have been more variable; (b) children's knowledge and skills increase more following participation in programs that incorporate modeling and rehearsal compared with programs that rely primarily on individual study or passive exposure; (c) although older children score higher than younger children on knowledge and skills measures, even preschoolers benefit substantially from these programs; (d) the feelings-based approach for teaching children to identify inappropriate sexual touching is ineffective with preschoolers; (e) knowledge and skill gains have been maintained for up to one year; and (f) well-trained teachers are as effective as outside consultants in presenting prevention concepts to third and fourth graders.

TOWARD STAGE-THREE STUDIES

*Beyond Main Effects.* J. Kagan (1979) has accused developmental researchers of operating with an obsession to find "absolute principles which declare that a particular set of external conditions is inevitably associated with a fixed set of consequences for all children" (p.886). With CSA prevention research, this tendency to operate with main effect models is illustrated in the vast majority of studies reviewed in this chapter. For the most part, these studies have attempted to demonstrate that prevention programs either are or are not effective in teaching children personal safety knowledge and skills. What has often been overlooked is why some children learn the concepts and skills, but others do not. We argue that the effects of different types of programs must be examined with respect to individual differences among children (e.g., age, sex, intelligence, self-concept, abuse-nonabuse status, initial skill and knowledge level) and variations in the family microsystem (e.g., socioeconomic level, parent-child relationship, extent of sexuality education at home, parents' attitudes about prevention programs). In addition, characteristics of the macrosystem (i.e., sociocultural factors such as values regarding the worth of children, acceptance of adult-child sexual relationships) may also mediate effects of the programs. Employing this framework for conducting research demands that we expand our research question from "Does this prevention program work?" to "What type of prevention program works with what type of children in what type of setting?" More sophisticated research designs will be necessary initially to answer this question and to determine ultimately the overall impact of CSA prevention programs.

*Expanding to a More Diverse Child Population.* CSA programs have been evaluated with normal, (presumably) nonabused children, who range in age from 3 to 12. We do not know how these programs affect already victimized children or those children who may be victimized in the future. Nor do we know what program-related benefits might accrue to adolescents or to exceptional children (e.g., children with visual or hearing impairments), although both groups are considered to be at risk for sexual exploitation.

Both crime reports and surveys suggest that a significant number of adolescents have experienced sexual assault, either as victims of molestation by adults or by their peers in acquaintance rape (Ageton, 1983; American Academy of Pediatrics, 1983; Burgess, 1985; Hall & Flannery, 1984). Furthermore, as explained in chapter 1, many molesters begin offending during or before adolescence, and adolescents also commit sexual offenses against their peers and younger children. As it is quite likely that an adolescent audience contains both victims and current or potential victimizers, adolescent-focused prevention programs face a dual challenge. Although sexual abuse prevention curricula and materials have been developed for adolescents (e.g., Adams, Fay, & Loreen-Martin, 1984; Anderson-Kent, 1982; Children's Self-Help Project, 1988; Downer & Beland, 1985; Fay & Flerchinger, 1982; Fortune, 1984; Hughes & Sandler, 1987; Kassees & Hall, 1987; Network

Against Teenage Violence, 1987; Strong, Tate, Wehman, & Wyss, 1986), published evaluations of these programs are rare (see Barth & Derezotes, 1990, for an exception).

Most adolescent-focused programs are geared toward potential victims of acquaintance abuse (especially females) and rarely focus on preventing adolescents from becoming abusive with peers or younger children. In addition to teaching program participants to *say* "no" to abuse, we must teach them to *accept* "no" from others. Toward this goal, Committee for Children (1989) has recently developed the Second Step curriculum, which aims to reduce physical and sexual aggression by teaching potential perpetrators empathy, impulse control, anger management, and decision-making skills. Clearly, classroom-based prevention programs need to be expanded to incorporate and evaluate efforts aimed at preventing individuals from becoming abusers, particularly at the adolescent stage. Not to do so overlooks the fact that the offender (*not* the child victim) is responsible for the abuse.

It has also been proposed that special needs children are at higher risk for sexual abuse because their handicapping problems (e.g., mental retardation, communication problems, physical handicaps) make it difficult for them to protect or defend themselves or to report maltreatment. Their social and sexual naïveté, low self-esteem, desire to be accepted, greater dependency on caretakers, inability to differentiate basic assistance with personal care from sexual exploitation, and unquestioning compliance may also make them vulnerable (Brookhauser, Sullivan, Scanlan, & Garbarino, 1986; S. S. Cole, 1984–1986; Cruz, Price-Williams, & Andron, 1988; Moglia, 1986; Ryerson, 1984; Tharinger, Horton, & Millea, 1990). Characteristics of their care facilities may also place them at risk (e.g., geographical isolation, limited parental involvement: Whittaker, 1987).

To be effective with these children, program modifications that recognize their special needs are required (e.g., children with language impairments may not be able to say "no" and therefore need to be taught alternative self-protective strategies; children with hearing impairments need access to interpreters if they are to disclose abuse; children with visual impairments require translation of printed material). Prevention curricula have been developed for preschoolers, latency-aged children, and adolescents with various disabilities (Dreyer & Haseltine, 1986; Krents & Atkins, 1985; LaBarre, Hinkley, & Nelson, 1986; O'Day, 1983; Seattle Rape Relief, 1980). Unfortunately, these programs have been infrequently subjected to proper scientific evaluation (see Haseltine & Miltenberger, 1990, for an exception).

### Effects of CSA Prevention Programs

Are prevention programs effective? The evidence can be viewed from a number of perspectives. For example, one can study changes in process or proximal measures (i.e., immediately observable changes such as gains in knowledge or skills), or changes in distal outcomes (i.e., delayed changes such as reduced incidence). In addition, prevention researchers can attend to the cost-benefit ratio of prevention programming. In the following sections, we will analyze the question of effectiveness from these different perspectives.

DISTAL OUTCOMES
*Reducing Incidence.* Have these programs reduced the incidence of CSA? To answer this question would require following very large samples of trained and untrained children and documenting a lower incidence of abuse among the former. Although these are methodologically, pragmatically, and ethically difficult studies to conduct, demonstrating a reduction in incidence represents the most demanding yet necessary challenge facing the prevention researcher. At this point, the degree to which programs actually reduce the incidence of CSA is an unanswered empirical question. This does not mean that the programs are not achieving this goal, only that their efficacy in meeting this objective has not been demonstrated.

*Increasing Disclosures.* Do these programs encourage disclosure of past or ongoing abuse (a secondary prevention goal)? An important percentage of program participants say they would tell if they

were involved in an abusive situation. Findings are mixed, however, as to whether victimized children actually disclose their
abuse. There are ample anecdotal reports of children disclosing
such abuse. We conducted an informal survey of prevention programmers and all reported receiving disclosures, mostly from
older children regarding past abuse.[3] Published reports of disclosures are rare, however, and when they do occur, rates tend to be
low. Disclosure rates have varied from a low of 0% (Gilbert et al.,
1989) to a high of 7% of program participants (Hazzard et al.,
1990; Kolko et al., 1987). These figures would suggest that prevention programs are minimally effective in enhancing immediate
disclosure. Alternatively, it may be that children are disclosing but
researchers are not documenting or reporting these findings. Such
information is important to better determine whether these programs are encouraging disclosure and thereby reducing the duration of the disorder. Nor do we know if these programs promote
false reporting of abuse (as suggested by Krivacska, 1989; Wakefield & Underwager, 1988), although fictitious allegations of sexual abuse in general appear to be rare (Everson & Boat, 1989;
Goodwin, Sahd, & Rada, 1982; D. P. H. Jones & McGraw, 1987).

PROXIMAL OUTCOMES
*Knowledge Acquisition.* If the word *effective* is used to mean enhanced knowledge about sexual abuse prevention concepts, then
both school- and preschool-aged children benefit from participating in these programs. Maintenance of knowledge gains has been
documented for up to one year. Older children know more initially
compared with younger children, and a few researchers have
found differences on knowledge tests according to subject sex
(e.g., Garbarino, 1987; Hazzard et al., 1990; Hazzard et al., 1991).

3. Contributors to the survey included: Mel Bulman (Women's Services Inc.),
Joan Cole Duffell (Committee for Children), Jaime M. Grant (Susquehanna Valley
Women in Transition), Carol Grimm (Rape & Abuse Crisis Center), Crystal Hurn-
don (Rape Crisis Center), William F. Schenck (Project PAAR), Jeannette M. Adkins
(Project PAAR), Gayle M. Stringer (King County Rape Relief), and Don Yost (The
Bridgework Theater).

Children appear to make equivalent knowledge gains whether taught by teachers or expert consultants. Certain concepts, however, seem difficult to grasp (e.g., that victims are not to blame; that abuse could be perpetrated by family members; or such abstract concepts as "stranger," "safe," "confusing touches," or "secrets" vs. "surprises"). In light of these findings, several curriculum experts have revised their presentations to include less abstract and more concrete concepts and rules for young children (e.g., Committee for Children, 1987).

*Skill Acquisition.* If the goal of sexual abuse prevention programs is to teach behaviors so that when a potential perpetrator makes a sexual advance toward a child, the child will act in a protective fashion by recognizing the abuse, saying "no," and escaping, then there is no direct evidence that programs have been effective.[4] Indirect evidence, based on children's responses to written, verbal, or videotaped vignettes, shows that these programs can enhance children's personal safety skills. Skill gains have been inconsistent across studies, however, possibly because of the limited duration of the programs and the way skills have been taught. Programs that provide mastery experiences (e.g., practicing self-protective skills in response to role plays) are more effective compared with those that rely primarily on passive exposure or individual study (e.g., films, comic books).

Of course, being able to respond appropriately to hypothetical perpetrators described in vignettes does not guarantee that children would use the skills in real-life abusive situations. In order to test whether or not a program has achieved this goal, in vivo as-

4. An attempt to collect success stories from participants in Child Assault Prevention (CAP) programs in California has begun (K. Kain, personal communication, May 10, 1990). A toll-free hot line has been established for children to call in their success stories, and a sample of the 4.3 million California children who have received prevention training in their school classrooms will be queried as to their experiences following the training. Although this is a step in the right direction, without a matched sample of control children, it will be difficult to put these findings into perspective, as children's successes may have happened without training.

sessments would need to be employed. In vivo assessments have been used to determine how children respond to the lures of potential abductors (Fryer, Kraizer, & Miyoshi, 1987a, 1987b; Miltenberger & Thiesse-Duffy, 1988; Poche, Brouwer, & Swearingen, 1981; Poche, Yoder, & Miltenberger, 1988) and have recently been employed by Kraizer et al. (1989) to measure children's responses to a potential molester.

These simulations are very difficult to construct without raising major human subject protection issues (see Conte, 1987). Important concerns are whether children will assume all inappropriate touch requests are simply "experimental tests," along with the potential emotional upset these situations might cause. As an alternative, we encourage the assessment of children's responses to hypothetical scenarios describing both appropriate and inappropriate requests to touch or view the child's genitals. Children can be asked to identify the request as appropriate or inappropriate, and if the latter, to describe their intended verbal and behavioral responses. Even though such a method relies on self-report, this procedure can provide a wealth of information because it can help identify children who lack these perceptual and behavioral skills and can assess children's abilities to generalize their newly learned skills to novel, personal situations.

*Untested Proximal Effects.* Some argue that enhancing knowledge or self-protective skills is only part of what these programs achieve. Perhaps program effectiveness would be better demonstrated if we measured whether they enhance children's awareness of their rights to live free from abuse, or whether they "empower" children, although this latter concept is difficult to define or operationalize (Swift & Levin, 1987). Perhaps these programs enhance children's sense of self-protective efficacy, as has been found among adults who participate in self-defense programs (Ozer & Bandura, 1990). Consistent with the ideology of prevention that includes health promotion, perhaps these programs have such positive indirect outcomes as enhanced self-esteem, assertiveness, or decision-making skills. These are important but unanswered questions.

COST-BENEFIT ANALYSIS

In the previous section, we found evidence (using proximal measures) suggesting that children do benefit from participating in classroom-based CSA prevention programs. But at what costs are these benefits achieved? Given the lack of evidence about whether these programs actually prevent abuse (using distal outcomes), the costs must be minimal to nonexistent to justify their continuation, let alone their expansion. Cost-benefit analyses of social service programs are extremely complex (Barnett, 1986; K. R. White, 1988). As a starting point, we will include as costs, expenses to the school and negative consequences for the participants.

From our informal survey of prevention programmers, it appears that the dollar cost is minimal. As prevention programs can be implemented with groups of children, the per child cost can be kept low. Rates in our survey ranged from $0.00 (free) to $2.50 per child. Such expenses are substantially less than those associated with the costs of abuse (e.g., social service intervention, therapeutic services for the child and perpetrator, prosecution and incarceration of offenders).

But what about negative unintended consequences of these programs on the child participants? Several researchers have attempted to answer this question. Some asked parents if their children had shown any adverse reactions after participating in the programs and few parents typically report observing problems (e.g., 5% in Swan et al., 1985; 7% in Nibert, Cooper, & Ford, 1989). Similarly, neither teachers nor parents noticed signs of increased emotional distress in Binder and McNiel (1987). Others have assessed children's fear levels of various people and situations potentially affected by a personal safety program (e.g., receiving physical affection from parents) and found no significant increases in children's fear ratings subsequent to program participation (Wurtele & Miller-Perrin, 1987). Unfortunately, none of the above studies included control groups, nor did they employ standardized instruments to assess children's emotional reponses to prevention programs.

When Hazzard et al. (1991) used a standardized measure of anxiety, they found no differences between treatment and control children's self-reported anxiety levels, nor were there differences in the frequency of treatment and control parents' reports of child behaviors indicative of emotional distress. Compared with controls, personal safety program participants in Wurtele et al. (1989) showed no significant increases in how fearful they were, nor did their parents perceive them as becoming more fearful. In addition, no significant teacher-rated changes in the frequency of negative behaviors for personal safety program participants were observed. Similarly, no significant increases in teacher- and parent-reported problematic behaviors were obtained in Wurtele (1990b). In this study, children were also asked how much they liked their "private parts" and if it is "OK for kids to touch their own private parts." No significant differences between treatment and control groups were found on these questions, suggesting that the program did not negatively affect program participants' views on these aspects of sexuality.

In contrast, two studies have reported negative effects. Garbarino (1987) found that half of the fourth graders who read the *Spiderman* comic book dealing with sexual abuse indicated that they felt "worried" or "scared" that "it" might happen to them. This heightened fear level may have been the result of providing children with information about sexual abuse but not providing opportunities to discuss their concerns or to learn self-protective skills. In addition, those children who read the comic with their parents were more likely to worry than those children who read the book alone. Parental reaction to the topic may have been a factor in how these children reacted to the material (perhaps parents became uncomfortable, which resulted in heightened anxiety levels in their children).

In a study that has had a major impact on the field because of its claim that participants are "worse off" as a result of these programs, Gilbert et al. (1989) found that after training, preschoolers were more likely than before to identify pictures of bunnies being bathed and tickled with feelings of sadness (although the findings on the tickling picture did not reach significance and the psychometric properties of this measure are unknown). On the basis of this finding, these authors suggested that the programs heightened children's sensitivity to negative feelings about physical contact. The methodological problems of this study described earlier suggest that this conclusion is overstated. A more parsimonious explanation for their finding is that some preschoolers do not like to take baths.

Furthermore, several researchers have found what might be considered positive side effects of program participation. For example, Binder and McNiel (1987) reported that 64% of the children in their study said that the program made them feel much safer and 72% felt better able to protect themselves. Others have found that after participating in a program, children are more likely to discuss the contents of the program with their parents, further reducing the secrecy surrounding sexual abuse (Binder & McNiel, 1987; Hazzard et al., 1991; Swan et al., 1985; Wurtele, 1990b; Wurtele & Miller-Perrin, 1987).

Even though negative side effects have been measured in many different ways and across many different programs, the bulk of the research suggests that prevention programs are associated with no or minimal short-term negative effects. Furthermore, no study has documented any long-term negative effects as a result of personal safety education. There is a strong possibility that they may even produce positive indirect effects (e.g., increased discussion at home). Perhaps the measures used in these studies have not been sensitive to all potential negative effects. Researchers have yet to explore whether these programs cause increased guilt about past, ongoing, or future abuse; how they affect children's attitudes toward sexuality and male-female relationships; or whether they result in heightened mistrust of adults, decreased sense of security, or increased sexual curiosity (Wurtele, 1988). Given the current data base, we believe the benefits of these programs outweigh their costs. However, to reassure parents and school administrators, we recommend that researchers continue to assess for unintended consequences and if negative effects are identified, it becomes incumbent upon the programmer and/or researcher to correct or treat the problem.

## Recommendations for Classroom-Based Prevention Programs

From our review of programs and their evaluations, it appears that we have come a long way in a relatively short time toward educating children about body safety, even though we have yet to develop the ideal program. Toward that goal, we offer the following recommendations. These recommendations are pertinent to those who develop, implement, and evaluate prevention programs.

### EVALUATE

We believe that evaluation is crucial to the success of the CSA prevention movement. Although the value of classroom-based programs may be crystal clear to workers in the field, the rest of society, including major funders, must be convinced of it. We join with Zigler and Black (1989) in proposing that "evaluation is our most effective marketing tool" (p.16). Without evaluating prevention attempts, we risk giving children, parents, and professionals a false sense of security, because exposure to the prevention program may not equip children to adequately protect themselves from potential molesters. In addition, if we prematurely assume that these programs work, then other, perhaps more effective efforts to address the problem will not be pursued. Conversely, if a program is evaluated improperly, it may be incorrectly and prematurely dismissed as a failure.

To build a solid knowledge base regarding program effects, researchers are encouraged to develop and employ developmentally appropriate, psychometrically sound assessment instruments that reflect program goals. Ideally, outcomes would be determined using multiple methods and information obtained from multiple sources (e.g., children, teachers, parents, child protective services; see Wurtele, 1990a). Beyond measuring program effects on children, a major challenge for prevention researchers will be to include outcome measures that reflect an ecological focus (e.g., how different persons and systems are affected by the implementation of classroom-based programs).

### USE ACCURATE LABELS

Rather than mislead the public and create a false sense of security about what these programs can do, we suggest referring to them as "body safety programs" or "personal safety programs." Compared with the descriptor "child sexual abuse prevention program," these labels more accurately (and humbly) reflect the content and outcomes of these programs. The importance of these types of programs is not lessened by a change of name; enhancing children's sense of body importance and personal safety are important goals in their own right. Given our current data base, any program that claims to prevent CSA should be viewed as suspect. A more realistic descriptor is that a program teaches knowledge and strategies that *may* prevent CSA.

### TRAIN PARTICIPANTS IN THE FOUR *R*S

At the minimum, classroom-based curricula should emphasize training in the four *R*s (Remember, Recognize, Resist, and Report). Of the three skill objectives (i.e., Recognize, Resist, and Report), we believe that recognizing and reporting are the most important to emphasize since these are two skills children can learn and feasibly implement. Preventing the continuation of abuse (through reporting) seems more plausible and realistic for children than preventing the initiation of abuse.

*Remember.* A typical goal of a body safety program is to enhance knowledge about and retention of sexual abuse prevention concepts (e.g., that secrets about touches should not be kept). Most researchers use true-false or multiple-choice tests composed of items specific to the program being evaluated. More work is needed to create items that are difficult enough so that not all children respond correctly at pretest, yet are simple and clear enough for the child's developmental status or reading level.

*Recognize.* How program participants are taught to recognize abuse should be geared to the cognitive limitations and abilities of the audience members. Materials that emphasize feelings as a guide to identifying inappropriate touch requests should not be used with young children. Instead, the definition employed with young children should be narrow, concrete, and specific to sexual behaviors (e.g., teaching children to protect their genitals). As they get older, definitions can be broader and more abstract. For example, with adolescents, discussions about perpetrators' motivations, intentions, and manipulations would be appropriate.

*Resist.* When teaching self-protective skills, modeling and role playing should be employed. Children need opportunities to exercise their personal safety skills and receive feedback on their performance. Program impact on resistance skills may be enhanced by extending the training and including periodic reviews (e.g., booster sessions).

Given young children's egocentric tendency to ascribe self-blame for bad outcomes, there is a strong possibility that children will feel guilty if they either fail to use the resistance strategies or use them but are still abused. Children should not be made responsible for protecting themselves or to feel guilty when they do not respond effectively. To reduce the likelihood of self-blame, presenters should offer resistance techniques as *options* for responding to the abuse (e.g., things they *can* do, instead of *should* do).

*Report.* Program participants should be given permission to disclose abuse (ongoing and previous), taught how to report and about the need to persevere in seeking help, and provided with opportunities to disclose. Given that victims of CSA sometimes disclose their experiences to peers (L. G. Schultz & Jones, 1983), youths should be informed how to respond to their friends' disclosures as well. Prevention researchers must begin documenting the frequency and type of disclosure (i.e., past vs. ongoing abuse; sexual vs. physical abuse) and provide corroborating information (e.g., from parents, school officials, child protection agencies; see Kolko et al., 1989, for an example). Most importantly, the system must be prepared to sensitively handle such disclosures.

## EXPAND THE FOCUS

As suggested in chapter 1, there are several characteristics of children that may make them vulnerable to abuse. One characteristic, addressed by current personal safety programs, is their naïveté about inappropriate sexual contacts. What is needed are efforts to address the other potential risk factors (e.g., low self-esteem, limited decision-making and problem-solving skills, unassertiveness). We suggest that a comprehensive, multiyear curriculum focusing on "human relations training" be included in all children's education. This curriculum would focus on various realms:

- Affective (identifying emotions in self and others, sensitivity to others' feelings, empathy, stress and anger management, impulse control)
- Behavioral (social skills, heterosocial skills, assertiveness, conflict resolution, verbal / nonverbal communication, help-seeking behavior)
- Cognitive (accurate self-appraisal, perspective taking, decision making, problem solving, self-control, self-management, identifying and challenging irrational beliefs)

Given the frequent finding of low self-esteem among both victims and perpetrators, school programs to enhance self-esteem among students would be a valuable addition to this curriculum (e.g., A. W. Pope, McHale, & Craighead, 1988). The curriculum should be designed in a building-block fashion, with lessons and activities for older adolescents being built upon skills and experiences introduced earlier. Multiple educational opportunities should be provided to children as they develop and encounter more complex social interactions. Learning should also take place in a culturally relevant fashion (e.g., Zambrana & Aguirre-Molina, 1987). Training in these skills could also help program participants avoid problems facing many children and youth today (e.g., substance abuse, AIDS, suicide, rape, unwanted pregnancy, assault). Several models already exist for teaching many of these skills (e.g., Botvin, 1983; Camp & Bash, 1981; Clabby & Elias, 1987; Committee for Children, 1989; Elias & Clabby, 1988; Feis & Simons, 1985; Gazda & Pistole, 1986; Guerney, 1977; Kendall & Braswell, 1985; Rotheram-Borus, 1988; Shure & Spivack, 1988; Vernon, 1989a, 1989b).

Developing this orientation will require that schools make a dramatic shift from a "traditional reactive, remedial, orientation to one with a proactive, primary prevention focus" (Zins, Conyne, & Ponti, 1988, p.548). Meyers and Parsons (1987) offer some useful suggestions for overcoming resistance to prevention programs in the schools. In addition to overcoming philosophical resistance, there may be resistance to this approach based on practical concerns (e.g., time, expertise). We recognize that this is an onerous task for schools to undertake and encourage joint school-community partnership efforts to share the responsibilities. For example, New Jersey has adopted a model where schools and community agencies work together to provide services to teenagers in their School-Based Youth Services Program (Kean, 1989).

## PROMOTE HEALTHY SEXUALITY

We concur with Krivacska (1990) that attempts "to divorce education about CSA from any discussion of sexuality are doomed to failure" (p.94). Children and adolescents require instruction that promotes healthy sexuality. They need information regarding normal sexual behavior, thoughts, and feelings, presented at times when they are ready (developmentally) to assimilate the information. For example, adolescents need information about the kinds of sexual feelings they may have for younger children, family members, or same-sex peers, and they need opportunities to discuss how to deal with them. By opening up the channels of communication about sex, we might be able to identify youths who are distressed about sex and also provide remediation before any exploitive behaviors occur. Sexuality education must begin early and continue through high school, with students given progressively sophisticated and detailed information as they develop. In addition to providing factual information, the constant theme of these lessons must be the principle of *respect* for self and others. An underlying message should be that all types of people, regardless of sex, age, race, or culture, have special value and should be treated with respect, dignity, and equality. They need to be taught that force and coercion are not legitimate ways to gain compliance in sexual relationships, and the importance of sexual consent and mutuality of needs must be stressed (see Sparks & Bar On, 1985).

The harm resulting from sexual abuse must be emphasized. With this approach, the focus shifts to preventing the development of sexually exploitive behaviors, which is ultimately the only way we can ever hope to eliminate CSA.

## Summary

Our review of the limited number of published evaluations of prevention programs suggests that these programs can teach children to distinguish between abusive and nonabusive situations, increase their knowledge about sexual abuse, enhance their personal safety skills, and can do so without producing negative side effects. Regardless of these positive findings, these programs should not be viewed as a panacea to the problem of CSA for several reasons. First, the range of factors that contribute to CSA makes the classroom-centered approach a much too simple solution for this complicated problem. Second, the goal of teaching children to successfully fend off a sexual perpetrator is also unrealistic, given the sheer size and power differentials. Third, this literature review reveals that not all program participants show perfect understanding of program concepts, nor do they all display criterion performance during role-play assessments. In addition, consensus is lacking as to whether children should even be educated about sexual abuse. In a nurturing, nonexploitive society, children would not need lessons on self-protection. In our society, however, many dangers exist for children. It would seem inhumane and socially irresponsible not to teach children about a harm that occurs somewhat frequently and is often associated with traumatic consequences. Children and adolescents have a right to be enlightened about sexuality and sexual abuse and to know about their right to live free from such abuse. The more pertinent question is not *whether* to educate children about sexual abuse but rather *how* to do so in an effective, sensitive manner.

Our conclusion is that personal safety education, as currently implemented, is a necessary but insufficient step toward preventing the sexual abuse of children. Classroom-based programs should only be supported when they operate in the context of multilevel preventive efforts (e.g., parent, community, and population-centered approaches), each of which should be viewed as making a contribution toward CSA prevention.

*As a parent, I feel I could benefit from the education of a body safety program, too ... this subject needs the caring support of a parent to be effective.* —ANONYMOUS PARENT, 1990

In chapter 2, child-focused prevention approaches were reviewed and critiqued. We concluded that although classroom-based programs are a promising avenue for prevention efforts, the problem of CSA is too complex to be approached in a unidimensional way. To truly combat this problem, multidimensional approaches are necessary. The present chapter focuses on an additional target group with the potential of playing a critical role in preventing this problem: parents. This chapter is written not only for parents, but also for those who work with parents (e.g., researchers, psychologists, prevention programmers, teachers, etc.).

## Rationale

There are several potential advantages of parent-focused efforts. For example, such efforts may indirectly affect the success of classroom-based prevention programs. Parents' first role in prevention efforts involves permitting their children to participate in the programs. In addition, the success of prevention lessons taught at school depends on the support of parents at home, both to clarify concepts and to help children apply their new knowledge in daily life (Conte & Fogarty, 1989). In contrast, uninformed parents may not be able to answer questions, may contradict accurate information, and may not know how to correct any misconceptions their children may have (Adams & Fay, 1986). Furthermore, if parents could be trained to be prevention educators, then children would receive repeated exposure to prevention information in their natural environment, thus providing a series of booster sessions to supplement other prevention efforts. Discussing sexual abuse with a parent might also make it easier for a child to disclose to that parent if abuse has already occurred, or if it occurs in the future (Finkelhor, 1984; Reppucci & Haugaard, 1989). Finally, because of their frequent contact with children, parents are in a position to aid secondary prevention efforts by identifying child victims and responding to victim disclosures.

Regardless of the advantages of parent-focused prevention efforts, relatively few parents opt to discuss CSA with their children. Recent studies indicate that although the majority of parents report teaching their children general safety rules, very few discuss personal safety in particular. For example, in 1981, Finkelhor (1984) surveyed 521 parents of children aged six to 14 years in Boston and found that fewer of them (29%) had discussed CSA than other difficult topics (e.g., death, pregnancy, homosexuality, abortion). Likewise, the majority of the 86 parents of first and second grade students surveyed by Porch and Petretic-Jackson (1986) indicated that they had discussed difficult topics such as death, kidnapping, and drugs with their children (84–94%), whereas fewer parents (60%) had discussed CSA. Less than half (47%) of the 47 parents of kindergartners surveyed by Wurtele and Miller-Perrin (1987) indicated that they had discussed the topic of CSA with their children.

In a more recent study conducted by the Berkeley Family Welfare Research Group (Berrick, 1988; Gilbert, 1988), preprogram interviews with 116 parents of preschoolers indicated that when discussing "dos and don'ts" with their children, most emphasized "stranger-danger" (72%) rather than general safety rules (45%) or CSA (22%). In contrast, 59% of the 375 parents of preschoolers in Wurtele, Kvaternick, and Franklin (in press) said they had discussed CSA with their children. These findings reveal considerable variability in the percentage of parents reporting discussions of

CSA with their children, ranging from 22% to 60% depending on the particular study in question. This variability may be the result of surveying parents of different-aged children (e.g., preschool vs. school-age children), the method of data collection (e.g., survey vs. interview), and/or the method of subject recruitment (e.g., random sampling vs. parent volunteers). Despite these methodological differences, these data clearly demonstrate that large numbers of parents do not discuss CSA with their children.

Why might parents be reluctant to discuss CSA with their children? Some researchers have asked parents what made it difficult for them to discuss this topic. Table 3 includes some reasons why parents fail to discuss CSA with their children. In addition, lack of confidence in their ability to discuss CSA with their children was mentioned by 31% of the parents in Porch and Petretic-Jackson (1986). Other reasons endorsed by parents in Wurtele, Kvaternick, and Franklin (in press) included a lack of knowledge, vocabulary, or materials. A comparison of these studies indicates that parents in more recent surveys endorse fewer reasons for failing to discuss CSA with their children. The discrepancies between the studies might be the result of methodological differences between the studies and/or a result of changes in parental attitudes occurring over the decade from 1981 to 1991 (see Table 3). Perhaps parental attitudes have become more favorable regarding the discussion of CSA as a result of increased public awareness of the problem.

Results from two recent parent surveys lend further support to the notion that parental attitudes toward CSA prevention are improving. Conte and Fogarty (1989) conducted a survey designed to measure parental knowledge, attitudes, and beliefs about CSA prevention among 376 parents of elementary school–aged children selected from a stratified random sample of counties throughout the 48 contiguous United States. Parent responses indicated a supportive attitude toward prevention, as few believed that prevention programs would harm their children. The large majority indicated that they would be very likely (80%) or somewhat likely (15%) to allow their children to attend a prevention program. In addition, parents "strongly agreed" that CSA prevention should be part of all elementary school curricula and "slightly agreed" that

## Table 3: Reasons Endorsed by Parents for Not Discussing Child Sexual Abuse

| Reasons for Not Discussing | Percentage of Parents | | |
| --- | --- | --- | --- |
| | (a) | (b) | (c) |
| Difficult subject to discuss | 68 | 49 | 6 |
| Topic might frighten child | 44 | 27 | 15 |
| Need for discussion has not occurred to parent | 35 | 13 | 48 |
| Child too young for discussion | 30 | 10 | 42 |
| Child in little danger of abuse | 38 | 8 | 13 |
| Child reluctant to discuss topic | 36 | 1 | 11 |

*Note.* (a) = Finkelhor (1984); (b) = Porch & Petretic-Jackson (1986); (c) = Wurtele, Kvaternick, & Franklin (in press).

children should be exposed to prevention programs in preschool. Over half of the respondents requested additional information on CSA prevention and several asked how they could begin a prevention program in their own community. Although these findings are quite positive, given the poor response rate (7.7%), they may not generalize to all parents and likely reflect the attitudes of proprevention parents. A positive attitude toward CSA prevention, however, was also found in Wurtele and colleagues' survey of 375 parents of preschoolers (50% response rate; Wurtele, Kvaternick, & Franklin, in press). Parents supported the inclusion of CSA prevention programs in preschools, and few believed that prevention programs would harm their children. The majority (84%) indicated that they would be either somewhat or very likely to allow their children to participate in a CSA prevention program. Parents also expressed a strong desire to be involved with their children in prevention efforts. Taken together, these surveys suggest that parents are receptive toward CSA prevention efforts and are interested in assisting such education.

Although historically parents have been included in some prevention efforts (e.g., attending school meetings to preview classroom-based prevention curricula), the time for more expanded parent involvement in prevention efforts has come. That child-focused programs as presently implemented are necessary but not sufficient in the fight against CSA is one indication. In addition, survey research indicates that parents need to acquire more information about CSA as well as guidance in disseminating this information to their children. Finally, recent studies indicate a shift in parental attitudes toward greater acknowledgment of the CSA problem and interest in its prevention.

## Objectives

There are numerous prevention efforts that attempt to involve parents in the prevention movement (see annotated bibliographies of materials by Finkelhor & Araji, 1983; Hallingby & Brick, 1984; Schroeder, Gordon, & McConnell, 1986). Parent-directed prevention efforts vary according to the method used to reach parents. One of the most common parent-focused approaches is to reach parents through orientation meetings where parents are introduced to classroom-based curricula. Other approaches attempt to reach parents through books on CSA and its prevention (e.g., Adams & Fay, 1981; Kraizer, 1985; Sanford, 1980), brief pamphlets on the subject (e.g., DHHS, 1984), or audiovisual methods such as filmstrips and films (e.g., ODN Productions, 1985). More recently, parent-directed prevention efforts have expanded to include prevention training programs, similar to training programs for children, usually referred to as parent workshops (e.g., Porch & Petretic-Jackson, 1986).

Parent-focused approaches also vary according to their objectives. A perusal of these programs reveals a variety of goals, some common to all, some unique to a few innovative programs. The level of sophistication and comprehensiveness of the information varies from those approaches designed simply to inform and reassure parents about the content of classroom-based programs, to those designed to help parents educate their own children. The major objectives as reflected in the literature and available programs include: (a) informing parents about the problem of CSA,

(b) educating parents about how to teach their children CSA prevention, (c) assisting parents in identifying CSA victims, and (d) teaching parents appropriate responses to the disclosures of victims. In the following sections, a review of efforts toward achieving these objectives will be presented.

INFORMING PARENTS ABOUT CHILD SEXUAL ABUSE

We asserted in chapter 1 that the development and implementation of CSA prevention should be guided by a comprehensive understanding of the problem. Information about CSA can likewise help parents gain a deeper understanding of the problem and assist them in protecting and educating their children (primary prevention). Parent-focused prevention approaches need to introduce parents to the multiple dimensions of CSA: the definition of sexual abuse, the pervasiveness of the problem, the characteristics of victims (e.g., age, sex) and perpetrators (e.g., age, sex, relationship to child), and the dynamics of abuse (e.g., type of sexual activity, inherent secrecy of abuse situations).

Most programs and materials for parents include some information about the parameters of CSA. Available materials provide definitions (e.g., Adams & Fay, 1981; Carver County Program, 1980; Lieff & Parker, 1981), report statistics (e.g., Cooper, Lutter, & Phelps, 1983), dispel myths (e.g., Carver County Program, 1980; Cooper et al., 1983), present facts about child abuse (e.g., Carver County Program, 1980), and discuss the dynamics of CSA (e.g., Hagans & Case, 1988). The degree to which different approaches include this information, however, varies. Some approaches merely discuss prevalence statistics (e.g., Children's Self-Help Project, 1981), others cover an intermediate amount of information (e.g., Adams & Fay, 1981), whereas a few notable exceptions are quite comprehensive (e.g., Carver County Program, 1980; Cooper et al., 1983; Hagans & Case, 1988).

Recent studies evaluating parental knowledge of CSA indicate that parents need to receive information about CSA and its prevention. For example, Conte and Fogarty (1989) found that half of their random sample of parents believed that most offenders were under 21 years of age; over one-third believed offenders were "unmarried, immature and socially inept" (p.7). Berrick (1988) found that the majority of parents she interviewed either overestimated or underestimated the prevalence of sexual abuse and less than half (42%) knew that most abuse is committed by someone known to the child. In several studies, parents were found more likely to warn their children about strangers touching their private areas than about other possible perpetrators (Finkelhor, 1984; Wurtele, Kvaternick, & Franklin, in press; Wurtele & Miller-Perrin, 1987). Thus, parent-focused efforts might play an important role in dispelling myths and providing accurate information about CSA.

In addition to informing parents about the parameters of the CSA problem, prevention efforts directed at parents should include other topics that to date have been neglected. Materials for parents might help them explore and clarify how their values and knowledge related to sexuality, as well as their own sexual experiences, might influence their prevention attitudes and behaviors. In addition, it would be helpful to familiarize parents with CSA risk factors, particularly what they can do to keep their child safe (i.e., reducing risk factors and increasing protective factors; see chapter 1). For example, by educating them about high-risk situations, parents can become more effective in reducing an offender's access to their children by increasing supervision, rearranging sleeping conditions that might be conducive to inappropriate sexual behaviors between family members, and checking day-care and baby-sitting arrangements. Educating parents about protective factors and specific actions they can take to enhance such factors (e.g., teaching their children such MegaSkills [see Rich, 1988] as confidence and problem solving, building their child's self-esteem, communicating openly within the family and discouraging secrets, enhancing healthy sexuality, stressing the importance of personal body safety and privacy in the home) might also reduce the risk of abuse. Finally, in this age of enhanced concern about the sexual touching of children, parents also need to be reassured that non-sexual touching is a natural and essential part of parenting.

Two studies have evaluated the effects of interventions on parents' knowledge about CSA and related prevention skills. Porch and Petretic-Jackson (1986) evaluated the effectiveness of Child

Assault Prevention Project's parent education workshops by pre- and posttesting 85 parents on their knowledge about sexual abuse and skills in initiating prevention behaviors in the home. Following their participation in the workshop, parents showed an increase in knowledge about CSA, which was maintained at the four-week follow-up. In addition, parents reported an increase in prevention behaviors, including warning children about specific situations (e.g., someone removing their clothing and touching their genitals) and possible perpetrators (i.e., known adults), and recommending responses to abusive encounters (i.e., saying "no", screaming). Discussions with their children about sexual abuse increased from pretest (57%) to posttest (84%). However, increases were observed for only 50% of knowledge items and 28% of prevention behaviors. Unfortunately, the researchers did not employ a control group, making it unclear whether the observed changes (however minimal) were indeed a result of the parent workshop.

More recently, Berrick (1988) evaluated the effect of workshops on parents' attitudes toward CSA prevention, knowledge about the parameters of abuse, identification of behavioral signs of abused children, and reporting behavior. The parent components of seven preschool programs operating across California were evaluated using pre- and posttest interviews with parents. Results indicated that attendance at the parents' meeting had little impact on parents' perceptions of the rate of child abuse or perpetrator identity, perhaps because parental knowledge was reasonably accurate before they attended the meeting. For example, 42% of parents at pretest believed that the offender is most often known to the child. At posttest, parents were unable to identify many indicators of sexual abuse, and minimal change was observed in the average number of people or agencies to whom they answered they would report cases of abuse. Results also indicated that parents who attended meetings were as likely to discuss CSA prevention with their children as nonattenders. The author concluded, "It is difficult to see the particular benefits parent meetings offer in terms of child abuse prevention" (p.551).

We believe such a conclusion is premature, however, given the methodological limitations of this study. For example, only 34%

of parents attended the meetings and there was a 19% rate of attrition from pretest to posttest. The design of this study was flawed because of its small sample, lack of a control group, and use of nonstandardized assessment procedures. In addition, the effects of seven different parent workshops were combined. Although the workshops were similar in content, they differed on a number of dimensions, including comprehensiveness, presentation, and duration, among others.

Although both studies are limited by methodological problems, they do indicate that parents are able to acquire some prevention knowledge and skills as a result of parent-focused programs. Much work is needed, however, to improve the content, process, and evaluation of parent workshops. One objective to be addressed is how to involve more parents (especially fathers). Others have noted the difficulty in enlisting parent's cooperation, especially interest and participation (Berrick, 1988; Garbarino, 1988; Peterson, Mori, Selby, & Rosen, 1988). Less-interested parents might become more involved if prevention proponents found more convenient meeting times and places for them (e.g., after work hours, lunchtime meetings in the workplace, meetings at social or religious organizations) or used innovative instructional media (e.g., television, videos, newspapers, or magazines). These various alternatives also have the potential of reaching a greater number of males, thereby increasing the likelihood of deterring potential perpetrators.

## EDUCATING CHILDREN

In addition to providing parents with a comprehensive understanding of the CSA problem, parent-focused efforts could help those parents who want to be more actively involved in educating their children about CSA. As noted in chapter 2, educating children about CSA is a primary prevention goal. Many parent-focused approaches encourage parents to teach specific body safety skills that children can use to protect themselves (e.g., say "no," get away, and tell someone; Council on Child Abuse, 1982; S. Gordon & Gordon, 1984; Hyde, 1984). Others take a broader approach by teaching children assertiveness training and physical self-defense (e.g., Colao & Hosansky, 1987) or by suggesting how parents might build their children's self-esteem in order to prevent abuse (e.g., Sanford, 1980).

Prevention approaches also vary in their suggested methods of imparting information to children. For example, several approaches offer general guidelines on how to discuss this difficult topic with children (e.g., Adams & Fay, 1981; Carver County Program, 1980; Cooper et al., 1983; Council on Child Abuse, 1982; Hart-Rossi, 1984; Project SAAFE, 1984; Schaefer, 1984). Others suggest that parents use role-play exercises, activities, or games (e.g., Adams & Fay, 1981; Carver County Program, 1980; Children's Self-Help Project, 1981; Hart-Rossi, 1984; Kraizer, 1985; Porch & Petretic-Jackson, 1986; Sanford, 1982).

Other important issues should be addressed when training parents to educate their children about abuse. For example, parent-directed prevention efforts need to address the potential guilt that parents might experience should their children be victimized, despite their prevention efforts. Programs that describe the complexity of the CSA problem and emphasize the shared responsibility for prevention might reduce parental perceptions of their sole responsibility for the incident. In addition, parent-directed efforts might serve to inform parents about how they can clarify and reinforce what is taught in school. Parents are in a pivotal position to support classroom-based prevention efforts and, conversely, are in a prominent position to thwart such prevention attempts. For example, parents may punish their children for asserting the rights sometimes taught in personal safety programs (e.g., the right to say "No" to adults). Parent-directed approaches should address what is taught in classroom-based prevention programs and the rationale behind these concepts, so that the lessons learned at home and at school do not contradict each other.

As noted in the beginning of this chapter, there are several barriers keeping parents from discussing CSA and its prevention with their children. It is important for prevention efforts to address these barriers with parents. To help parents feel more comfortable discussing CSA and its prevention, parent-directed efforts should provide parents with vocabulary as well as practice in discussing

CSA. Parents should be encouraged to use teaching aids such as books, videos, or puppets. These materials help take the focus off parents and may reduce their fears of appearing ignorant or tongue-tied.

A few studies have attempted to evaluate the efficacy of parents as educators of their children. Although early studies suggested that parents are ineffective trainers of their children's personal safety skills (e.g., Miltenberger & Thiesse-Duffy, 1988; Miltenberger, Thiesse-Duffy, Suda, Kozak, & Bruellman, 1990), more recent work suggests that parents can be very effective instructors (Wurtele, Currier, Gillispie, & Franklin, 1991; Wurtele, Gillispie, Currier, & Franklin, 1992; Wurtele, Kast, & Melzer, in press). In studies conducted by Wurtele and colleagues, parents were provided with the Behavioral Skills Training (BST) program, which included background information on CSA along with a script (to overcome parents' concerns about lacking the vocabulary to discuss the topic). Children received pictures to accompany the stories in the program, along with a "token time" packet, which contained the objectives of the BST program. As each concept or skill was mastered, the child placed a sticker next to the description of the objective. (This device was included to help parents track their children's progress, to maintain their children's attention, to provide self-reinforcement for their children, and to check on parental compliance in teaching the program.) Parents taught personal safety skills via instruction, modeling, rehearsal, and praise.

Results from Wurtele et al. (1991) suggested that when using a developmentally appropriate program that employs a behavioral approach, middle-class parents are indeed effective teachers, as their children (aged 3½ to 5½ years) significantly improved their knowledge about CSA and their abilities to recognize inappropriate touch requests and respond appropriately in these situations.

Similar results were obtained in two studies in which parents of children enrolled in a Head Start program were asked to teach the BST program at home. In Wurtele, Gillispie, Currier, and Franklin (1992), 61 low-income preschoolers were pretested and participated in either a home-based program, a school-based program (taught by the classroom teachers), or an attention control program. At posttesting, no significant differences were found on knowledge and skill tests between groups of children taught by parents or teachers, and children in both groups demonstrated greater knowledge about sexual abuse and higher levels of personal safety skills than children in a control group. Knowledge and skill gains were maintained at the two-month follow-up.

In Wurtele, Kast, and Melzer (in press), 172 Head Start preschoolers were taught the BST program by their teachers, parents, both teachers and parents, or they participated in a general safety control program. Following program participation, children taught the BST program by their teachers, parents, or both demonstrated greater knowledge about sexual abuse and higher levels of personal safety skills than children in the control group. Gains in knowledge and skills were maintained at the five-month follow-up. Children taught by their parents showed greater improvements in recognizing inappropriate requests to touch their genitals and in their personal safety skills than children taught by their teachers. Children who received the program both at home and school were better able to recognize appropriate requests to touch their genitals and demonstrated higher levels of personal safety skills than children taught only at school.

Although the findings of these studies are specific to preschool-aged children and cannot be generalized to other age groups, they do demonstrate the potential of parents as effective disseminators of CSA prevention information. We recognize that any large-scale approach of asking parents to teach their children about CSA may not be reasonable or feasible, particularly with abusing and/or severely dysfunctional families, for whom classroom-based interventions would be required. Much work is needed to determine what types of parents are most receptive to, and effective at, teaching their children.

## IDENTIFYING VICTIMS

Parents, because of their frequent contact with children, are in an excellent position to detect when abuse is occurring (a secondary prevention goal). Victim identification is a critical component of parent-focused prevention programs, because many cases of victimization are not brought into awareness. As noted in chapter 1, only a small percentage of children who are victimized will report the abuse themselves, and even smaller numbers are actually detected and reported by professionals. In that chapter we reviewed the many reasons why children fail to disclose when they have been sexually abused (e.g., pressure for secrecy, fears that they will not be believed, etc.). Another reason why many cases go undetected is that parents and professionals are simply not aware of the signs and symptoms associated with abuse, making it difficult to accurately identify CSA cases and implement proper intervention to terminate the abuse and protect child victims.

Guidelines for identifying signs of CSA vary from general caveats to "be alert to any unusual stress in a child" (Strasser & Bailey, 1984, p.38) to detailed lists of possible symptoms (e.g., Downer, 1985; Krugman, 1986; MacFarlane, 1986). Experts generally group the symptoms of victimization into physical, emotional, and behavioral indicators of abuse. Little emphasis, however, has been placed on understanding how these physical, emotional, and behavioral patterns vary across different ages of children, or on viewing these symptoms within the context of normal development. Indeed, it is only recently that the field of child psychology has recognized the importance of understanding normal development when discussing aberrations in child behavior (Gelfand & Peterson, 1985). In this section, we will present developmentally specific behavior patterns that might indicate the occurrence of abuse and emphasize that these indicators must be viewed in the context of normal development.

*Sexual Abuse Indicators.* As noted in chapter 1, symptoms of CSA do not follow a set pattern, nor do all child victims display the same kinds of behaviors. In some cases, there are no demonstrable changes in behavior. Yet because watching for and noting changes in children's behaviors may be one of the only ways parents can identify the problem, it is important for parents to be aware of the possible signs of abuse. Recent research indicates that parents need such information. For example, when Berrick (1988) asked a group of parents prior to their participation in a CSA prevention workshop, "What might make you think a child had been sexually abused?," an average of only 1.85 indicators were mentioned. Instead, parents frequently depended upon their intuition or referred to one generalized change in their child's behavior as an indicator of abuse (e.g., "I'd just know by the way he acts"; or "she'd just act different, but I would know", p.549). Parents need to be informed of specific and concrete signs indicating the possibility that a child has been sexually abused. Various behavioral, emotional, and physical indicators of sexual abuse are listed in Table 4 according to the developmental level (age) of the child.

Among preschool-aged children, several behavioral indicators have been noted. For example, sexualized behavior in preschoolers is one of the most common indicators of abuse and includes preoccupation with sexual matters and atypical knowledge of sexual acts, excessive masturbation, exposure of genitals, seductive behavior, sexual aggressiveness, requests for sexual stimulation, and sexual victimization of other children. Other indicators noted in preschoolers include withdrawal; regressive behaviors such as bed-wetting, thumb sucking, and baby talk; and difficulty separating from adults. Emotional indicators frequently noted in preschoolers include guilt, depressive symptomatology, anger and hostility (e.g., tantrums, aggressive behaviors), and most commonly, general anxiety (e.g., clinging behavior, nightmares) and specific fears (e.g., of adults). Physical effects observed in preschoolers include sleep and appetite disturbances, somatic complaints (e.g., enuresis, encopresis, stomachaches, headaches), bruises, genital bleeding, pain and itching of the genitals, unusual genital odors, and problems walking or sitting.

In school-aged children, behavioral indicators are similar and include sexualized behaviors (preoccupation with sexual matters, masturbation, exposure of genitals, sex play with others, sexual language, seductiveness, and victimization of other children) and social withdrawal, with less fear of separation and regression to infantile behavior. School-aged children, however, frequently exhibit school-related problems such as learning difficulties and declining grades, difficulties with concentration and attention, and poor peer relations. In addition, acting-out behaviors such as delin-

**Table 4: Behavioral, Emotional, and Physical Indicators of Sexual Abuse According to Level of Development**

| Sexual Abuse Indicators | Developmental Level | | |
| --- | --- | --- | --- |
| | Preschool (0–5 yrs) | School-Age (6–12 yrs) | Adolescence (13–16 yrs) |
| BEHAVIORAL | | | |
| Regression | X | | |
| Social withdrawal | X | X | X |
| Preoccupation with sex | X | X | X |
| Knowledge of sexual acts | X | X | X |
| Seductive behavior | X | X | X |
| Excessive masturbation | X | X | |
| Sex play with others | X | X | |
| Sexual language | X | X | X |
| Genital exposure | X | X | |
| Victimizing others | X | X | X |
| Promiscuity / prostitution | | | X |
| Difficulty separating | X | | |
| Delinquency | | X | X |
| Stealing | | X | X |
| Running away | | X | X |
| Early marriage | | | X |
| Substance abuse | | X | X |
| Truancy | | | X |
| Dropping out of school | | | X |
| Learning difficulties | | X | X |
| Poor concentration / attention | | X | X |
| Declining grades | | X | X |
| Poor peer relations | | X | X |
| | | | |
| EMOTIONAL | | | |
| Anxiety | X | X | X |
| Clinging | X | | |
| Nightmares | X | X | X |
| Fears of adults | X | X | |

**Table 4, continued**

| Sexual Abuse Indicators | Developmental Level | | |
|---|---|---|---|
| | Preschool (0–5 yrs) | School-Age (6–12 yrs) | Adolescence (13–16 yrs) |
| Phobias | | x | x |
| Obsessions | | x | x |
| Tics | | x | |
| Depression | x | x | x |
| Guilt | x | x | x |
| Suicidal ideation | | | x |
| Suicide attempts | | x | x |
| Low self-esteem / confidence | | | x |
| Hostility / anger | x | x | x |
| Tantrums | x | | |
| Aggression | x | x | |
| Family / peer conflicts | x | x | |
| | | | |
| PHYSICAL | | | |
| Bruises / genital bleeding | x | | |
| Genital pain / itching / odors | x | x | x |
| Problems walking / sitting | x | x | x |
| Sleep disturbance | x | x | x |
| Appetite disturbance | x | x | x |
| Somatic concerns | x | x | x |
| Enuresis | x | x | |
| Encopresis | x | x | |
| Stomachaches | x | x | x |
| Headaches | x | x | x |
| Pregnancy | | | x |

*Note.* The information in this table was provided by the following sources: Adams-Tucker, 1981, 1982; S. C. Anderson, Bach, & Griffith, 1981; Becker, Cunningham-Rathner, & Kaplan, 1986; Brassard, Tyler, & Kehle, 1983; Burgess, Groth, & McCausland, 1981; Cavaiola & Schiff, 1988; J. A. Cohen & Mannarino, 1988; DeFrancis, 1969; Deisher, Robinson, & Boyer, 1982; Einbender & Friedrich, 1989; Elwell & Ephros, 1987; Friedrich et al., 1986; Gale et al., 1988; Gomes-

## Table 4, continued

Schwartz, Horowitz, & Sauzier, 1985; Gomes-Schwartz et al., 1990; Goodwin, 1981; Groth, 1977; Harrison, Hoffman, & Edwall, 1989; Hillman & Solek-Tefft, 1988; R. L. Johnson & Shrier, 1985; T. C. Johnson, 1988; Kempe & Kempe, 1984; Kohan, Pothier, & Norbeck, 1987; Kolko, Moser, & Weldy, 1988; Lewis & Sarrel, 1969; Lindberg & Distad, 1985; Livingston, 1987; Lusk & Waterman, 1986; MacVicar, 1979; Mannarino & Cohen, 1986; Massie & Johnson, 1989; Meiselman, 1978; Mian et al., 1986; Miller-Perrin & Wurtele, 1990; Paperny & Deisher, 1983; Pascoe & Duterte, 1981; Peters, 1976; Riggs, 1982; Rimsza, Berg, & Locke, 1988; Rosenfeld, Nadelson, Krieger, & Backman, 1979; Silbert & Pines, 1983; Tong, Oates, & McDowell, 1987; J. Weiss, Rogers, Darwin, & Dutton, 1955; S. White, Halpin, Strom, & Santilli, 1988.

quency, stealing, running away, and substance abuse have been noted. School-aged victims also show such emotional problems as guilt, depression, anxiety and phobias, and hostility and aggression. The behaviors associated with these affective states, however, differ somewhat for school-aged children and include suicide attempts, tics, and obsessions. Physical effects in school-aged children are similar to those in preschool children and include sleep and appetite disturbances and somatic complaints. Physical signs such as bruises and genital bleeding tend to be less frequently noted in school-aged children than in preschoolers, although school-aged children may exhibit pain and itching of the genitals, unusual genital odors, and problems walking or sitting.

The behavioral, emotional, and physical indicators characteristic of adolescent victims are similar to those of school-aged children with several slight deviations. Similar sexualized behaviors are present in the adolescent victim of sexual abuse, but additional behaviors such as promiscuity and prostitution are also evident. Social withdrawal is another adolescent indicator, as are early marriages by adolescent victims. Antisocial behaviors (e.g., running away, drug abuse, delinquency) continue to be an indicator for adolescent victims. For the adolescent victim, school problems take a different form and include dropping out of school and truancy. Emotional effects also include guilt, depression (including suicidal ideation and attempts), and anxiety, as well as lowered self-esteem and confidence. Physical indicators are similar to those observed in school-aged children, although early pregnancy can be an additional complication for adolescents.

It must be stressed to parents that none of the above presentations is pathognomonic of CSA. Many of these indicators can result from stress in general and are not specific to CSA (Legrand, Wakefield, & Underwager, 1989). How then, is one to determine cause for alarm or suspicion? Several guidelines have been suggested. For example, parents are warned to be alert for any radical changes in behavior (Hagans & Case, 1988; Meddin & Rosen, 1986). A key consideration is whether these behaviors are a dramatic change from a child's usual pattern of behavior.

Children molested over a long period of time, however, may have a long history of one or more of these indicators, which will not stand out as a recent change. Such cases might be identified using an additional guideline: When symptoms are chronic and fail to respond to usual methods of management, CSA should be considered (Krugman, 1986). In addition, rarely does the presence or absence of a single factor confirm whether or not CSA has occurred. A pattern of these symptoms and behaviors, however, will more likely indicate harm or risk to the child (Meddin & Rosen, 1986; Miller-Perrin & Wurtele, 1988). The severity of the symptoms presented has also been suggested as important by Krents, Schulman, and Brenner (1987), who state, "When one or more of these indicators appears in extreme or repeatedly, there is enough justification for suspecting abuse." (p.85). Finally, it is important to keep in mind that although the appearance of such indicators does not absolutely indicate CSA, it does suggest the need to search for the cause of the behavior (Tennant, 1988).

Materials for parents have appeared informing them about specific indicators of sexual abuse, including several books (e.g., Hagans & Case, 1988; MacFarlane et al., 1986), pamphlets (e.g., Lieff & Parker, 1981), and parent workshops or meetings (e.g., Project SAAFE, 1984). Many materials for parents neglect this area, however, and even programs that do discuss CSA identification do not always include comprehensive coverage of indicators (i.e., physical, emotional, behavioral) and in most cases fail to inform parents about developmental variations. In addition, there is a dearth of attention to developmentally appropriate behaviors, although some efforts to provide this information are beginning to appear (e.g., Hagans & Case, 1988; Parent Education Center of Yakima, 1984; Waterman, 1986).

*Age-Appropriate Sexuality.* As noted in both chapter 1 and the previous section, one of the symptoms of abuse cited most often is sexualized behavior. In order to identify sexualized behavior in child victims of molestation, parents must first know what constitutes normal, developmentally appropriate sexuality, including age-appropriate knowledge and behavior. Parents who are aware of children's sexual knowledge and behavior and how these characteristics change over the course of development should be better equipped to identify child victims. Unfortunately, little work has been conducted to guide an understanding of the sexual nature and experiences of children (Haroian, 1983; Martinson, 1981). In the following sections, we will review our current understanding in this area, outlining normative behavior for children of different ages in terms of sexual knowledge and behavior.

*Age-Appropriate Sexual Knowledge.* Table 5 shows what children of different ages typically know about sexuality. Several sources have provided information about normative childhood sexual knowledge including retrospective reports from adults, observations made by parents or teachers, interviews with children, and children's drawings.

Gebhard (1977) compared unpublished Kinsey data with a small college sample to examine the acquisition of basic sex information. Knowledge of intercourse steadily increased from early childhood until near puberty where there was a marked acceleration in knowledge. For example, few students reported that they understood about intercourse before they were 5 years old (less than 1% of Kinsey's sample and none of Gebhard's sample). The

## Table 5: Age-Appropriate Sexual Knowledge

| | Developmental Level | |
| Preschool (0–5 yrs) | School Age (6–12 yrs) | Adolescence (13–16 yrs) |
| --- | --- | --- |
| GENDER IDENTITY By the end of this period, majority have well-developed sense of gender identity, but not all children understand that they will always be that gender | Gender identity and gender constancy firmly established; can identify maleness and femaleness by genitalia | Firmly established gender identity |
| BODY PARTS Largely unaware of correct terminology for genitals; use primarily slang terms | Use primarily slang terms until age 10 | Know correct terms for sexual body parts |
| BODY FUNCTIONS Some preschoolers mention elimination functions for sexual body parts; most are unaware of sexual functions | Children aged 6–9 are aware of sexual functions as they are related to pregnancy; otherwise describe elimination functions for the penis, vagina, and anus and nursing functions for the breast | Knowledgeable about sexual functions |
| SEXUAL BEHAVIORS Minority are aware of sexual activities and behaviors; very limited knowledge of intercourse or other adult behaviors; knowledge of masturbation is also limited until ages 4–5, when one-third become aware | Early school-aged (6–9 yrs) children's knowledge is related to kissing and hugging; by ages 10–12, 50% are aware of sexual touching, masturbation, and intercourse; from ages 10–11 yrs, males also become aware of penile erections | By age 13 most children are knowledgeable about sexual intercourse and masturbation; most females become knowledgeable about penile erections from 12–15 yrs |

majority of Kinsey's sample reported learning about intercourse when they were between 10 and 13 years old; more than half of Gebhard's sample were knowledgeable by the end of their tenth year. When asked when they first learned about penile erections, one-third of females in Kinsey's study were knowledgeable by age 15, with most (53%) reporting knowledge acquisition between 15 to 18 years. Females in Gebhard's sample obtained this information at a much earlier age, as 80% of females were knowledgeable by age 15 with the majority (62%) obtaining such knowledge between 12 to 15 years. The majority of Gebhard's male subjects knew about penile erections by age 11.

Janus and Bess (1981) analyzed the picture drawings and essays of 3,200 children (aged 5 to 12 years) to examine their knowledge of gender identity and sexual activity. They found that 97% of both boys and girls in kindergarten and first grade had a well-developed sense of their gender identity. (Others have found that children acquire a firm gender identity, or an awareness that they are either a boy or a girl, by the age of 2½ to 3; Thompson, 1975.) A minority of kindergartners (16–24%) mentioned sexual activities or behaviors, which included kissing different areas of the body (e.g., mouth and neck), creating babies, and feelings of "liking" and "loving." Approximately 18–35% of second and third graders mentioned such sexual activities as kissing, hugging, and dancing with the opposite sex. By fourth through fifth grade, 39–44% of children were aware of touching and its connection with sex, nude magazines, and more intimate sexual activity and vocabulary. Just over half of the sixth graders displayed sexual knowledge about such topics as menarche, pregnancy, intercourse, masturbation, and sexual desire.

Goldman and Goldman (1989) asked 1,000 children (aged 5 to 15 years) in five different countries (Australia, United States, Canada, England, and Sweden) a standardized series of questions regarding their sexual knowledge. They found that children 5 and 6 years old relied on nonsexual physical characteristics in determining sex differences (e.g., clothes, hair styles). Children aged 7 to 9 years made identifications based on slang terms for genitalia and mentioned elimination rather than sexual functions for genitalia. Children 10 years and older were able to identify sexual organs with their correct terms.

These researchers also investigated the age at which children knew about sexual intercourse. Knowledge varied by country. By

9 years, 100% of Swedish, 48% of English, 40% of Australian, and only 17% of North American children were aware of intercourse. By age 11, percentages increased to 95% of Australian, 80% of English, and 50% of North American children. By age 13, all children across all countries had knowledge about sexual intercourse. However, 50% of these children saw having babies as the sole reason for sexual intercourse.

More recently, B. N. Gordon, Schroeder, and Abrams (1990a) interviewed 130 2- to 7-year-old children to assess their knowledge about sexual body parts and behavior. Knowledge acquisition showed a distinct developmental progression. For example, almost all (97%) of the older children (ages 6 and 7) but only 45% of the younger children (ages 2 through 5 years) knew that babies grew inside the mother. Few at any age knew about the sexual aspects of pregnancy. Indeed, only 8 children demonstrated a knowledge of sexual intercourse (mostly 6- and 7-year-olds). Knowledge of masturbation was limited in children under 5 years of age, although 58% of the older children knew about the topic.

Knowledge of genital terminology also varied across ages. Although the majority (78%) of older children knew the correct label for *penis*, only 32% of younger children had such knowledge. For *vagina*, 42% of the older children knew the correct label compared to only 11% of the younger children. As found by Schor and Sivan (1989), children at all ages were more knowledgeable about male than female genitalia. None of the children knew the correct term for *anus*, but the majority of 3- to 7-year-olds gave a slang name for this body part. About half (55%) of the older children knew the correct label for *breasts*, whereas few (26%) younger children did; most used slang terms. Only 7 children (primarily 5 years or older) gave sexual functions for these body parts; for those that did, they discussed functions related to pregnancy and birth. Most of the children gave elimination functions for the penis, vagina, and anus, and nursing functions for the breast.

*Age-Appropriate Sexual Behaviors.* Table 6 shows those sexual behaviors that have been observed among children of different ages. Four studies provide the majority of information about de-

## Table 6: Age-Appropriate Sexual Behavior

| Age Range | Sexual Behaviors |
| --- | --- |
| PRESCHOOL (0–5 YEARS) | Sexual language is used frequently and is primarily related to anatomical differences, elimination processes, and pregnancy and birth; use of sexual words and discussion of sexual acts is uncommon; masturbation at home and in public is common; contact experiences with other children are rare; exhibitionistic and voyeuristic behaviors are common; adultlike or aggressive sexual behaviors are rare |
| SCHOOL AGE (6–12 YEARS) | Questions center around menstruation, pregnancy, and sexual conduct; use of sexual words and discussing sexual acts is more frequent than during preschool years although still uncommon (10–20%); masturbation is common in the home or other private places but rare in public; contact experiences with other children are very common and typically occur during "games" with same-age peers involving primarily heterosexual encounters including kissing, hugging, fondling, exhibitionism, and role playing; adultlike or aggressive sexual behaviors are rare |
| ADOLESCENCE (13–16 YEARS) | Questions focus on concerns about decision making, social relationships, and sexual mores; masturbation is common and restricted to socially appropriate settings; contact experiences with peers are common and include open-mouth kissing, fondling, simulated intercourse; voyeuristic behaviors are common; sexual intercourse occurs in approximately one-third of this age group |

velopmentally appropriate sexual behavior: (a) questionnaire data from Kinsey's large-scale retrospective studies on sexuality (Kinsey, Pomeroy, & Martin, 1948; Kinsey et al., 1953); (b) observational data from 60 Norwegian preschool teachers who were interviewed about the sexual behavior of 400 children aged 3 to 7 years (Gundersen, Melas, & Skar, 1981); (c) questionnaire data collected by Goldman and Goldman (1989) from 1,000 first-year students (aged 18–23 years) in Australian universities and colleges regarding sexual experiences before age 17; and (d) behavioral ratings provided by mothers of 880 children aged 2 to 12 years (Friedrich, Grambsch, Broughton, Kuiper, & Beilke, 1991). Following is a description of the findings from these and other studies that have investigated sexual language and questions, masturbation, homo- and heterosexual play, and intercourse.

Gundersen and colleagues (1981) queried teachers about the sexual language used and questions asked by their preschool students. Half of the teachers reported that sexual words (e.g., for sex organs or elimination processes) were used "occasionally"; the other 50% said they were used "often" or "very often." Children rarely asked questions related to sexual matters; most of the questions were about anatomical sex differences, pregnancy, and childbirth. Similarly, Broderick (1969) found that many preschool children showed an interest in sex differences, both physical and behavioral. In addition, children at this age expressed interest in where babies come from, especially if a new baby was part of their experience. Preschool-aged children rarely asked questions about sexual intercourse or conception, however, unless these were raised by older children or adults. Children aged 6 to 12 years asked questions about menstruation, pregnancy, and sexual conduct, whereas adolescents asked questions about decision making, social relationships, and sexual mores. Friedrich et al. (1991) found the use of sexual words and discussions of sexual acts to be infrequent among young children (aged 7 to 12 years), as only 12% of females and 20% of males used sexual words and less than 11% of both sexes talked about sexual acts.

Masturbation appears to be quite common in children and begins at an early age. For example, a baby discovers its area of sexual pleasure at about six months of age (Calderone, 1983), and by his or her first birthday, sporadic self-stimulation becomes more intentional (Roiphe & Galenson, 1981). Almost all of the respondents (94%) in Gundersen et al. (1981) stated that the children, aged 3 to 7 years, showed marked interest in their own genitals, indicated by fondling and showing them to others. In addition, masturbation was observed (24% said it occurred "often" or "very often") by 85% of the participants in the study; 23% of the teachers had observed orgasm in masturbating children.

Parents in Friedrich et al. (1991) indicated that masturbatory behaviors (e.g., masturbating with hand, touching sex parts in public, touching sex parts at home) were quite common (15–46%) in the children they studied and decreased with age. For example, 19% (girls) to 36% (boys) of young children (aged 2 to 6 years) were reported by mothers to touch their sex parts in public, whereas only 3% (girls) to 16% (boys) of older children (aged 7 to 12 years) did so. Goldman and Goldman (1989) asked college students about their first sexual experiences and found that from ages 2 to 4, students reported masturbating for comfort, whereas from ages 3 to 9 years, fondling became more deliberate, often done for pleasure. By age 10, subjects reported masturbating to orgasm. Bell, Weinberg, and Hammersmith (1981) found that by the age of 13, 63% of boys and 32% of girls had already begun masturbating (with boys masturbating sooner, more frequently, and more often in the company of same-sex peers than girls).

Other researchers have investigated children's heterosexual and homosexual behaviors. Goldman and Goldman (1989) asked students to describe their early childhood experiences with other children; over 64% reported some type of sexual experience with another child. The peak ages for such experiences were between 6 and 12 years. Experiences were with children about the same age (within one or two years) and primarily occurred in heterosexual twosomes, usually with friends, although some experiences occurred with cousins and siblings. The students reported playing games such as "cowboys and Indians" (involving kissing, hugging, fondling), "mothers and fathers" (dressing for dinner, undressing for bed, getting married), and "doctors and nurses" (body examination). Sexual activities included kissing and hugging, exhibiting sexual organs, and fondling or touching sex organs. Few (18%) reported participating in sexual intercourse without penetration (e.g., mutual masturbation, rubbing sex organs together), and even fewer (1%) reported intercourse or attempted intercourse. Similar results were obtained by Gundersen et al. (1981) who reported that all teachers observed some game playing in their preschoolers, including doctor/nurse/patient games and family role playing. Fifty percent of them said that this play contained some direct sexual behavior, such as exploring bodies and genitals and coitus training.

Precise estimates of children's homosexual behaviors are difficult to obtain, although experts suggest that homosexual experimentation occurs frequently during later childhood, particularly among males. According to R. E. Jones (1984), approximately half of preadolescent boys and a third of girls engage in some form of homosexual play. Male students in the Kinsey studies indicated that 30% were involved in homosexual play and 40% had experienced heterosexual play (including exhibition and looking, as well as touching) by the age of 12 years. Among female respondents, about 20% remembered childhood homosexual experiences and 30% reported heterosexual childhood experiences (including looking and exhibition) by the age of 12 years.

To determine types of sexual activity, Friedrich et al. (1991) obtained mothers' ratings of the occurrence of various sexual behaviors in children and found sexual touching of others' genitals to be relatively rare (6%). Touching of others' breasts, however, was quite common (31%), particularly for younger children (44–48%). (Others have likewise found that touching a parent's genitals [especially mothers' breasts] is not uncommon among children aged 2 to 10; see Rosenfeld, Bailey, Siegel, & Bailey, 1986). Younger children also displayed exhibitionistic and voyeuristic behaviors (e.g., showing sex parts to other children or adults, watching others undress, sitting with crotch exposed, undressing in front of others) more frequently than older children.

In contrast, adultlike sexual behavior (e.g., putting mouth on others' sex parts, asking to engage in sexual acts, masturbating with objects, inserting objects in vagina or anus, imitating intercourse, and French kissing) as well as aggressive sexual behaviors (e.g., coercive fellatio) were very rare in both younger and older children (0–4%). By age 13, 68% of girls and 65% of boys reported they had kissed or been kissed in Vener and Stewart (1974). Goldman and Goldman (1989) asked college students about their initial intercourse experiences and found that only 2% had participated before 11 years, with proportions steadily increasing thereafter (6% between 11–13 years; 39% from 14–16 years). By age 16, more than 31% of females (Zelnik & Kantner, 1980) and 38% of males (Sonnerstein, Pleck, & Ku, 1989) have experienced coitus.

*Summary.* Young children (ages 2 to 5) are most interested in where babies come from and in physical differences between boys and girls. Almost all children can accurately label themselves as boys or girls (i.e., gender identity) by 2 or 3 years of age. They begin to understand that sex is an unchanging quality (i.e., gender constancy) between the ages of 5 and 7 (or even earlier; see Bem, 1989). Children at this age are largely unaware of the correct terminology for genitals (especially females'), although they frequently use slang terms. As far as what the genitals are used for, preschoolers often mention elimination functions but remain unaware of sexual functions. Knowledge about sexual intercourse or other forms of adult sexual behavior (other than kissing and holding hands) appears to be very rare in preschool children, although awareness of masturbation develops by the end of this period. For the most part, sexual experiences are consistent with knowledge levels and include masturbation as well as exhibitionistic and voyeuristic behaviors, whereas adultlike and aggressive sexual behaviors are rare.

School-aged children (ages 6 to 12) have a more developed understanding about and interest in sexuality. At this age, children are quite curious about the physiology of sex and desire concrete and accurate information about sexuality. Children at this age are aware of gender differences and can identify maleness and femaleness by genitalia. They provide primarily slang labels for genitals until age 10, when they begin using correct labels. Younger school-aged children (ages 6 to 9) are aware of sexual functions as they are related to pregnancy but otherwise provide elimination functions for genitals. Knowledge regarding sexual behaviors is also variable among school-aged children. For children aged 6 to 9, their knowledge is limited to kissing and hugging; by ages 10 to 12, about half of school-aged children have some knowledge about sexual intercourse, sexual touching, and masturbation. As children turn 6 or 7 their sense of modesty becomes stronger, although a natural sexual curiosity may be expressed through game playing with same- or opposite-sex peers during the school years. Masturbation is common throughout this period and is restricted to more socially acceptable settings by early adolescence. Adult-like or aggressive sexual behaviors remain rare.

Children entering adolescence possess more of an adultlike understanding of sexual matters and are primarily concerned with social relationships and sexual mores. Adolescents are knowledgeable about sexual body parts and functions and are able to use correct sexual terms. In addition, by age 13 most teens are aware of sexual intercourse as well as masturbation. Masturbation is common during the adolescent period and restricted to socially appropriate settings. Other sexual behaviors are consistent with level of knowledge as adolescents begin experimenting with adultlike sexual behaviors including open-mouth kissing, fondling, and intercourse.

In conclusion, sexual knowledge and behaviors vary considerably across different ages. Developmental information regarding sexual knowledge and behavior must be considered when "sexualization" is noted in children. Such frequently mentioned behavioral indicators of abuse as excessive sexual curiosity, precocious sexual knowledge, excessive masturbation, and sexual play with other children must be interpreted in the context of these developmental trends. For example, although excessive masturbation can be of diagnostic value in CSA cases, one must be careful not to assume abuse only on the basis of masturbation, given its frequency across all ages (although its public expression by older school-aged children and adolescents is atypical). In addition, experts have suggested that masturbation that has a compulsive quality (i.e., the child cannot stop), occurs several times in a day, or is unresponsive to redirection (e.g., asking a child to restrict masturbatory activities to private areas) should be regarded as a sign of abuse (Faller, 1990; Sgroi, Bunk, & Wabrek, 1988). Parent-focused prevention attempts should not only inform parents about behavioral indicators of abuse (e.g., sexualized behavior) but also developmental norms related to these indicators and provide them with guidelines for understanding the interaction between the two. Such information could also play an important primary prevention role by helping parents understand and support their children's developing sexuality.

Unfortunately, our understanding regarding normative childhood sexual knowledge and behavior is limited by the minimal amount of research in this area. Research has been hampered by subjects' (and researchers') reluctance to discuss sexual topics. Furthermore, studies of normative childhood sexual behavior and knowledge have failed to screen samples for sexually abused children (with one exception; see Friedrich et al., 1991), which might contaminate findings. Future studies should address these issues and might also compare abused and nonabused children's sexual knowledge and behavior across developmental levels. In addition, researchers need to consider other factors that might influence sexual knowledge and behavior. For example, Friedrich et al. (1991) found the sexual behaviors of the children they studied to be related to the extent of family nudity. Other factors that might affect sexual knowledge include: sexual information offered by parents, witnessing sexually-related material on television or in person, peer-group functioning, parental and family values, exposure to pornographic materials, and demographic variables (e.g., socioeconomic status).

RESPONDING APPROPRIATELY TO VICTIM DISCLOSURES
Providing parents with information about CSA and the signs of victimization is not enough; parents must also be equipped to respond appropriately to a child victim's disclosure of abuse. Increasing evidence suggests that disclosure events (e.g., experiences

that occur subsequent to the revelation that CSA has taken place, such as the reactions of other individuals toward the child victim, intervention by the courts, and intervention by social service agencies) are very influential in shaping the impact of CSA upon its victims (Conte & Schuerman, 1987; DeFrancis, 1969; Elwell & Ephros, 1987; Gomes-Schwartz et al., 1990; Pelletier & Handy, 1986; Wyatt & Mickey, 1987). If victims encounter positive and therapeutic responses when they disclose, then their feelings of self-blame, isolation, or anger may be reduced (a secondary prevention goal). As Esquilin (1987) suggests, "It is the family's reaction in the aftermath of identification of abuse that may be one of the most important factors in determining the child's ultimate resolution of the event" (p.106). Parents need to understand the importance of their reactions to abuse in responding to victims, reporting abuse, and seeking treatment services for their children as well as themselves.

*Reactions Toward the Child.* Recent descriptions of parental reactions toward their children after disclosure indicate the need for parents to receive information about appropriate responses toward child victims. Research in this area has investigated parental responses to both intrafamilial (e.g., responses of nonoffending parents) and extrafamilial abuse (e.g., responses primarily of mothers of victims), with most research focusing on responses to intrafamilial abuse. For example, Scott and Flowers (1988) queried 24 adolescent and 26 adult female victims of father-daughter incest about their mothers' responses. Twenty-nine percent of adolescent and 50% of adult victims believed their mothers knew of the incest but failed to intervene. It is important to keep in mind, however, that these results reflect retrospective accounts as well as victim perceptions.

Everson, Hunter, Runyon, Edelsohn, and Coulter (1989) evaluated parental reactions within two weeks of victim disclosure. Parental reactions toward 88 child victims (ages 6 to 17 years) were determined by combining clinical ratings in three areas, including: (a) emotional support (ranging from commitment and support of child, to threats, hostility, and abandoning the child psychologically); (b) belief of child (ranging from making a clear, public statement of belief, to totally denying that the abuse occurred); and (c) action toward perpetrator (ranging from actively demonstrating disapproval of the perpetrator's abusive behavior, to choosing the perpetrator over the child). Results indicated that 44% of mothers were rated as providing consistent support, 32% inconsistent support, and 24% were rated as unsupportive or rejecting. Maternal support was not related to victim characteristics (i.e., gender, age, race) or mother's educational level, but was related to the offender's relationship with the mother. Mothers were most supportive of their children when the offender was an ex-spouse and least supportive when the perpetrator was a current boyfriend.

DeJong (1988) evaluated the reactions of mothers of 103 children returning for a follow-up visit two to three weeks after an initial evaluation at a hospital-based sexual assault center. Mothers responded to a questionnaire designed to assess their: (a) expressed attitude (supportive vs. nonsupportive), and (b) reactions toward their children and the perpetrator. Sixty-nine percent of the mothers were classified as supportive (e.g., believed child; believed perpetrator was responsible) and 31% as nonsupportive (e.g., disbelieved and blamed child). Reactions toward their children differed according to mothers' supportiveness. Nonsupportive mothers were frequently angry at their children but not the perpetrators, whereas supportive mothers rarely expressed anger at their children but were often angry at the perpetrators. Supportive mothers were also more likely than nonsupportive mothers to express anxiety about the effects of the abuse on their children.

Factors associated with maternal support were also examined. No differences were observed between supportive and nonsupportive mothers with regard to the victim (i.e., age or sex) or abuse characteristics (i.e., intercourse vs. nonintercourse; single vs. recurrent episodes), but responses did vary according to characteristics of the perpetrator. For example, 44% of mothers whose children were abused by fathers or paramours were nonsupportive, compared with 27% of mothers whose children were abused by others.

Sirles and Franke (1989) also investigated factors that might influence maternal reactions to victim disclosures. Interview responses of 193 mothers whose children were involved in intrafamilial sexual abuse were analyzed. Results indicated that 78% of mothers believed their children's reports of abuse and that several variables were associated with maternal beliefs. Mothers were most likely to believe the report if the offender was an extended family member, less likely to believe the report if the offender was the biological father, and least likely to believe the report if the offender was a stepfather or live-in boyfriend. Mothers were also more likely to believe reports when the nature of the abuse was less severe (digital contact vs. genital-genital contact) and when they were not present in the home when the abuse occurred. Results also indicated a developmental trend in mothers' beliefs: mothers believed 95% of preschool-aged children, 82% of latency-aged children, and 63% of teenage victims. Mothers were less likely to believe disclosures when their children were also physically abused by the perpetrator and when the sexual offender also abused alcohol. In contrast, mothers' reactions were not related to the frequency of abuse, the type of pressure used, the offender's reaction to the report, a history of physical abuse in the mother, or the sex or race of the victim.

In the most comprehensive study of this issue to date, researchers at the Tufts New England Medical Center Hospital (Gomes-Schwartz et al., 1990) evaluated mothers' reactions toward their victimized children. Clinicians rated the attitudes and behaviors of all mothers at the beginning of treatment. From these ratings, three scales were developed to describe mothers' actions after disclosure (reassuring and protecting the child; scolding or punishing the child; and removing the offender from the home) and three to gauge mothers' attitudes (concern for the child's well-being, including absence of protectiveness toward the offender; preoccupation with the effects of the abuse on herself, including self-pity; and anger toward the child).

Results indicated that 44% of the mothers consistently took some form of action to protect their children (e.g., talking to the child about the abuse, preventing the offender from having contact with the child), 38% took inconsistent protective action, and only 18% failed to take any protective action. Most mothers (70%) did not resort to punishing the child, although 30% reported using some type of punishment. In situations where it was possible for a mother to demand that the offender leave, only 22% did so.

Attitudes toward the sexual abuse showed somewhat similar trends. The majority of mothers (90%) demonstrated at least a moderate degree of concern for the child (10% slight, 37% moderate, 53% strong). Interestingly, a relatively large number of mothers (45%) were either moderately or strongly preoccupied with the effects of the abuse on themselves. Although the majority (77%) expressed no hostility or anger toward the victimized child, 23% did. Results also indicated that mothers' attitudes and actions were related to their relationships with the offenders. Mothers were least protective and most angry at the child when the abuser was a stepfather or boyfriend. The researchers suggest that mothers who feel conflicted in their allegiance between their children and their abusing partners may attempt to resolve the conflict by blaming their children for the abuse.

Studies evaluating parental responses to extrafamilial abuse are limited. Regehr (1990), however, recently reported on the clinical observations of parents of 33 extrafamilial child victims treated by a sexual assault team at a community hospital. Parental responses were categorized by whom emotional reactions were directed toward. Parents displayed a number of negative feelings toward themselves including guilt, fear of reprisals, and embarrassment. Negative reactions directed toward the child included anger at the child for not preventing the abuse, failing to tell the parent about it, or disrupting the parent's life. Finally, negative feelings toward the offender were also evident if parents desired revenge or retribution or were concerned about the impact of the abuse on the offender's career and family.

In conclusion, the majority of mothers surveyed do believe their children's reports of abuse (e.g., 78% in Sirles & Franke, 1989) and do take some form of protective action (69–82% across studies). These findings challenge the notion that mothers are co-conspirators in the abuse or are emotionally distant from their children. Maternal support was also found to be inversely related to the recency and intensity of the mother's relationship with the perpetrator. It appears to be difficult for mothers to be supportive of their children when the abuser is a current spouse or paramour. Maternal response was also associated with type of sexual contact and victim age in one study (Sirles & Franke, 1989) but not in others (DeJong, 1988; Everson et al., 1989). Additionally, mothers in Sirles and Franke (1989) were less likely to believe victims when mothers had been present in the home when the abuse occurred, if the child was also the victim of physical abuse, and if the offender abused alcohol. Varying maternal responses do not appear to be associated, however, with victim characteristics such as race and sex or elements of the abusive situation (e.g., type of pressure used or duration or frequency of abuse). Differences in rates across studies may result from differences in the definitions of "supportive," the methods of data collection (survey or questionnaire data vs. clinical observations), or variable response rates (e.g., 45% in DeJong's 1988 study vs. 85% in Sirles & Franke's 1989 study).

Future research should address these issues as well as other factors that may influence maternal reactions, such as fear of reporting, previous emotional or behavioral problems in the victim, financial reliance on the perpetrator, and maternal coping responses. Understanding the factors that influence maternal responses would enable prevention proponents to better target supportive efforts to victims and families in general, as well as those at risk for responding inappropriately. Finally, future research should also investigate the reactions of siblings and other nonoffending relatives toward victims of CSA.

Clearly, the results of these studies indicate the need to address this issue in parent-focused prevention efforts. Prevention programs directed at parents should address both general and specific responses parents can make when a child discloses CSA victimization. One of the most commonly suggested adaptive responses is to convey a belief in the child's report (C. Anderson, 1979; Esquilin, 1987; Hagans & Case, 1988; MacFarlane et al., 1986). In contrast, maladaptive responses would be to doubt the veracity of the child's report or to deny that the abuse has occurred. Esquilin

(1987) distinguishes between two levels of denial: (a) parents may acknowledge the assault but deny that the child understands what occurred, or (b) parents may deny that the assault occurred at all. In addition, we would include a third level of denial: Parents may deny that the event has had any impact upon the child, and thus fail to seek therapeutic assistance.

It is also important for parents to convey to the child that the assault was completely the responsibility of the perpetrator, instead of becoming angry at the child or blaming him or her for the event (C. Anderson, 1979; Brooks, 1982; Esquilin, 1987; Hagans & Case, 1988; MacFarlane et al., 1986; Tennant, 1988; Tormes, 1972). Staying calm and avoiding overreactions is another suggestion (Hagans & Case, 1988; MacFarlane et al., 1986; Tennant, 1988). Overreactions can contribute to children's sense of stigmatization or feeling as though they are different from others or "damaged goods." Instead of emphasizing the child's victim status, it is important to stress that the child is a survivor (Esquilin, 1987). In fact, many experts suggest that parents should underreact (MacFarlane et al., 1986; Tennant, 1988) and try to respond to the event in a matter-of-fact manner while continuing the child's normal routine. It is also helpful for parents to reassure children that no lasting harm will result from their experiences (MacFarlane et al., 1986).

Other suggested reactions have included protecting the child from further harm, acknowledging the courage it took for the child to disclose, accepting the child's feelings about the event, and reinforcing the child's disclosure by praising him or her for "doing the right thing" (Browning & Boatman, 1977; Esquilin, 1987; Hagans & Case, 1988; MacFarlane et al., 1986). In contrast, inappropriate reactions include overprotectiveness (e.g., restricting usual activities), which may have the paradoxical effect of making children more vulnerable to abuse by disrupting their lives and lessening their ability to control their environment (Regehr, 1990). In addition, parents may be reluctant to touch child victims, which may reinforce the child's sense of being "damaged goods." Parents should be encouraged to provide normal expressions of affection to prevent these negative outcomes and to reassure victims that normal affection is quite different than abusive touching.

Unfortunately, few parent-focused prevention approaches address this issue thoroughly. We know of one film (*Not in my Family*; Lawren Productions, 1980) that includes a discussion about emotional responses between five mothers whose children were sexually abused. Occasionally, parent workshops address reactions to disclosure in their discussions (e.g., Cooper et al., 1983; Project SAAFE, 1984), but typically they provide limited information; for example, by offering only vague encouragement to "believe and support the child" (Children's Self-Help Project, 1981). Parent-focused prevention efforts need to comprehensively address this issue by including the following information: (a) a rationale explaining why parental responses to disclosure are so important (e.g., importance in mitigating the effects of abuse; significance in reinforcing self-protective skills); (b) inclusive and detailed material of helpful as well as harmful responses; (c) examples of specific behaviors that constitute positive and negative responses (e.g., "protecting the child" should be translated into specific behaviors such as contacting the appropriate authorities, eliminating the perpetrator's access to the victim); and (d) examples of specific verbal statements that correspond to positive and negative responses.

Table 7 displays examples of appropriate and inappropriate parental responses to disclosure for possible inclusion in parent-focused material. Encouragingly, some recent parent-focused prevention efforts (primarily books and pamphlets) are including such information (e.g., Hagans & Case, 1988; Hart-Rossi, 1984; Kile, 1986). It would also be helpful for parent-directed approaches to give parents opportunities to practice using such information (e.g., by responding to hypothetical disclosures).

*Reporting.* In addition to specific parental reactions toward child disclosures, parent-directed prevention approaches can also address another potential response parents may initiate: reporting the incident(s). Subsequent to a child's disclosure of abuse, parents are confronted with the often difficult decision of whether or not to report the abuse to authorities. Parents must consider their sense

**Table 7: Examples of Appropriate and Inappropriate Parental Responses to Disclosure**

| Type of Response | Behavior and/or Verbal Statement |
| --- | --- |
| APPROPRIATE | |
| Believe child | "I'm sorry this happened to you." |
| | "Thank you for telling the truth about what happened to you." |
| | Make public statements (to professionals who are involved such as social workers, physicians, mental health professionals) that endorse belief of victim. |
| Perpetrator responsible | "She/he knew she/he was doing something wrong; it wasn't your fault." |
| | "You didn't do anything wrong." |
| Stay calm | Follow regular routines; seek professional assistance for self. |
| Emphasize survivor status | "You were so brave to tell what happened and because you told, we can make it stop." |
| | "There are safety rules we can learn so that this won't happen again." |
| | Model positive coping strategies. |
| Reassure no lasting harm | Seek professional assistance for child (e.g., physical exam to ensure integrity) |
| | "Your scared/hurt feelings will go away soon." |

**Table 7, continued**

| Type of Response | Behavior and / or Verbal Statement |
| --- | --- |
| Protect victim | "We'll tell someone about what happened so that this will never happen again." |
| | Report to appropriate authorities. |
| | Eliminate perpetrator access to victim. |
| Praise victim disclosure | "I'm so proud of you for telling me what happened." |
| | "You did the right thing by telling me about this." |
| Accept victim's feelings | "You feel _____ now but will feel better later." |
| | "It sounds like you're feeling _____ toward [perpetrator]." |
| | Encourage victim to discuss abuse. |
| | Acknowledge child's feelings. |
| Expression of affection | "I still love you and will always love you no matter what." |
| | Continue typical displays of touch and affection. |
| | Allow child to control type and frequency of touch. |

INAPPROPRIATE

| | |
| --- | --- |
| Deny that abuse occurred | "This can't be true." |
| | "Are you sure?" |

**Table 7, continued**

| Type of Response | Behavior and/or Verbal Statement |
| --- | --- |
| Deny that abuse occurred (continued) | "There must be a misunderstanding." |
| | "Don't make up stories like that." |
| Blame victim for abuse | "Why did you let him do it?" |
| | "Why didn't you tell me sooner?" |
| | "How could you let this happen?" |
| | "Why didn't you say no, scream, fight?" |
| | "What a mess you've made of things!" |
| | Scold or punish victim. |
| Overreact | "You'll never be the same!" |
| | "Now you're ruined!" |
| | Express anger at child or perpetrator. |
| Emphasize victim status | Verbally refer to child as victim. |
| | Avoid touching or hugging child. |
| Overprotect victim | Restrict normal activities. |

of social responsibility to protect other children, desire for retribution, and fears that the court process will further traumatize the child (Regehr, 1990). Few parent-focused approaches incorporate reporting issues into their materials, although there are some notable exceptions (e.g., Children's Self-Help Project, 1981; State Documents Center, 1982). Some encourage parents to report sexual assaults against children, although parents are not legally mandated to report CSA in all states.

To help them make the decision, parents should be informed of the consequences of reporting and of nonreporting (e.g., authorities cannot prosecute offenders, thereby precluding the mandating of treatment and increasing the risk of victimization for other children). Parents should also be provided information regarding reporting laws, legal protection for children, and the process of reporting (e.g., reports can be filed with the local Department of Social Services or child protective branch of that agency; parents also have the option of notifying their local police department and/or filing suit against the offender on behalf of the child).

Recent studies evaluating parental reporting behavior demonstrate the necessity for providing such information to parents. For example, Berrick (1988) asked parents, "If one of your child's playmates told you s/he had been abused by a stranger, what do you think you would do?" (p.547). Responses were scored on a scale of zero to two depending on whether parents mentioned the police or Child Protective Services (CPS) as agencies to whom they would report. Parents' mean score was .21, indicating that few parents would report the event to authorities. When parents were asked to describe their responses depending on whether the abuse had been committed by a stranger or by the child's parent, different reporting patterns emerged. When the perpetrator was a stranger, most parents (54%) believed that the most appropriate response would be to handle such matters privately, by discussing the issue with the child's parents. Few parents indicated that they would report the incident to a public agency such as CPS (14%) or the police (14%). When the perpetrator was a parent, respondents were more likely to report to CPS (33%), the police (25%), or the child's teacher (16%). However, 10% still indicated that the problem would best be dealt with by talking with the abusing parent or his or her spouse.

*Service Seeking.* A final parental response to a child's sexual victimization is obtaining services from community resources. The belief that professional therapy for victims and their families is vitally important is receiving increasing attention and support

(DeJong, 1988; Hagans & Case, 1988). Experts agree on the importance of referring children and families into therapy as soon as possible. First, therapeutic intervention is essential for child victims because it helps to alleviate the initial and long-term complications of CSA (Gelinas, 1983). In addition, studies confirm that families are most receptive to help during the crisis/disclosure stage of CSA (Hagans & Case, 1988), and the establishment of an effective counseling relationship is facilitated at that time. Although few parent-focused prevention approaches address this issue, some inform parents about the need for treatment, in addition to acquainting parents with various community services available and providing them with names and telephone numbers of contact people and community agencies (e.g., Cooper et al., 1983, Hagans & Case, 1988). In addition, one exceptional parent resource provides a discussion of guidelines for selecting a therapist (Hagans & Case, 1988).

Unfortunately, a common initial reaction to learning about the abuse is to deny the need for outside help, feeling that the situation can be handled within the family unit (Hagans & Case, 1988). Research evaluating service-seeking behavior in parents demonstrates the need to address this issue in parent-focused efforts. For example, DeJong (1988) found that nonsupportive mothers rarely sought counseling for themselves or their children. In addition, maternal perceptions of the need for treatment were influenced by the presence or absence of emotional and behavioral changes in the mother. For example, supportive mothers without emotional changes rarely believed they needed counseling (6%) and only half (53%) sought counseling for their children. The supportive mothers who were themselves experiencing behavioral symptoms, however, were most likely to seek counseling for themselves (74%) and their children (82%).

Parent-focused materials should address the importance of treatment for victims. In addition, parents should be informed about the potential for negative effects in themselves (e.g., guilt and anger), how to obtain services for themselves (e.g., looking in telephone book under crisis intervention, counseling, sexual assault center), of the existence of support groups for parents of victims, and about signs in themselves that may indicate the need for assistance (e.g., sleep or appetite disturbances, recurrent crying).

## Summary

Ten years ago, this chapter could not have been written. It is clear that the prevention movement has expanded rapidly to include parent-focused efforts. There are now available a number and variety of prevention materials that attempt to include parents in the struggle against the CSA problem. Prevention efforts have attempted to educate parents about the CSA problem in terms of the parameters of abuse, methods of preventing abuse, the identification of abuse victims, and specific responses to make if and when CSA is disclosed. Although such efforts and objectives are commendable, the potential of parent-focused prevention efforts has not been realized in terms of parent involvement, the content included in prevention programs and materials, or in the research addressing the effectiveness of these programs.

Efforts to encourage parents who are less interested to become involved in the prevention movement are needed (e.g., convenient meeting times and places; innovative instructional media). Future parent-directed prevention efforts should also attempt to expand the breadth of content covered in prevention programs and materials to include the objectives identified in this chapter (i.e., educating children, identifying victims, reporting abuse, supporting victims). Finally, more efforts to evaluate the effectiveness of parent-focused programs and materials are needed. If we continue to endorse parent-focused efforts without evaluating their impact, we risk potentially harming the families that use such materials, as well as creating a false sense of security as parents assume that their children are prepared to protect themselves when in reality they may be ill prepared.

Parents are a valuable resource waiting to be recognized as contributors to the CSA prevention movement. Although parents are an important target group in prevention efforts, they alone cannot prevent this widespread, complex social problem. Multiple methods and targets are needed to accomplish the prevention of CSA. Other individuals and groups must share the burden of responsibility; parents are but one of many target groups to be enlisted as partners in prevention.

*No single profession can handle a problem so deeply embedded in our
societal values as sexual abuse.*—ANNE COHN, 1986

In chapter 3, parent-focused prevention approaches were reviewed
and critiqued. We concluded that parents have much to offer the
prevention movement. Other target groups with prevention potential include professionals. As no single professional group can handle a problem as widespread and complex as CSA, we will focus
on the prevention roles and responsibilities shared by several
professional groups including (but not limited to) educational
professionals, day-care workers, social-work professionals, law-
enforcement personnel, and mental and medical health professionals. These are professionals who are most likely to have direct
contact with children; in the next chapter we will explore the roles
played by other professionals whose actions impact children indirectly.

## Rationale

There are several advantages to targeting professionals in prevention efforts. For example, these individuals often have ongoing
contact with children and unique opportunities to educate them
(vis à vis primary prevention) and can also assist in uncovering and
reacting appropriately to disclosures of abuse (secondary prevention). They also have the opportunity as well as the legal obligation
to report suspected victims of sexual abuse.

Certain professional groups play pivotal roles in preventing CSA. For example, teachers and day-care personnel, with their daily accessibility to children, special skills in communicating with children, and knowledge of child development, can notice behavioral changes that might indicate a child has been abused. Furthermore, teachers are likely recipients of child disclosures given their stable and consistent relationships with children, as well as their identification in classroom-based programs as resource persons. Teachers are also in a pivotal position not only to implement prevention programs in the classroom, but also to reinforce children's applications of the prevention concepts taught in both classroom- and home-based programs.

Medical and mental health professionals are also in significant positions to aid prevention efforts. Medical professionals can, in their regular well-child visits, discuss with parents and children sexual development as an integral part of normal development. Given their knowledge of the human body and its functioning, physicians can raise questions concerning the possibility of sexual abuse as reflected in physical signs and symptoms. In addition, because they are frequently involved in the physical examination of suspected abuse victims, they play an important role in documenting physical findings, responding to victim disclosures, and reassuring victimized children about their physical integrity. Mental health professionals who work with troubled children (a population at high risk for abuse; Finkelhor & Araji, 1983) are in a strategic position to uncover abuse in this population. Like physicians, mental health professionals may also be asked to assess for the possibility of sexual abuse.

Police officers, social workers, and child protective services staff all play pivotal roles in prevention efforts. These professionals are often involved in the investigation of sexual abuse and therefore have frequent contact with alleged CSA victims. Their responses to these children may be critical in terms of mitigating the effects of abuse. In addition, law-enforcement personnel are also involved in the teaching of classroom-based prevention programs (e.g., Conte et al., 1985) and are often identified in these programs as potential resource persons, increasing the likelihood of their receiving victim disclosures.

Despite the numerous advantages of including professionals in prevention efforts, their involvement has been limited. In the past, professionals were willing to leave the responsibility for sexually abused children primarily to child welfare professionals (Kempe & Kempe, 1978) and the obligation of abuse prevention to child-focused, classroom-based programs. Their limited involvement in the prevention movement has resulted for a variety of reasons, one being that professionals generally lack education and training about all forms of child maltreatment, including CSA.

For example, teachers have been noted to have several concerns regarding their responsibilities for identifying, reporting, and preventing CSA because of inadequate education and training. In a survey of teachers in Illinois, T. C. McIntyre (1987) found that only 19% of teachers reported receiving child abuse information during college and only 34% received education about abuse during in-service training. Similarly, although 49% of the teachers surveyed in the National Teacher Survey (Abrahams, Casey, & Daro, 1989) reported that their schools provided in-service workshops on child abuse, only 34% felt that this education was sufficient in enabling them to identify cases of abuse.

Lack of education and training has also been a problem for psychologists, social workers, and physicians. For example, Hibbard, Serwint, and Connolly (1987) surveyed medical professionals (nurses and physicians) and social workers about their training in the medical evaluation of sexual abuse victims. Sixty-four percent of these professionals (including 71% of nurses and physicians) had no previous training despite having been in their respective professions an average of six years. Likewise, Hibbard and Zollinger (1990) found that about half (51%) of the physicians, nurses, attorneys, law-enforcement officers, psychologists, and social workers they surveyed reported no previous formal training in the evaluation of alleged sexual abuse victims. Less than half (47%) of the school psychologists surveyed by Tharinger, Russian, and Robinson (1989) reported receiving information about CSA during college. Finally, in her national study of 1,196 mandated reporters (including principals, psychiatrists, psychologists, social workers, medical professionals, and child care providers), Zellman (1990b) found that only 26% of the professionals surveyed had received 10 or more hours of formal child abuse training; 38% had received none.

Thus, it appears that professional schools are doing little in the way of educating professionals in the identification, reporting, and prevention of CSA. It would be important to evaluate the curricula of professional training programs to determine the type and quality of training professionals receive, how much time is spent on training, and whether or not such training is a mandatory part of their education. Only then can the specific training needs be determined and addressed.

Another reason why professionals have had limited involvement in the CSA-prevention movement may be related to the emotional discomfort that this topic often engenders. The reality that adults sexually misuse children produces emotional reactions (such as horror, repulsion, dread, fear, anger, and anxiety) that are difficult for professionals to overcome (Ladson, Johnson, & Doty, 1987; Levin, 1983; Paulson, 1978). In addition, consideration of CSA unavoidably involves the difficult task of sorting through personal values and feelings about sexuality and sexual behavior (Tharinger & Veveir, 1987). Furthermore, given the large proportion of abuse victims in the general population, professionals must also contend with their own personal histories of sexual abuse and accompanying feelings. These onerous thoughts and feelings may lead to minimizing the seriousness or extensiveness of the problem or doubting the credibility of the child's report (Conte & Berliner, 1981).

Another possible obstacle is lack of support for prevention activities. Pelcovitz (1978) reported that teachers often feel unsupported by their superiors (i.e., principals) in dealing with abuse cases, as might also be true of other professionals who work in agency settings. A large percentage of school psychologists surveyed by Tharinger et al. (1989) perceived little or no support for identifying or reporting child sexual victimization, and they perceived only moderate support for providing information about

CSA to other school personnel, implementing sexual abuse education programs for students, or providing sexuality education for children.

Professionals may also fear the turmoil that can result from calling attention to the possible existence of CSA for the victim, his or her family, and the professional. Lynch (1975) reported that many teachers were afraid of parental reprisal resulting from reports of abuse or were afraid of the legal system in general. In addition, professionals may doubt the ability of legal and social service agencies to effectively address the needs of child victims. Indeed, it is possible that further abuse of the child may result from the post-report process (e.g., multiple interviews, court proceedings, etc). Several authors have also called attention to the professional's dilemmas regarding the conflict between reporting and maintaining client confidentiality (K. Pope, Tabachnick, & Keith-Spiegel, 1987), as well as the ethical obligation to inform parents of such reports (Racusin & Felsman, 1986). Others have suggested that physicians' unwillingness to become involved in CSA issues is related to fears of disrupting family-physician relationships and reluctance to become involved in the court system (Saulsbury & Campbell, 1985).

A final reason why professionals might fail to become involved in sexual abuse prevention is associated with role ambiguity. As Finkelhor and his colleagues note, "Sexual abuse falls into competing professional and institutional domains . . . it is a serious child welfare problem . . . it is a serious crime . . . it is also a mental health and, in some cases, even a medical problem" (Finkelhor et al., 1984, p.201). Because the problem of CSA falls within the domain of multiple professions, the roles of each professional group are not easily distinguishable. As a result, professionals can experience confusion as to their respective responsibilities in responding to and preventing CSA. Some areas of confusion include: Who is mandated to report abuse? Who should conduct prevention education? Whose responsibility is it to investigate?

In summary, although professionals serve as a potential target group for prevention efforts, several barriers to more extensive participation exist, including lack of education, the emotional discomfort that surrounds the topic of sexual abuse, concerns over mandatory reporting, and role ambiguity. Despite these obstacles, professionals are becoming more receptive to involvement in CSA prevention. Professionals not only agree that sexual abuse is a major issue that deserves their attention but also desire more information and instruction in this area (Tharinger et al., 1989).

## Objectives

Several objectives of professional-focused approaches are similar to those described for parents and include informing professionals about the CSA problem, educating children, identifying sexual abuse victims, and responding appropriately to victim disclosures. Although parent- and professional-focused prevention efforts share similar goals, there are differences in emphasis. Because professionals are likely to come into contact with alleged or undisclosed victims, they need to know about symptoms indicative of abuse; child, family, and environmental risk factors of abuse; therapeutic responses to disclosures; and reporting obligations and procedures. In addition, the prevention roles and responsibilities of different professional groups vary, corresponding to their special abilities and the nature of their contact with CSA victims or children at risk for victimization. In the following sections we will describe the common objectives of professional-focused prevention efforts while highlighting the potential roles and responsibilities specific to various professional groups.

### INFORMING PROFESSIONALS
### ABOUT CHILD SEXUAL ABUSE

The first objective is to equip professionals with a comprehensive understanding of the CSA problem. Armed with information about the parameters of CSA (as described in chapter 1), professionals can become familiar with the true nature of the problem and disregard the myths surrounding the topic. Such information can also help professional groups clarify their prevention-related roles and responsibilities.

For example, professionals must be educated regarding the various definitions of sexual abuse. Not only is this information important in identifying victims (see Mazur & Pekor, 1985), but it is also essential to allay fears associated with appropriate touching. L. L. Davis (1986) has noted, "Fear of touching children works at cross purposes to our efforts to eliminate child sexual abuse and creates, for both adults and children alike, a greater probability of victimization" (p.89), because the child's need for physical contact may be met through inappropriate touching. Information about the incidence and prevalence of CSA is also important to convey an accurate perception of the magnitude of the problem. Low incidence expectations may lead to an insensitivity about the possibility of CSA, whereas overly exaggerated expectations might lead to overreporting. Knowledge of the characteristics of victims is also important so that professionals working with children are alert to the fact that victims can be males as well as females of a variety of ages. Information about the dynamics of abuse can help professionals understand that child victims may not readily disclose because of the secrecy inherent in sexual abuse, and can familiarize professionals with the risk factors associated with abuse.

Recent studies indicate the need for professionals to receive up-to-date and accurate information about CSA. For example, Hazzard and Rupp (1986) assessed professionals' (i.e., pediatricians, mental health professionals, teachers) knowledge about the definitions, characteristics, causes, reporting requirements, treatment options, and effects of child abuse. Their 34-item scale included questions about abuse in general, as well as physical abuse, neglect, and sexual abuse. Knowledge scores varied according to professional-group membership. Mental health professionals appeared to be the most knowledgeable (80% correct) followed by pediatricians (73% correct), whereas teachers were correct only as often as college students (68% correct). Unfortunately, the authors did not report separate scores for the sexual abuse items. Although these results appear to indicate a reasonable amount of knowledge among professionals, they should be regarded as tentative because of the variable response rate (33–97%). Indeed, these findings may overestimate the knowledge of the average professional, as respondents with more knowledge and/or interest may have been more likely to respond. One conclusion is definite, however: Teachers are a clearly overlooked and undertrained professional group.

Others have surveyed various professionals about their knowledge specific to CSA. For example, Attias and Goodwin (1985) found that both pediatricians and psychiatrists were less knowledgeable about incest compared with psychologists or mental health counselors, although most professionals were fairly knowledgeable, answering over 75% of the items correctly. Specific knowledge deficits appeared to be associated with particular professional groups. For example, compared with pediatricians, fewer mental health professionals recognized the need for physical exams for sexual abuse victims. Psychiatrists were most likely to overestimate the likelihood that children's accusations were fantasies and were least likely to refer a case to Protective Services after the child's retraction.

When Hibbard and Zollinger (1990) surveyed social, legal, mental health, and medical professionals about CSA, they found the respondents to be fairly knowledgeable about CSA (averaging 80–86% correct), although there were several areas where professionals exhibited knowledge deficits. For example, they were unaware that sexual abuse does not always involve physical force or intercourse, that victims may have positive feelings about the experience, that running away is a sign of CSA, and that victims may have normal physical exams. Once again, differences in knowledge scores were noted between professional groups. For example, social workers received higher scores than all other professional groups (except psychologists). Psychologists and physicians scored higher than attorneys and law-enforcement professionals. In addition, nurses were most likely to know that CSA victims might have a normal physical exam, whereas law-enforcement professionals were most knowledgeable regarding reporting and immunity.

Although it would appear that professionals are fairly knowledgeable about CSA, results of these studies indicate deficits in some areas for some professionals. Knowledge deficits are evident regarding the necessity and implications of physical exams, characteristics of abuse (e.g., typical sexual activity, likelihood of physical force, etc.), effects of abuse, and reporting issues. Additionally, certain professional groups appear to be more knowledgeable than others, with social and mental health professionals exhibiting the greatest knowledge, followed by physicians and psychiatrists, with teachers, attorneys, and law-enforcement officers displaying the least amount of knowledge. Not surprisingly, knowledge patterns among professional groups appear to be idiosyncratic to their specific areas of expertise (e.g., law-enforcement and legal professionals know about reporting legislation; medical personnel know about physical exams).

Professional education about CSA (as well as other forms of maltreatment) should be integrated into the standard undergraduate and graduate curricula for all professionals working with children and families. Furthermore, education and training directed at professionals should emphasize both multidisciplinary case management and the specific roles and responsibilities of different professional groups. Future studies might explore other areas of knowledge among professionals (e.g., prevalence of sexual abuse) as well as the most effective format and timing for training (e.g., during training in professional programs or through continuing education or in-service training).

### EDUCATING CHILDREN

Another prevention objective that has been identified within the realm of professionals' responsibility is that of educating children about sexual abuse and personal safety skills (Downer, 1986; Finkelhor & Araji, 1983; Miller-Perrin & Wurtele, 1988). Educational professionals have been most readily identified as potential educators of children. Teachers are in a unique position for educating children about sexual abuse and its prevention, given their special skills in educating and communicating with children and their consistent and longitudinal contact with children, which allows for both repeated exposure to prevention materials and reinforcement of protective behaviors. There has been a proliferation of prevention materials targeted at this group of professionals.

Some organizations that produce materials for children offer training workshops (Committee for Children; Seattle, WA) or have developed audiovisual aids for teachers who use their products. For example, the publishers of *My Very Own Book About Me* (Stowell & Dietzel, 1982) have created a 20-minute training videotape to help teachers present the program in a comfortable and sensitive manner (Lutheran Social Services, 1983). Others have produced written information to help teachers locate and select classroom prevention materials and activities (e.g., Braun, 1988; Fay, 1986; Tower, 1987).

Regardless of their potential as prevention educators, many teachers have expressed concerns about the area of sexual abuse and reservations about educating children on this topic. As we noted at the beginning of the chapter, teachers not only have deficits in their knowledge about important aspects of child abuse, but also do not perceive themselves as qualified to undertake this onerous task. Educators have also expressed concern that educational curricula should not include topics related to sexual matters, because such issues are best dealt with in the privacy of the home setting (Brassard et al., 1983). Teachers have also expressed a general reluctance to bring education about the taboo subject of sexual abuse into their classroom (L. L. Davis, 1986) and to intervene in what is perceived as a complex social problem (P. E. Fox, 1977).

Downer (1986) outlined several other concerns of teachers who implement prevention programs with children. Time is a critical issue for teachers. Because educators have little time for lesson planning, developing new materials, participating in training workshops, or searching through resource materials, programs that demand preparation or extensive teaching time are unrealistic. In contrast, Trudell and Whatley (1988) suggest, "Brief sessions that simply train teachers to use predeveloped materials are woefully insufficient and may actually contribute to overall teacher deskilling" (p. 107). An additional area of concern involves the types of prevention materials. Educators prefer materials that are developmentally appropriate and diverse enough to reach their entire class. Other critical issues for teachers involve concerns about reactions of parents to prevention education, fears of possible negative effects of prevention programs on children, as well as concerns about their own immunity from suspicion of abuse. Finally, teachers are in need of support for their prevention efforts from both fellow teachers and administrators.

Recent surveys of teachers suggest that these concerns may be lessening. For example, the majority of teachers (65%) in the National Survey of Teachers (Abrahams et al., 1989) had no reservations about teaching CSA prevention programs. Reservations expressed by the remaining teachers were similar to previous reports and included feeling unqualified to implement prevention programs, time constraints, and feeling uncomfortable with the subject matter. Very few were concerned about potential negative effects on children or the lack of school or community support for these programs. That so few teachers had reservations about teaching these programs is inconsistent with previous reports and may be the result of increased awareness of and knowledge about the CSA problem. The present findings may also reflect sampling bias (34% survey return rate), teaching experience (80% of teachers had six or more years of job experience), or prior experience with prevention materials (53% reported that their students had been exposed to a program within the past year).

An ongoing controversy has been who should present CSA prevention information to children. Typically, programs are either implemented by regular teachers who have received some special training or by expert consultants from outside the school system, usually mental health professionals or paraprofessionals with some expertise in sexual abuse. Each approach has potential merits and drawbacks. For example, because teachers have greater familiarity with their children, they may be better able to structure training to meet children's special needs, incorporate training into the regular curriculum, and review material periodically to ensure that children retain the information (Conte, Rosen, & Saperstein, 1986).

In contrast, bringing community people into the classroom may provide a welcome change for the children and emphasize the importance of the subject matter (Ray, 1984). In addition, experts may be more effective because of their greater knowledge of and comfort in discussing sexual assault (Hazzard, 1990). The one study that explored the relative effectiveness of teachers versus experts (Hazzard et al., 1990; see description in chapter 2) found no significant differences in the impact of type of trainer for third and fourth graders. Although the authors concluded that there do not appear to be any overriding advantages or disadvantages to having either teachers or experts present prevention programs, they did caution that their findings may be limited to teachers who receive extensive preparation before program presentations and who feel comfortable presenting such information (84% of teachers felt "somewhat" or "very comfortable" presenting the program).

In conclusion, it would appear that professionals (teachers in particular) can and do play critical roles in sexual abuse prevention efforts by educating children under their care. Comprehensive prevention training appears to be essential before instructing children. This training should address the many concerns teachers have expressed that may serve as barriers to prevention efforts. Future research is also needed to replicate the Hazzard et al. (1990) study on the type of trainer and also to assess the effects of trainer sex, ethnicity, and training qualifications on program outcome. It is also unclear whether children are more likely to disclose abuse to a teacher whom they trust versus a sympathetic outsider with whom they may feel less embarrassment (Hazzard, 1990). Future studies should address this issue to determine any potential advantages of one professional group over another. Finally, research should investigate any possible negative side effects incurred by those who deliver prevention programs to children, such as potential guilt feelings if the children they educate are subsequently abused.

## IDENTIFYING VICTIMS

CSA victims cannot be protected and assisted unless they are first identified. Thus, identifying victims of sexual abuse is an important secondary prevention goal and professionals are in a critical position to assist with such efforts, for several reasons. First, many

victimized children do not disclose the abuse on their own initia-
tive, necessitating detection by others. Second, involvement by
individuals outside the family is often necessary for detecting victims of intrafamilial sexual abuse. Third, many professionals have
frequent contact with children and their families or work in oc-
cupational settings where sexually abused children are frequently
encountered. It is therefore imperative that they be trained in victim identification so that they can accurately identify sexual abuse
cases and intervene to terminate the abuse and protect child victims.

*Defining Abuse.* The first step in identifying undisclosed victims is
to delineate a clear and concise definition of CSA. Professionals
must have a grasp of specific behaviors that fall under the umbrella
of what we term *sexual abuse* before they can become vigilant to
the problem. Unfortunately, as we noted in chapter 1, defining
CSA is not an easy task. Not only do definitions vary according to
activities and characteristics of victims and perpetrators, but they
also vary depending on professionals' perceptions of those characteristics, which in turn are influenced by the professionals' culture, training, and experience. For example, Herzberger (1988) has
outlined several biases that affect professionals' ability to accurately label abuse: gender and age of the perpetrator or child; race,
ethnicity, or socioeconomic status of the perpetrator; and gender
and occupation of the reporter.

Unfortunately, there is no consensus among those preparing
prevention materials for professionals on the most appropriate
definition to facilitate victim identification. A definition that is too
broad or vague may cause suffering for innocent individuals or
may be frustrating and confusing to those who are mandated to
report, whereas a definition that is too narrow or exclusive might
result in the underreporting of abusive acts. The definition of CSA
offered by the NCCAN (see chapter 1) is a useful one for professionals. This definition encompasses any sexual aggression toward
a child and emphasizes developmental inappropriateness and coercion as key elements of sexual abuse. It is also consistent with the

definition used by child protective service agencies, the organizations with both the power and responsibility to protect children.

Types of sexual behavior are usually included in an operational definition of sexual abuse. A particularly useful operational definition of sexual abuse is that used by Child Protective Services in the state of Washington, a forerunner in programming and policy on sexual abuse and its prevention (Washington State Department of Social & Health Services, 1988). These guidelines are depicted in Table 8 according to two categories of sexual maltreatment: (a) physical acts, and (b) sexual exploitation. Specific acts are described under each category. Prevention approaches directed at professionals should include similar precise definitions, along with a discussion of the need to consider perpetrator and victim characteristics (e.g., age discrepancy).

The guidelines of the Child Protective Services of Washington also mention other concerns that are not legally defined as sexual abuse but may lead to investigation, including: remarks, comments, or threats of a sexual nature to a child by a caretaker or other family member; a caretaker failing to provide or allow for privacy for older children; preadolescent youths acting out sexually or committing physical acts of sexual abuse; caretakers allowing children to watch sexual activities; and a caretaker sleeping with a school-aged child of the opposite sex. Special considerations should be made when investigating these types of concerns, such as the family's culture and living space, or age of the children.

In order to define sexual abuse, normal (or nonabusive) patterns of touching and physical contact must also be considered. Few studies have investigated typical sexual behavior in families (e.g., the degree to which families encourage nudity; sexual and/or hygienic activities involving children). Such information would be invaluable in helping professionals decide if abuse is occurring and whether or not a report to social services is necessary. Despite the dearth of information regarding these issues, professionals are making these decisions based on untested assumptions. For example, the majority of physicians surveyed by Ladson et al. (1987) believed that when children reached age 4 it was inappropriate for mothers and fathers to bathe or sleep with children of the oppo-

## Table 8: Operational Definition of Child Sexual Abuse

| *Physical Acts* | *Sexual Exploitation* |
|---|---|
| 1. Rape: any penetration of the vagina, anus, mouth, by any object, when committed on one person by another without consent | 1. Conduct or activities related to pornography depicting minors |
| 2. Digital Penetration: insertion of a finger in the vagina or in the anus | 2. Promoting prostitution by minors |
| 3. Exposure: the act of exposing one's sexual organs in an inappropriate way, such as exhibitionism | 3. Forcing child to watch sexual activities of others: e.g., (a) parents or others engaging in sexual intercourse, or (b) watching pornography |
| 4. Vaginal or anal intercourse with the penis | |
| 5. Anal or vaginal penetration with an object | |
| 6. Fondling: touching or handling the genitals of another . . . includes forced masturbation to any kind of sexual contact, excluding penetration | |
| 7. Sodomy | |
| 8. Oral genital contact | |
| 9. Forcing child to engage in sexual activity with animals | |

*Source:* Washington State Department of Social & Health Services (1988)

site sex and that when children reached age 6 it was inappropriate for parents to appear nude in front of their children of the opposite sex.

Fortunately, normative data regarding these familial behaviors are appearing. For example, Rosenfeld, Siegel, and Bailey (1987) surveyed 576 parents (primarily mothers) of 2- to 10-year-olds regarding family bathing practices. Results indicated that in general, as children grew older, they bathed alone more frequently. For example, as boys and girls reached age 7, bathing with siblings was rare. Parents rarely bathed with their children at any age and cobathing behavior steadily decreased through age 10. For the most part, mothers bathed more frequently with their daughters, and fathers more frequently bathed with their sons. Same-sex parent-child bathing was rare after age 8 for girls and age 3 for boys. In addition, it was uncommon for mothers to bathe with sons older than 4 years of age or for fathers to bathe with daughters older than 3 years of age.

In a different report about the same sample, Rosenfeld et al. (1986) questioned parents about family affectional and sexual patterns. Parents were asked if their children had recently tried to touch their mother or father's genitalia or mother's breasts. Results indicated that children touched their fathers' genitals less often than their mothers' breasts or genitals, with daughters touching their mothers more than sons. Touching both parents was common among preschoolers (90% of parents indicated that sons and daughters touched their parents' genitals at a frequency somewhere between "sometimes" and "always") and declined significantly with increasing child age (by 8 to 10 years of age, 45–52% of children touched their mothers' genitals and only 20–30% touched their fathers' genitals). Children's touching their parents' genitals was also positively correlated with cobathing behaviors.

These data of normative behavior should be regarded as tentative until replication studies with larger samples are conducted. In addition, the representativeness of the study sample is questionable, as parents were primarily white, upper-middle class, well educated, and predominantly middle-of-the-road or liberal in political orientation. Approximately half (47%) were single parents. It is reasonable to assume that family bathing and touching patterns might be influenced by some or all of these variables. Nonetheless, given the dearth of normative information about these patterns, the contributions of Rosenfeld and his colleagues are significant. These initial data indicate that same-sex parent-child bathing is more common (until age 8 for girls and age 3 for boys) than op-posite-sex parent-child bathing, which is quite rare in both sexes after 4 years of age. Children touching their mother's or father's breasts or genitalia is also fairly common (especially among pre-schoolers), most likely because of children's natural curiosity.

Future studies should investigate the typical occurrence of other familial behaviors including sleeping patterns, nudity, pri-vacy, and other types of touching (e.g., kissing, hugging). By iden-tifying and disseminating information about normative, nonabu-sive patterns of touching, we not only empower professionals with the ability to better distinguish sexual abuse victims but also might help reduce some of the anxiety and stigma surrounding the pro-vision of nurturing touch by professionals.

*Sexual Abuse Indicators: Child Factors.* To effectively identify victims, professionals need to know specific signs and symptoms of CSA. In chapter 3 we presented possible physical, emotional, and behavioral indicators of sexual abuse, emphasizing normal behavior and developmental variations. Recent research indicates the need for professionals to be made aware of this information as well. For example, Tharinger et al. (1989) surveyed school psy-chologists and found only moderate awareness of the emotional, behavioral, and physical signs suggestive of sexual abuse. Re-spondents were also unsure about their ability to differentiate de-velopmentally appropriate sexual behavior and child fantasy from that indicative of sexual abuse. Similarly, T. C. McIntyre (1987) randomly surveyed 440 teachers in Illinois and found that only 4% of teachers indicated that they were very aware of the signs and symptoms of sexual abuse; 76% reported no awareness of such information. Although relying on self-assessment, these stud-ies suggest that teachers may be in need of education regarding indicators of sexual abuse.

Studies evaluating medical health professionals' awareness of the indicators of sexual abuse also indicate knowledge deficits. For example, Eisenberg, Owens, and Dewey (1987) surveyed health visitors, nursing staff, and medical students about the types of problems experienced by victims of sexual abuse. Although most endorsed relationship problems, fear of sex, depression, marital problems, withdrawal, and later child-rearing problems, few professionals cited typical sequelae such as anger, aggression, delinquency, prostitution, alcohol and drug abuse, promiscuity, or suicidal behavior. Ladson et al. (1987) asked 129 physicians to identify behaviors and physical symptoms considered to be indicative of sexual abuse. Although the vast majority (82–92%) of physicians indicated pregnancy, running away, decreasing school performance, venereal disease, and poor self-confidence as possible indicators of sexual abuse, fewer were aware that sex play (57%) and masturbation (33%) could be signs of sexual victimization.

These researchers also investigated physicians' awareness that sexually transmitted diseases (STDs) and CSA are associated. With the exception of mycoplasma, over 70% of physicians surveyed reported they would suspect sexual abuse if a culture was positive for chlamydia trachomatis, herpes genitalis, trichomonas vaginalis, gonorrhea, syphilis, and chancroid. Less than two-thirds of these physicians, however, stated that they would subsequently report their suspicions to the proper legal authorities except in cases of gonorrhea and syphilis. These findings are particularly alarming given that STDs in children are most likely a result of sexual abuse (Asnes, Grebin, & Shore, 1972; Neinstein, Goldenring, & Carpenter, 1984; Paradise, 1990; Sgroi, 1977; Shore & Winkelstein, 1971).

From these studies, it is apparent that many professionals—including physicians, school psychologists, medical personnel, and teachers—report a lack of awareness about the behavioral, emotional, and physical indicators of sexual abuse. Prevention programs directed at these groups should include specific information about abuse indicators, including instruction about normal behavior and developmental variations (see chapter 3, and Tables 4, 5, and 6). In addition, professionals could benefit from receiving instruction in determining the type of symptom constellations that warrant suspicion, including radical changes in behavior, symptoms that are chronic and fail to respond to usual management methods, and multiple and severe symptomology.

*Sexual Abuse Indicators: Family and Environmental Factors.* In addition to victim behaviors, professionals need to be aware of other indicators of sexual abuse: for example, the functioning of other individuals within the victim's environment. By increasing the breadth of sexual abuse indicators to include characteristics of abusive families, the likelihood of successful victim identification is increased. Considering additional sexual abuse indicators is particularly important given that, at present, there are no pathognomonic indicators of sexual abuse victimization.

In chapter 1 we discussed a myriad of risk factors that appear to be present more often in the families of victims of sexual abuse (see also Table 2). These risk factors can be organized into specific categories including characteristics of the parents, home environment, and parent-child interactions. When specific characteristics of parents are present, including marital discord and/or power imbalances, lack of parental modeling of self-protective behaviors, parental history of abuse, absence of a natural parent, or presence of a father substitute, professionals should become vigilant to the possibility of sexual abuse. Home environments characterized by over- or undersexualization, lack of privacy or household crowding, stresses (e.g., unemployment, poverty), and social isolation also increase the chances that sexual exploitation might be present.

Finally, if professionals recognize parent-child interactions characterized by emotional neglect, inappropriate expectations regarding children's responsibilities, inefficient or sporadic supervision, weak or absent parent-child bonding, or exploitation serving adult needs, suspicions about CSA (as well as other forms of maltreatment) should be raised. As is true of child behavioral indicators, indicators related to the child's family and environment should also be viewed together, rather than in isolation, with patterns of multiple indicators suggesting the possibility of abuse. In addition, the presence of both child- and family-related indicators should be examined concurrently when evaluating for sexual abuse.

Recent studies indicate a lack of professional awareness of family and environmental risk factors. For example, the school psychologists surveyed by Tharinger et al. (1989) were only moderately aware of child behaviors indicative of sexual abuse and were even less aware of family signs that suggest sexual abuse. Ladson et al. (1987) found that of those physicians responding to a survey, 67% correctly understood that low socioeconomic status increased the risk of incest but incorrectly assumed that urban setting (54%) and families consisting of five or more children (42%) were risk factors. Although investigations of professionals' awareness of the risk factors associated with sexual abuse are few in number, the available data suggest that physicians' and school psychologists' knowledge about family and environmental risk factors is limited. Future prevention efforts directed at professionals should include a discussion of these additional risk factors when addressing victim identification.

RESPONDING APPROPRIATELY TO VICTIM DISCLOSURES
Along with understanding CSA and knowing how to identify victims, it is important that professionals be educated about their roles and responsibilities in responding to victims. If professionals are familiar with both appropriate and inappropriate responses before encountering victims of sexual abuse, they are more likely to respond in a therapeutic manner. Appropriate responses include reacting positively toward victims to prevent further trauma, reporting to the proper authorities to terminate the abuse and initiate the recovery process for the victim, and working collaboratively with other professionals to enhance service provision to victims and their families.

*Reactions Toward Victims.* Professionals' reactions and attitudes toward victims are important, not only because they might prevent further trauma but because appropriate reactions can be therapeutic for victims. Professional reactions can also affect decisions related to victims and their families in diverse ways, including whether the perpetrator or victim is removed from the home, whether or not criminal prosecution of the offender is pursued, and how treatment is conducted (Doughty & Schneider, 1987;

Hazzard & Rupp, 1986; Pierce & Pierce, 1985; Ringwalt & Earp, 1988).

In chapter 3 we discussed appropriate and inappropriate responses toward child victims in the context of parent-focused prevention approaches (see also Table 7). Professional-focused prevention approaches should also include guidelines for responding to abuse victims including: avoiding negative reactions such as shock, horror, disapproval, or anger; conveying a belief in the victim's statements; reassuring the child that he or she is not to blame and that every effort will be made to protect him or her; and acknowledging and praising the victim's courage in disclosing.

In addition, professional-focused prevention approaches should explore possible reasons for inappropriate reactions toward victims. One reason may be because of a lack of understanding about what constitutes appropriate or inappropriate reactions, a problem easily rectified by education. Professionals may also respond inappropriately to victims because of misconceptions about the nature of CSA and its victims. For example, some professionals inaccurately believe that male victims are infrequently abused or less affected by the experience compared with female victims; others believe that victims are in some way responsible for their abuse (Eisenberg et al., 1987; Finkelhor, 1984; Kalichman & Craig, 1990). Adhering to such beliefs can have devastating effects if professionals communicate disbelief, denial, or blame to victims. Finally, personal experiences with CSA might affect their responses toward victims. For example, unresolved anger at one's own perpetrator might be displaced to a client's perpetrator, resulting in inappropriate hostility, or one's own unresolved guilt may result in blaming child victims.

Recent studies evaluating professional reactions and attitudes toward sexual abuse victims indicate the need for professionals to receive such information. Most research in this area has focused on indirect measures of professionals' reactions by asking them to assign responsibility for the abuse (with the victim as one of the categories). Alarmingly, these studies have indicated that although most of the responsibility for the abuse is attributed to the perpetrator, a sizeable minority of professionals believe that children are responsible for their own victimization (Doughty & Schneider, 1987; Eisenberg et al., 1987; Galdston, 1978; Saunders, 1988; Wilk & McCarthy, 1986). For example, when Kelley (1990) examined the attitudes about abuse responsibility among 228 professionals (police officers, child protective workers, and nurses), she found that 20% of subjects attributed some portion of the responsibility to the child.

Similarly, when Hazzard and Rupp (1986) asked various professionals (pediatricians, mental health professionals, and teachers) to rate how they might feel when interacting with abusive parents or abused children (depicted in vignettes), they found that all professional groups admitted to having some negative emotions when thinking about an abused child, with mental health professionals having less negative reactions toward the child than other professionals. Overall, professionals tended to have generally negative emotional reactions toward abusive parents, with mental health professionals and pediatricians having less negative reactions toward abusive parents than teachers or college students. Wilk and McCarthy (1986) surveyed perceptions of blame in incest cases among law enforcement, welfare department, and mental health personnel using case examples that varied according to perpetrator characteristics (father vs. stepfather), whether or not the victim's mother was also abusive, and who reported the abuse. The majority of professionals believed the father was guilty (86–98%), although 14% believed the daughter was as guilty as the father when the victim was an adolescent and the mother was the reporter. In addition, law-enforcement officials were more likely than the other two professional groups to blame the adolescent abuse victim when she did not self-report.

Other studies have investigated the relationship between professionals' attitudes and their behaviors. For example, Ringwalt and Earp (1988) investigated 313 child protective service workers' preconceptions about the responsibilities of fathers, mothers, and daughters in father-daughter incest, and how such attitudes affected their choice of whether to incarcerate the father or place the daughter in foster care. Results indicated that the more joint responsibility workers attributed to the father and daughter and the less they attributed to the mother, the more likely they were to recommend the father's incarceration. The more responsibility they attributed to the father alone, the more likely they were to recommend that the daughter be placed in foster care. Kalichman, Craig, and Follingstad (1990) investigated the relationship between responsibility attributions of 467 mental health professionals and their likelihood of reporting CSA. Overall, most professionals tended to blame the father (upward from 80%), some blamed the mother (11–15%), few blamed society (3–4%), and very few blamed the victim (1%). Attribution of responsibility, however, did not explain a significant proportion of reporting variability in this study.

We are aware of only one study that has directly assessed professional reactions toward victims. Kohan et al. (1987) mailed 287 questionnaires to clinical care staff supervisors of accredited hospitals having child psychiatric inpatient units serving children under age 13. Respondents were asked to describe any difficulties encountered in caring for sexual abuse victims. Close to one-third of supervisors reported that their staff had difficulties managing the care of children with sexual abuse histories. For example, many reported feeling personal distress or discomfort (including anxiety, fear, shock, and surprise) in response to the behaviors of sexually abused patients (e.g., sexual acting-out symptoms such as exhibitionism, seductiveness, masturbation; being put off or distanced; and acting out behaviors). Other staff problems included feeling angry (at the parents of the victim, primarily the abuser) or uncomfortable about being touched by children who had been sexually abused. Inappropriate responses toward child victims reported in the survey included: withdrawal, avoidance, expression of disgust, restriction, punishment, involvement in power struggles, and overprotection. These personal reactions and attitudes were viewed as barriers to therapeutic relationships and communication between staff and children.

In conclusion, extant studies indicate that although most professionals hold perpetrators highly responsible and victims minimally responsible for abuse, there are professionals who assign some blame to child victims. The studies reviewed also indicate differences between professional groups in attributing responsibility to victims. Mental health professionals as a group have been found to be less likely to blame victims of sexual abuse, whereas considerable numbers of psychiatrists, medical personnel, law-enforcement officials, and students have been found to hold victims responsible for their molestation. Although these findings should be regarded as tentative given the variable response rates, both across the studies (61–75%) as well as between professional groups, they suggest that professional biases do color individuals' perceptions of perpetrators and victims and may affect their professional reactions to victims and other involved persons.

Unfortunately, it is unclear from the majority of these studies what contributes to the formation of such attitudes in professionals. Studies are beginning to appear, however, that attempt to identify factors affecting attribution of responsibility (e.g., victim age, disclosure behaviors, admission by the perpetrator) and to explore how such attitudes may affect victims in the decisions made by professionals (e.g., incarceration of the perpetrator, foster-care placement of the child). Research is needed to investigate other factors that might contribute to professionals' attitudes (e.g., their own personal histories of sexual abuse; characteristics of the abuse). Few studies have attempted to directly measure professionals' reactions toward sexual abuse victims, although available data suggest the possibility of negative emotional reactions toward victims. Research is needed to assess professionals' reactions and the effects of such attitudes on the victims and families who encounter them. Future studies should also investigate other professional attitudes (e.g., credibility of the child, positive expectations for recovery, etc.) and how such attitudes might be related to professionals' behaviors. Not until empirical efforts are directed at such issues can potentially harmful attitudes and behaviors be identified and corrected.

*Reporting.* Providing professionals with information about reporting suspected cases of CSA is another important objective of prevention efforts. Both primary and secondary prevention goals can be accomplished through reporting. For example, reporting suspected cases of abuse to the appropriate authorities contributes to the termination of ongoing abuse and facilitates treatment for victims (secondary prevention). Reporting suspected cases of sexual abuse can also contribute to primary prevention, as deterring and rehabilitating perpetrators would prevent the abuse of potential victims.

Between 1963 and 1967, all jurisdictions in the United States passed statutes requiring certain professionals to report suspected cases of child maltreatment. There is general consensus among legal scholars that required reporting of abuse is essential to deal with the problem of CSA (Comment, 1984; Note, 1982; Saltzman, 1985; Weisberg & Wald, 1984). However, the reluctance and failure of professionals to report suspected cases of child abuse (including CSA) have been well documented (e.g., Bailey, 1982; Collier, 1983; Green, 1975; Helfer, 1975; Mazura, 1977; McDonald & Reece, 1979; Zellman, 1990a). For example, in the second National Incidence Study (DHHS, 1988), only half of the maltreatment cases known to community professionals were officially reported to child protective services (Sedlak, 1990).

The extent to which different professional groups report suspected cases of child maltreatment varies. In Zellman's (1990a) national survey of mandated reporters, she found that almost 40% of respondents at some time in their careers had failed to make a report of suspected abuse or neglect, with failure-to-report rates ranging from 24% for child-care providers to 58% for child psychiatrists. In their survey of mandated reporters, Finkelhor and colleagues found that the reporting of suspected cases of CSA ranged from 43% for criminal-justice personnel to 76% for school personnel (Finkelhor et al., 1984). Overall, 36% failed to report sexual abuse cases, with mental health and criminal-justice professionals failing to report suspected cases most often. In Kalichman et al.'s (1990) survey of clinicians, 24% indicated that they would not report a child's disclosure of abuse. Interestingly, only 65% of these clinicians had reported a case of abuse even though all reported having seen an abuse case.

Why might professionals be reluctant to report suspected cases of sexual abuse? Several studies indicate that professionals may not fully understand their reporting responsibilities. For example, T. C. McIntyre (1987) found that only 34% of teachers were "very aware" of their reporting responsibilities, 60% were only "somewhat aware," and 4% indicated "no awareness." Similar findings were reported in the National Survey of Teachers (Abrahams et al., 1989), where 65% of teachers felt that insufficient knowledge was a significant barrier to consistent reporting of CSA. Wurtele and Schmitt (in press) found a group of child-care workers to be deficient in their knowledge regarding reporting rights and responsibilities. For example, although workers were aware that they are required by law to report suspected cases of CSA, they were more likely than a group of sexual abuse experts to believe that it was their responsibility to "prove" suspected abuse before reporting.

Reluctance to report CSA might also reflect professionals' concerns about the consequences of reporting for victims and their families. For example, professionals may fail to report because of the harm they believe it causes the family, both in additional problems for the victim (e.g., premature removal from home) and interference with the ability of abusing parents to deal with their problems and reintegrate their families (James et al., 1978; Muehleman & Kimmons, 1981; E. H. Newberger, 1983; Swoboda, Elwork, Sales, & Levine, 1978; Watson & Levine, 1989). For example, of the 279 licensed psychologists surveyed by Kalichman et al. (1989), 37% believed that reporting would have a negative effect on the family.

Clinicians are sometimes hesitant to report cases of child abuse because of the potential disruption to treatment that reporting may cause (Finkelhor, 1984; Helfer, 1975; Kalichman & Craig, 1990; Kalichman et al., 1988; Muehleman & Kimmons, 1981; K. Pope et al., 1987; Swoboda et al., 1978; Watson & Levine, 1989; Zellman, 1990a). For example, K. Pope et al. (1987) surveyed members of the American Psychological Association's Division 29 (Psychotherapy) and found that approximately one-third of the therapists responding would be unwilling to break confidentiality to report a case of child abuse. Miller and Weinstock (1987) surveyed 51 therapists working with sex offenders and reported that 65% of the therapists considered the conflict between reporting and confidentiality to be a significant problem. Forty-two percent of the psychologists surveyed by Kalichman et al. (1989) believed that reporting would result in negative consequences for family therapy.

Concern over negative personal consequences is another potential obstacle preventing professionals from reporting. Wurtele and Schmitt (in press) found that child-care workers were more likely than a group of CSA experts to believe (incorrectly) that they could be successfully sued if a case they reported was not substantiated. Likewise, 63% of teachers in Abrahams et al. (1989) indicated that fears of the legal ramifications for false allegations increased their reluctance to report. In Zellman (1990b), professionals who perceived that reporting would result in negative personal consequences (e.g., lost time from work, personal upset, court appearance, loss of income) were less likely to report all suspected cases of abuse that came to their attention.

Other obstacles to reporting endorsed by the teachers surveyed by Abrahams et al. (1989) included: reprisal against the child and damage to parent-teacher and teacher-child relationships (endorsed by 52%); parental denial and disapproval of reports (45%); interference in parent-child relationships and family privacy (35%); lack of community or school support in making allegations (24%); and school board or principal disapproval (14%). Other reasons for nonreporting outlined by Watson and Levine (1989) included: (a) broad reporting statutes or vague statutory definitions, (b) reporters' unwillingness to see parents as abusive, (c) worry about the effects that reporting will have on business practices, (d) egotistical inability to call in outside intervention, (e) fears that the parents who are the subjects of such reports will be handled in an "inept and punitive" fashion, (f) beliefs that reporting does not achieve what it should for the child, and (g) epidemics in reporting rising disproportionately to services available for children and their families.

Professionals may also fail to report because of a reluctance to become involved with the judicial system (Saulsbury & Campbell, 1985) or to testify (J. G. Jones et al., 1990). In addition, professionals may fail to report because they are unclear about the degree of certainty necessary to file a report of abuse. Indeed, those clinicians in Kalichman et al. (1990) with higher levels of confidence that abuse had occurred were more likely to make a report. Finally, as Kalichman and Craig (1991) have suggested, professionals may fail to report because of reporting biases, generated by idiosyncratic personal standards (e.g., following the law, professional guidelines, or personal values).

In summary, available evidence suggests that many professionals do not adhere to mandatory reporting laws. Several factors are thought to influence the reporting behavior of professionals (see additional factors in chapter 5), including: professionals' lack of knowledge about CSA and reporting responsibilities, fears of the consequences of reporting (e.g., harm to families, victims, and themselves), conflict between reporting and confidentiality, and uncertainty regarding whether or not a report is warranted. In order to enhance reporting compliance and gain the prevention benefits associated with reporting, professional-focused prevention efforts need to address reporting issues.

Prevention materials targeted toward professionals should include information about their reporting rights and responsibilities. First, professionals should be informed as to which groups of professionals are mandated to report. Table 9 shows the national legislature on mandatory reporting, including statutes passed through 1989. Although states vary in their specific requirements and regulations, most require that certain professionals report any cases where abuse is suspected. State statutes vary in what groups of professionals are required to report, from listings of specific occupations to general all-inclusive descriptions such as "any person" or "any persons responsible for the care or treatment of children." Typically, professionals who are mandated to report include medical personnel (physicians, dentists, nurses, chiropractors, medical examiners), educators (teachers, school counselors), mental health professionals (psychologists, drug and alcohol abuse counselors), social-service professionals (social workers), public-agency employees (law-enforcement officers, probation officers), and day-care personnel (day-care center staff, child-care workers). More recently, legislation has been passed in some states mandat-

## Table 9: National Legislation on Mandatory Reporting of Child Sexual Abuse

| Professional Group | States Required* |
|---|---|
| MEDICAL | |
| Chiropractors | All states except: AR GA KS MI MN ND OH SC VA WV |
| Coroners/medical examiners | All states except: AK GA IA KS MN OR VA WA WV |
| Dental hygienists | AK CA CO IL IA LA ME NY NV |
| Dentists | All states except: MN VA |
| Emergency medical technicians | CA IA IL KS KY** LA MA ME MI NV OR WI WV |
| Health practitioners/ professionals | AK CA HI IA KS KY** LA ME MD** MN MO** MT ND OH SC VA WA WI WV |
| Hospital/institution personnel | All states except: KS ME MI ND OH OR SC SD WI |
| Naturopaths | AK OR |
| Nurses | All states except: MN WV |
| Optometrists | All states except: AR GA IL MA ME MI MN OH VA VT WV |

* States with all-inclusive definitions (e.g., "any person"; "persons responsible for the care of children") or that do not refer to particular occupations are not specified in the table. States with all-inclusive definitions are: AZ, CT, DE, FL, ID, IN, KY, MD, MO, MS, NC, NE, NH, NJ, NM, OK, PA, RI, TN, TX, UT, WY.

** States with all-inclusive definitions that also specify particular occupations

## Table 9, continued

| Professional Group | States Required* |
|---|---|
| Osteopaths | All states except: CA KS LA MI MN ND NV OH OR SC VA WI WV |
| Pharmacists | AL CO HI WA |
| Physicians / surgeons | All states except: KS MN WV |
| Podiatrists | All states except: AK AR KS MI MN ND OR SC VA VT WI WV |
| Residents / interns | All states except: AK AL MI MN ND SC WA WI WV |

MENTAL HEALTH / SOCIAL SERVICE

| | |
|---|---|
| Alcohol / drug abuse counselors | CT** ND NV SD WI |
| Crisis intervention programs | AK IL |
| Marriage / family / child counselors | CA CT** LA MA MI NV |
| Mental health professionals | All states except: AK CA GA KS MA MI NV WA |
| Psychiatrists | AK CA IL LA MN NH** NV |
| Psychologists / counselors | All states except: AL AR MT ND SC VA WI WV |
| Social workers / technicians | All states |
| Supervisors / administrators of public assistance | CA HI IL SC WI |

## Table 9, continued

| Professional Group | States Required* |
| --- | --- |
| EDUCATIONAL / CHILD CARE | |
| Day-care providers | All states |
| School administrators / officials | All states except: CA IA IL MN NV OR SC VA WV |
| School counselors | All states except: AK AL AR CA CO HI IA IL KS LA MN MT NY OH OR VA WV |
| School personnel / employees | All states except: AK AL AR GA ME MI MN ND NV NY OH SC SD VT WI |
| Teachers / educators | All states except: CO HI IA IL NY OR |
| LEGAL / LAW ENFORCEMENT | |
| Attorneys | MS NV NY OH OR |
| Judges | All states except: AK AL AR CA CO GA IA KS LA ME MI MN MT ND NV NY OH OR SD VA VT WA WI WV |
| Parole / probation officers | CA HI IL KS LA MD MO** NV SD |
| Police / law enforcement | All states except: CA OH WA |
| OTHER | |
| Child abuse prevention programmers | AK CA |

## Table 9, continued

| Professional Group | States Required* |
|---|---|
| Christian Science practitioners | CO IL MD** MT NH** NV NY PA** SC VA WA WV |
| Clergymen | AZ** CT** MN NV NH** MS** OH OR |
| Commercial film/photo processors | AK CA CO GA IL LA MO** OK** OR SC WA |
| Firefighters/inspectors | KS OR ME MA |
| Funeral directors | PA** |
| Homemakers | IL ME |
| Neighbors/friends/relatives | TN** |
| Occupational therapists | WI |
| Parents/legal guardians/foster care providers | AZ** AR CA FL** HI IA IL LA MA MT NH** NV NY OR PA** TN** WI WV |
| Physical therapists | AK CO LA WI |
| Religious healers | All states except: AL AR CO GA HI IL IA LA ME MA MI MN MT NY OR VA VT WI |
| Speech pathologists/audiologists | AK MI OH WI |
| Veterinarians | CO |

*Source:* National Center on Child Abuse and Neglect (1989)

ing CSA reports from commercial film and photo processors and child abuse prevention programmers.

Additional reporting responsibilities professionals should be informed of are shown in Table 10. In general, reports are made to the division of the local department of social services (usually referred to as child protective services), law-enforcement agencies, or central state registries. Most states require reporters to contact the appropriate services "immediately" after suspicion has been aroused, and many states also require a written report to follow within a specific time period, usually 24 to 48 hours. Requested information typically includes the child's name, parents' or guardians' names and addresses, and the circumstances that led the reporting person to believe that abuse occurred. Professionals should also make an effort to document any incident or discussion that leads them to suspect abuse (e.g., date, time, description of the incident or discussion with the child; Stringer, 1986; Tharinger & Veveir, 1987; Tower, 1984).

Professionals should also be informed about the consequences of reporting, particularly about penalties for failure to report and their rights regarding immunity to civil liability and criminal penalty. Most state statutes contain penalties for failure to report suspected abuse, usually a misdemeanor subject to a fine and/or jail sentence. Some states include tort liability for harm done to the child (Brown & Truitt, 1978) and professionals may be subject to reprimands from ethical authorities (Meriwether, 1986). Laws in all 50 states provide for immunity to the reporter if he or she has reported in good faith with the intention of ensuring the safety of the child.

Professional-focused prevention programs should also allow participants to voice their concerns about reporting and discuss the difficulties inherent in determining when a suspicion becomes a reportable concern. Professionals should be encouraged to evaluate the following: (a) whether or not the child's experience meets the operational definition of sexual abuse, (b) possible indicators of abuse (including child behaviors or symptoms, family characteristics, and environmental factors), (c) developmental influences, and (d) cultural and family considerations regarding nudity or

## Table 10: National Legislation Related to Child Sexual Abuse Reporting

| Reporting Statute | Requirement | State |
|---|---|---|
| Agency to receive report | Department of Social Services | All states except: WI |
| | Law Enforcement | All states except: AR CT DE FL GA IA IL MA ME MI MS MO MT NC ND NH NJ NM NY OK PA RI VA VT WV |
| | Central Register | NY FL |
| Oral reports | Immediately / ASAP | AK AL AR AZ CA CO DE FL GA IL IN KY MA MD ME MI MN MS ND NH NJ NM NY OR PA RI SD TN UT WI WV WY |
| | Promptly | HI MT OK |
| | Within 24 hours | ID NV |
| | Within 48 hours | TX WA |
| | Time frame unspecified | CT IA KS LA MO NE NC OH SC VA VT |
| Written reports | Immediately / promptly | CO CT OK |
| | Within 36 hours | CA |
| | Within 48 hours | AR FL IA IL IN KY* MA MD ME* ND* NH* NY PA UT* WV* |
| | Within 72 hours | AZ MI MN |
| | Within 5 days | LA TX |

* Require reports "upon request"

## Table 10, continued

| Reporting Statute | Requirement | State |
|---|---|---|
| | Following oral report; time frame unspecified | AL DE GA* HI KS* MS NE NM OH RI VT WA* WI WY |
| | Not required | AK ID MO MT NC NJ NV OR SC SD TN WA |
| Content of report | Name / address of child | All states** |
| | Child's age | AZ CO CT GA HI IA IL IN KS KY LA MA MD ME MI MO MS MT NC NE NJ NM NV NY OH OK OR PA TN VT WA |
| | Child's sex | AR CO IN LA MA ME MO NV NY PA |
| | Child's race | AR CO LA MO NY |
| | Child's whereabouts | AL CA IA MD NC |
| | Parent's name / address | AL AZ AR CT GA HI IA IL IN KS KY LA MA MD ME MI MO MS MT NC NE NH NJ NM NV NY OH OK OR PA SD VT WA |
| | Guardian / caretaker | AL AZ AR CT GA HI IA IL IN KS KY LA MA MD ME MI MO MS MT NC NE NH NJ NM NV NY OH OK OR PA SD TN TX VT WA |
| | Reporter's name / occupation | AR CA CO IA IN LA ME MN MO NE NY PA VT |
| | Extent of injuries | All states** |

** Except for those states where content of report is not specified

## Table 10, continued

| Reporting Statute | Requirement | State |
|---|---|---|
| Content of report | Previous injuries | AL AZ AR CO CT GA IA IL IN KS KY LA MA MD MO MS NE NH NJ NM NV NY OH OK OR PA VT WA |
| | Injuries to siblings | CO CT IA KY ME MO NY PA VT |
| | Identity/address of person responsible | AL AR CO GA IA IL IN KS KY LA MA MD MN MO MS NE NH NJ NM NV NY OK OR PA WA |
| | Family composition | AR CO IA LA ME MI MO NY PA |
| | Source of report | AR CO IN LA MA ME MO MT NY PA WV |
| | Actions taken by reporter | AR CO IN MA ME MO NY PA |
| | Explanations for cause of injury/condition | LA ME OR |
| | Dependence of child on controlled substances | OK |
| | Where abuse occurred | PA |
| | Child's birth date/place | SD |
| | None specified | AK DE FL ID ND SC UT WI WY |

*Source:* National Center on Child Abuse and Neglect (1989)

touching. In addition, professionals should be encouraged to consult with other professionals about their suspicions. Professionals can even make an anonymous call to CPS to inquire whether or not a report should be made.

Finally, professionals should be informed that the report is simply a request for an investigation based on "reason to suspect" a child has been or is being abused. The reporting person does not have to be certain that a child has been abused in order to file a report. Determining whether or not abuse has occurred is the responsibility of trained investigators. Educating professionals about their reporting rights and responsibilities should help alleviate their fears and uncertainties, which in turn should enhance their compliance with reporting laws, help terminate ongoing abuse, and prevent the possible occurrence of future abuse.

*Enhancing Collaborative Efforts.* As we noted at the beginning of the chapter, sexual abuse is a complex problem that falls into the domain of multiple professions. As a result, many professionals experience confusion about their responsibilities, as well as a lack of cross-disciplinary networking with other agencies (McCaffrey & Tewey, 1978). Such confusion contributes to failures in reporting, improper case management, delays in providing assistance to victims, and a reluctance to refer victims to other professionals. For example, only about half of the school psychologists surveyed by Tharinger et al. (1989) referred child victims to mental health services in the community. Finkelhor et al.'s (1984) survey of 790 professionals (from social work, psychology, medicine, law, education, nursing, and law enforcement) found that in general, these professionals tended to handle sexual abuse cases in an isolated way within their own restricted professional network. For example, 40% of mental health, 47% of educational, 38% of medical, and 45% of social service professionals consulted no one about CSA cases, indicating a low level of interagency cooperation and communication.

To deal with CSA effectively, multidisciplinary efforts are necessary, requiring cooperative networking among a variety of professional groups and agencies. Professional-focused prevention efforts should emphasize the advantages of collaboration between professional groups and outline the respective roles and responsibilities of different professionals in managing CSA cases. For example, the optimal treatment of CSA cases entails close cooperation between the criminal justice system (responsible for coordinating the investigation of abuse and the arrest of perpetrators), the legal system (responsible for the prosecution of cases and/or the custody of the child victim), the medical system (responsible for gathering corroborative evidence of the assault and treating the physical effects of abuse), the school system (responsible for access to, and ongoing monitoring of the child), and the mental health system (responsible for providing treatment services to victims). By educating professionals about the importance of multidisciplinary case management and each professional group's roles and responsibilities, confusion and insularity will be reduced, thereby enhancing professionals' feelings of competence and ultimately benefiting victims and their families.

## Evaluating Training Programs Directed at Professionals

In the previous sections we identified several critical objectives for professional-focused prevention efforts, including disseminating sexual abuse information, educating children, identifying victims, and responding appropriately to victim disclosures. Unfortunately, research evaluating the effectiveness of programs and workshops aimed at enhancing professionals' knowledge and skills in these areas has been limited. In the past, most evaluation research focused primarily on teachers and neglected other professional groups. Not until recently have studies of day-care professionals, physicians, and mental health professionals appeared. In the following sections we will review and critique studies assessing the effectiveness of CSA prevention training programs for various groups of professionals.

### TEACHERS
Several studies have examined the impact of sexual abuse prevention programs on teachers' knowledge, attitudes, and/or behav-

iors. For example, Allsopp and Prosen (1988) evaluated a comprehensive sexual abuse prevention training program for elementary school teachers consisting of didactic presentations, role plays, and discussion. One hundred eighty teachers completed a 10-item true-false questionnaire both before and after receiving the program. At posttest, knowledge increases were observed on all items. For example, before the program, only 30% of teachers were aware of their immunity to liability in suspected cases, which increased to 87% at posttest.

In addition, teachers indicated that the program increased their awareness of victims and offenders, gave them a clearer understanding of the school system's procedures for reporting CSA, and increased their knowledge of county services available to victims. Teachers also believed they were better prepared to deal with a situation in which a child had been abused. Unfortunately, these researchers failed to include a control group and made limited attempts to assess actual knowledge (rather than opinion). In addition, the nonstandardized and brief true-false questionnaire limited the researchers' assessment in both the breadth and depth of content addressed in the workshop. It is also unclear from the present study what effect the workshop had, if any, on teachers' prevention behaviors or on the actual prevention of sexual abuse.

McGrath, Cappelli, Wiseman, Khalil, and Allan (1987) evaluated a two-hour workshop presented by social workers to 184 teachers. Teachers were pretested, randomly assigned to one of two groups (immediate teaching or a delayed teaching control group), and posttested (both immediately after the program and two months later). Comparisons between experimental and control teachers at the two-month follow-up assessment revealed that experimental teachers identified a greater number of indicators for sexual and emotional abuse, were more knowledgeable about reporting and legal issues, and were more aware of school board policies regarding abuse. Even after participating in the workshop, however, teachers still lacked knowledge in important areas (e.g., penalties for failing to report abuse, protection from legal suit when reporting abuse, conditions requiring that a report be made to Child Protective Services, who is responsible for making reports, and child characteristics that may increase the probability of abuse). The limited duration of the workshop (two hours) may not have provided sufficient time to cover all areas. Although gains in knowledge were assessed in this study, the possible effects of the workshop on teachers' prevention behaviors were not determined.

Recent studies conducted by Hazzard and her colleagues (e.g., Hazzard, 1984; Hazzard et al., 1990; Kleemeier, Webb, Hazzard, & Pohl, 1988) have overcome many of the methodological limitations of previous teacher-evaluation studies. For example, Kleemeier et al. (1988) evaluated the impact of a six-hour training workshop with 45 teachers. The workshop was thorough; it addressed incidence and dynamics, indicators of abuse, short- and long-term effects of abuse, basic interviewing techniques, reporting, treatment resources, and primary prevention. Teaching techniques included didactic presentations, videotapes, experiential exercises, role plays, group discussion, and a question-and-answer session with a Child Protective Services worker. Relative to controls, trained teachers increased their knowledge about the scope of the problem, dynamics of sexual abuse, behavioral indicators, reporting procedures, treatment alternatives, and prevention concepts. In response to hypothetical vignettes, trained teachers were better able than controls to identify specific indicators of sexual abuse and to respond to hypothetical victims in helpful, supportive, and appropriate ways.

Trained teachers also exhibited changes in their attitudes relative to controls. For example, they were more willing to acknowledge the severity of the CSA problem, less blaming of the victim, more likely to see community agencies such as Child Protective Services as helpful, more supportive of child-focused prevention programs, and more confident of their own role in addressing the problem. At the six-week follow-up, however, trained teachers were not significantly different from controls in self-reported preventive behaviors (e.g., conducting classroom prevention activities, discussing child abuse issues with a friend or colleague, discussing potential abuse with individual students, or reporting suspected abuse cases). The authors suggest that the absence of behavioral changes may have been a result of the limited follow-up period, or an increase in control teachers' motivation to deal with the issue of abuse as a result of completing the measures. It is unclear what effect the workshop had on other targeted behaviors such as the identification of abuse victims or appropriate responses to actual child disclosures. Although responses to hypothetical situations indicated that teachers were capable of applying their knowledge, it is unclear to what extent this knowledge would translate into actual behavior. Further research is needed on how to enhance actual preventive behaviors by teachers.

### DAY-CARE PROFESSIONALS

As the number of children in day care expands as a result of the increasing number of mothers in the work force (Hofferth & Phillips, 1987), day-care personnel need to be recognized for their potential role in prevention efforts. As mentioned in chapter 2, classroom-based approaches have only recently addressed pre-school-aged children, and efforts to educate those who work with this age group are also beginning to appear. For example, Barber-Madden (1983) evaluated a workshop for day-care personnel, the purpose of which was to impact their knowledge, attitudes, and skills associated with abuse and neglect intervention and prevention. The workshop covered the identification of victims, reporting policies and procedures, community referral, prevention activities, and treatment. Assessments were conducted before and after the workshop and at a one-year follow-up. Results indicated knowledge increases, attitudinal changes, and improved skills at posttest for staff who participated in the training workshop. At the one-year follow-up, trained staff engaged in more prevention activities (e.g., conducted parent or staff training) and more often referred high-risk families to community resources in comparison with untrained staff. In addition, more trained personnel reported developing a written policy for handling abuse cases.

When the adequacy of policies was rated, however, significant between-group differences were not observed. Unfortunately, this study was not designed to evaluate sexual abuse prevention efforts specifically and is limited by methodological problems (e.g., the small number of participants; the voluntary nature of the study; prior training in prevention). Despite these limitations, this study indicates the importance and feasibility of training day-care personnel. With many children receiving substitute care in preschools, child-care centers, and day-care homes, it is imperative that substitute caregivers receive education about CSA and their legal rights and responsibilities so that they can become an increasingly effective resource for young children.

## MENTAL HEALTH PROFESSIONALS

We have been able to locate only one published article addressing an educational program on sexual abuse for mental health professionals. Krenk (1984) reports on the outcome of a five-month inservice program that was developed to train direct care staff members of a residential treatment facility in the identification, assessment, and treatment of CSA victims. Staff members were taught about the dynamics of incestuous families, behavioral and psychological characteristics of incest victims, interviewing techniques, and treatment. In addition, the program provided opportunities for staff members to explore their own attitudes and feelings about sexual abuse and to examine potential roles for each staff member in meeting overall treatment goals. Although no systematic evaluation was conducted, the program was viewed as desensitizing staff members and improving their attitudes toward sexual abuse victims, offenders, and other family members. In addition, mental health professionals' abilities to identify victim symptomatology and determine the treatment needs of victims and other family members improved. Increased numbers of referrals to social service resources to supplement treatment were also noted. The results of this study indicate that prevention training for mental health professionals is a viable prevention activity worthy of further investigation.

## MEDICAL AND OTHER PROFESSIONALS

Evaluations of educational programs directed at medical professionals are also beginning to appear. For example, Swift (1982) evaluated CSA training workshops for 71 professionals who were primarily nurses, although several other professional groups were included (child protection caseworkers, school counselors, police officers, community mental health center staff). Overall, posttest scores were significantly higher than pretest scores. In addition, there was a 500% increase in reported CSA cases in the year following the intervention. The findings of this study are limited because of the lack of a control group and unsystematic workshop presentation (i.e., workshops varied considerably in terms of content and length). In addition, the percentage of unfounded reports contained in the increased reporting rates was not determined, and differences between professional groups in knowledge gains and reporting behaviors were not examined.

Hibbard et al. (1987) evaluated a symposium designed to educate professionals in the evaluation and care of CSA victims. Forty professionals (22 caseworkers, 10 physicians, 8 nurses) attended a program that covered: (a) behavioral and physical indicators of CSA, (b) how to interview an alleged sexual abuse victim, (c) how to use dolls and drawings as interviewing aids, (d) the components and expected findings of the medical evaluation, and (e) legal responsibilities and possible legal sequelae when CSA is suspected. Educational methods included didactic presentations and discussions, role playing, and demonstration.

Participants completed questionnaires before the symposium and at two weeks and six months postsymposium. Results indicated that knowledge about reporting, abuse dynamics, epidemiology of abuse, and abuse evaluation improved at two weeks postsymposium and these gains persisted at six months. Although the average improvement in knowledge scores was small, the authors' impression is that this change represents more confidence in knowledge (from slightly to strongly agree or disagree). As an interview technique, dolls were used by only 6% of medical professionals before training, which increased to 66% at the six-month follow-up. Drawings were initially used as an interviewing tool by 26% of the respondents, with no significant changes after training. Unfortunately, these researchers did not assess actual interview or identification skills, reporting behaviors or statistics, or other prevention behaviors.

CONCLUSIONS

Teachers, day-care personnel, mental health professionals, and medical professionals have been identified as valuable resources in preventing CSA. The research reviewed in this section suggests that after participating in prevention training programs, professionals' knowledge levels are increased, skills are enhanced, and attitudes toward victims and their families are modified. In addition, several studies indicate that as a result of prevention training, professionals' confidence in their abilities is increased. Enhancing professionals' perceived competence, knowledge, and skills are important goals for professional-focused prevention efforts, given that deficits in these areas have impeded their involvement in the prevention movement in the past. Unfortunately, many of the studies reviewed are limited by methodological problems including a lack of standardized assessment, short follow-up periods, an absence of control groups, and small samples. Future studies should address these limitations and also include assessments of actual prevention behaviors and skills. The impact of such training programs on reporting, identifying, and assessing victims; responding to victims; and prevention behaviors (e.g., implementing child-focused programs) needs to be systematically assessed. Studies are also needed of other professionals who have contact with children (e.g., police officers, religious leaders, social workers, etc.), and to determine the most effective educational methods and materials for training professionals.

**Summary**

With their skills, knowledge, and unique contacts with children, professionals are important collaborators in the CSA prevention movement. Yet, as a target group for prevention efforts, professionals have been largely underutilized. Several reasons for their limited involvement were identified and include lack of education and training, fears associated with reporting CSA, the emotional discomfort that this topic engenders, lack of support for prevention activities by superiors and/or the community at large, and confusion as to what roles and responsibilities they have in CSA prevention. Suggestions for overcoming these barriers were offered (e.g., enhancing their knowledge of the CSA problem and improving their ability to educate children, identify CSA victims, respond appropriately to victims and their disclosures of abuse, and work effectively with other professionals). Several training programs that have been developed for professionals were reviewed. Although most of these studies are preliminary investigations and limited methodologically, they appear to affect professionals' knowledge and skill levels, along with their attitudes toward victims and families. Adequate training to increase knowledge and skills appears to help break down many of the barriers limiting the involvement of professional workers in prevention efforts. Other obstacles, however, such as poor community support, have impeded the involvement of professionals and restricted prevention efforts in general. In the next chapter we will address this final target component of prevention: society.

# The Roles of Policymakers, Researchers, and the General Public

*It is all of society, not just those immediately affected, that protects the secret of child sexual abuse.* —ROLAND SUMMIT, 1988

We concluded in chapters 3 and 4 that parents and professionals have much to offer the CSA prevention movement. Yet, given that these target groups are embedded within their communities and society at large, it is imperative to consider the impact of this broader level. Our intent in this chapter is to suggest possible roles and directions that various groups within our society might take to combat the CSA problem. These groups include policymakers, researchers, and the general public.

## Rationale

As noted in chapter 1, one approach to primary prevention is to change the environment so that negative conditions do not produce pathology. From an ecological perspective, cultural and societal levels (i.e., the macrosystem; Bronfenbrenner, 1979) subsume the values and belief systems that foster the sexual abuse of children and exert an influence on individuals and their environments. Given the extensiveness and etiological complexity of CSA, it is important to focus on the macrosystem in order to fully understand and ultimately combat this widespread problem. Such macrosystem interventions could in the long run have a much greater effect on reducing the incidence of this social problem compared with prevention efforts targeted at individuals (de

Young, 1987). Many of these values and beliefs, however, are deeply embedded in American culture and thus will be difficult to change.

## Policymakers

Policymakers include legislators and administrators at the local, state, and national levels. These individuals have both the power and authority to affect change within our society and thus have the potential for contributing greatly to the prevention of CSA.

### LEGISLATORS

Legislators can play key roles in promoting prevention efforts, both by allocating funds and by lobbying for laws and regulations related to children's welfare in general, and CSA more specifically.

*Allocating Funds.* Almost all states (49 as of 1989; National Committee for the Prevention of Child Abuse, 1990) provide monies for child abuse and neglect prevention efforts via Children's Trust and Prevention Funds. Funds are allocated for a variety of prevention strategies including, but not limited to, support programs for new parents, public awareness campaigns, and community organization efforts. Additional state and federal monies are needed to expand prevention research and programs. The willingness to devote monies to prevention (especially when the funding needs for investigation and treatment are so great) depends upon a commitment toward children's welfare, which is another area where legislators can play a key role in furthering prevention efforts.

*Promoting Child Welfare.* In 1988, an estimated 20% of American children under the age of 18 lived in poverty (U.S. Bureau of the Census, 1988). That we allow 12.6 million children to live in economically impoverished environments suggests that children are not highly valued in our society. Not only are more children being raised in households with limited financial resources, but the social support services available to assist low-income families are declining. Limited public support for medical and nutritional programs, along with the absence of a comprehensive national policy to provide health care for children, reflect a lack of commitment to children's welfare. Likewise, the absence of public or publicly funded child care suggests that our country does not value promoting children's development or the health of their families (although the recent passage of the child-care bill in the 101st Congress is a step in the right direction). All of these realities increase the vulnerability of children to all kinds of maltreatment, including sexual abuse.

Policymakers concerned about providing a higher standard of living for children could benefit from reviewing reports of a number of successful child and family support models being implemented in this and other countries (e.g., A. J. Kahn & Kamerman, 1988; Schorr, 1988). By pushing for a higher standard of living, policymakers would be promoting the view that children are persons with dignity who deserve to be protected. Policymakers could also benefit from a review of recent efforts on behalf of the United Nations to recognize the rights of children in general and specifically their right to be protected from all forms of sexual exploitation and abuse (see Castelle, 1990; C. P. Cohen & Naimark, 1991; Melton, 1991; United Nations, 1989).

Disruptive, dysfunctional families also put children at risk, not only for mental health problems but for CSA as well (see chapter 1). American families need to be supported and strengthened so they can nurture and protect their children. Measures to reduce stresses facing families (e.g., poverty, unemployment, homelessness, substance abuse, family violence and discord) will potentially eliminate some of the direct or indirect causes of child maltreatment. A range of social services geared toward enhancing the competencies of families are needed as well. Important areas for consideration include: affordable housing; day-care facilities at public housing complexes and at the workplace; guaranteed access to health care for pregnant women, infants, and children; paid maternity and paternity leaves; equitable pay for women; adequate income maintenance; substance-abuse treatment for parents (and mothers-to-be); and welfare benefits that do not require the father's absence from the home. Federal, state, and local governments might be encouraged to increase funding for the family support movement, a grassroots effort to support effective family functioning (see S. L. Kagan, Powell, Weissbourd, & Zigler, 1987; H. B. Weiss, 1989; H. B. Weiss & Jacobs, 1988; Zigler & Black, 1989). Although we would advocate that organized services be made available to all families because of the difficulty of raising children in a stressful world, we acknowledge that this strategy would be difficult to implement because of limited resources. If society wants to prevent all types of child maltreatment (including sexual abuse), however, then economic changes must be made.

Attempts to assume more public responsibility for children have also been constrained by our lack of "public love" (Grubb & Lazerson, 1988) for children. This lack of public commitment to children stems from an adherence to several ideologies. As Grubb and Lazerson (1988) explain, the English legal doctrine of *parens patriae* has evolved into a conception of limited public responsibility for children; public action is justified only in cases of parental failure or voluntary request for services. This doctrine has labeled public intervention an abnormal activity and has consequently limited the scope of public responsibility for children. Adherence to the ideology of parental determinism—the notion that parents alone determine the futures of their children—has also limited public responsibility.

Along with the 19th-century conception that the family is private and should be interfered with only when it breaks down, these ideologies have resulted in a reluctance to make a public commitment to children's welfare and a tendency to blame parents for children's problems, while ignoring the real origins of their problems (i.e., unemployment, poverty, sexual and racial discriminations, and class divisions). Grubb and Lazerson (1988) argue that replacing the doctrine of *parens patriae* with a set of public responsibilities toward children, along with transforming our economic and political systems, will ultimately be required if society is ever to establish a sense of collective responsibility and fulfill its public promises to children. Certainly, policymakers play a key role in struggling with the nature of the state and its role in addressing these social and economic problems.

*Modifying Child Abuse Statutes.* Legislators can play important roles by supporting legislation to protect children from child pornography, increase funding for child protective services, and develop clearer reporting statutes. They can also mandate prevention education, require background checks for adults who work with children, advocate court reforms, and enforce mandatory prison sentences for perpetrators. We will briefly describe these recommended modifications.

As explained in chapter 1, child pornography is a social force supporting the sexual victimization of children. There have been several state and federal statutes enacted to protect children from this type of exploitation. In 1978, the Protection of Children Against Sexual Exploitation Act was enacted to halt the production and dissemination of pornographic material involving children. The Child Sexual Abuse and Pornography Act of 1986 provides for federal prosecution of individuals engaged in child pornography, including parents who permit their children to engage in such activities (Otto & Melton, 1990). Using the final report of the 1986 U.S. Attorney General's Commission on Pornography, Howell, Lloyd, Schretter, and Stevens (1989) suggest that states should consider amending, if necessary, their child pornography statutes in these ways: (a) make the knowing possession of child pornography a felony; (b) make child selling for the production of sexually explicit visual depictions a felony; (c) make child pornography in the possession of an alleged child sexual abuser sufficient evidence of molestation for use in prosecuting that individual, whether or not the child involved is found or is able to testify; (d) eliminate the requirement that the prosecution produce testimony from the child, if proof of age can otherwise be established; (e) permit judges to impose a sentence of lifetime probation for convicted child pornographers, include enhanced penalties for repeat offenders, and provide a civil remedy for minor victims; (f) use seized profits to fund training of law-enforcement and social service personnel, community awareness and prevention programs, or treatment programs for sexually victimized children; (g) create an offense for advertising, selling, purchasing, giving, or receiving information as to where sexually explicit materials depicting children can be found; and (h) require photo-finishing laboratories to report suspected child pornography.

Another area where legislators can have an impact is CSA reporting legislation. As noted in chapter 4, all 50 states have enacted mandated reporting of CSA by various professionals. We also noted, however, that professionals often underreport suspected CSA cases. There are a variety of barriers to reporting that legislators can address (see also chapter 4 and Maney & Wells, 1988).

For example, professionals may fail to report because of concerns about how the child welfare system handles these reports. In the face of declining federal and state funds for social services, many child protective service (CPS) agencies are unable to respond adequately to the increasing number of reported cases or to provide services to sexually abused children (Faller, 1985). Indeed, a recent evaluation of the nation's CPS system concluded that child abuse and neglect in the U.S. now represent a national emergency and that the CPS system is failing in its response to the problem (U.S. Advisory Board on Child Abuse and Neglect, 1990). Policymakers must strive to improve the appropriateness, quality, and consistency of the child welfare response to reports of CSA. Creating legislation to increase the availability of treatment services should also reduce professional reluctance to report.

Another legal reform that might encourage reporting is a requirement that CPS agencies provide feedback to the reporter on the actions taken as a consequence of their report (Davidson, 1988). Although most agencies have policies to provide feedback to reporters, Zellman's (1990b) national study of mandated reporters indicated that only 25% of reporters regularly receive feedback; 27% never do. Furthermore, those professionals who received feedback had more positive perceptions of CPS and were more likely to report. Such feedback may serve to enhance a sense of collaboration between reporters and the CPS agency and would also serve an educational purpose for reporters (Conte, 1988).

State confidentiality laws and policies would need to be altered to allow for the benefits of this information exchange.

Given that a major determinant of a professional's likelihood of reporting CSA cases is his or her judgment about the law's demands (Zellman, 1990c), failure to report may be a result of the vagueness of state child abuse reporting statutes. For example, professionals have a duty to report when there is "suspicion," "cause to believe," or "reasonable cause to know or suspect" that a child is being sexually abused. What constitutes "reasonable suspicion" is not defined in reporting statutes. Is it when the thought first comes to mind? Does it mean when the abuse is "more likely than not" to have happened? Although vague statutory definitions allow judges considerable discretion in reaching decisions concerning state intervention into family life, they fail to serve as effective guidelines for those faced with reporting suspected cases of CSA. Indeed, uncertainties about what constitutes reasonable suspicion were believed to contribute to the tendency for professionals in Zellman's (1990a) study of mandated reporters to not report abuse cases in which there was insufficient evidence or the abuse did not seem serious enough. Mandated reporters need to know exactly what is and is not reportable, so they do not fail to report when they should and do not overwhelm an already overburdened child protection system with unfounded reports (Besharov, 1985, 1986, 1988; Faller, 1985; Meriwether, 1986). It would behoove policymakers to develop clearer statutes and guidelines to obviate the problems described above, thereby increasing reporting compliance. For us to make specific suggestions for solving this complex problem would be beyond the scope of this book. We would, however, suggest that this be done via a collaborative process with other interested constituencies (e.g., American Bar Association; American Psychological Association).

Legislators can also play an important role with regard to state laws concerning CSA prevention education. State legislation can be used to mandate that education and prevention programs be available or required for both children and professionals. Although some states have enacted legislation requiring education and prevention programs for children in the schools (e.g., Washington, Florida), the majority of states have not. By legally requiring that all children be exposed to such materials, society will be increasing protective factors thought to militate against the occurrence of CSA. This legislation would be particularly important for incest victims who may not receive parental permission to participate in such programs. Several states have also instituted legislation requiring professionals to receive training in CSA and its prevention. Programs have been established to educate professionals involved in evaluation, investigation, treatment, and legal management of sexual abuse cases. Questions still remain, however, about when such training should take place (preservice vs. in-service), how the quality of such training can be assessed, and who should be required to participate (e.g., all professionals or only those seeking licensure or certification). As suggested in chapter 4, it would seem reasonable to assume that professionals who are well trained in this area would be more likely to acknowledge the existence of CSA, identify and respond therapeutically to victims, know how to deal with abuse disclosures, engage in prevention efforts, and communicate more effectively with other professionals.

Although most people who work with children are deeply concerned about their welfare, there are those who exploit their positions of power and seek to harm children under their care. Included in this category would be school personnel; child-care personnel (and family members who may be present at a site); foster parents; staff and volunteers in youth organizations; and personnel in juvenile detention, correction, or treatment facilities. A critical step toward preventing CSA in institutions is the careful screening of personnel.

One important legislative step in this direction would be to require that criminal-history background checks (through state and federal law-enforcement information systems) be conducted on all persons who apply for employment or volunteer for a position in which they would have supervisory or disciplinary power over a minor. Some states (e.g., California, Illinois) require potential employees and volunteers in these settings to provide criminal-history record information and be fingerprinted; other states (e.g., Arizona) also require a sworn statement affirming that the applicant has not been previously convicted of a felony crime involving a minor. Although the number of perpetrators apprehended and fingerprinted is low, a background check can at least ensure that known offenders will not have access to children. Such screening might also have a deterrent effect, as molesters may not apply for such positions if they know they will be identified. In addition to these precautionary procedures, others have recommended the use of screening devices and particular interviewing strategies (e.g., using vignettes to determine how the applicant would deal with sexually charged situations) to assess applicants with regard to CSA (e.g., McCormack & Selvaggio, 1989; Siskind, 1986).

Closely related to the need for background checks of personnel is the need for the licensing of child-care facilities, including home-based child care. Although obtaining a license does not preclude abusing children, it can provide for the screening of employees, volunteers, and family members who may be present on a regular basis (see A. J. Cohen, 1988, for additional suggestions).

Legislators can also play an important role in promoting legislation that has secondary prevention benefits: reducing system-induced trauma for victims. Many have expressed the belief that the legal system unintentionally intensifies the emotional trauma suffered by victims of CSA (E. H. Weiss & Berg, 1982). There is concern that certain steps of the investigative process may be harmful to child victims. For example, subjecting children to repeated interviews about the crime (by child protection workers, law-enforcement officers, prosecutors, physicians, mental health professionals) can produce great strain on victims already under extreme stress. Others are concerned that court proceedings may have a detrimental impact on child witnesses (e.g., face-to-face testifying). If research shows that certain practices are associated with increased distress in child victims, then the solution is not to remove children from the legal process but to challenge those responsible for law enforcement to modify the process to better meet children's needs.

In the last decade, several procedural reforms have been suggested to reduce the stress faced by child victims of sexual abuse (see Berliner, 1985; Duquette, 1988; Maholick, 1986; Melton,

1985; Otto & Melton, 1990; Viinikka, 1989; Whitcomb, 1986). Among these changes are modifications in investigative interviewing (e.g., eliminating the uniformed officer interview except in emergency cases and substituting the detective interview; holding joint interviews to limit the number of times a child must describe what happened; and videotaping the interview for subsequent viewing at preliminary hearings or grand jury proceedings). Other changes include efforts to reduce the court-related stress on the child witness (e.g., providing him or her with a court-appointed advocate; restricting confusing interrogation by defense counsel; reducing continuances; employing "vertical prosecution," in which one prosecutor handles the case from the initial report through sentencing). It is also important to consider how children might be helped to prepare for courtroom testimony. Stress management and cognitive techniques might be used to teach children skills for coping with the stress of testifying (V. V. Wolfe, Sas, & Wilson, 1987). Others suggest "demystifying the courtroom," by providing children with tours and simple descriptions of the court process and people involved (Regehr, 1990).

Some states have allowed the use of out-of-court or hearsay statements, videotaped depositions in place of live testimony, testimony via closed-circuit television, the shielding of the child witness from the defendant, and limited courtroom access to spectators and the press during the child's testimony. These reforms not only may help reduce the potentially negative impact of the judicial process on child victims, but also may facilitate successful prosecution (i.e., children who feel more comfortable may provide more effective testimony, thereby strengthening the prosecution's case).

These procedural reforms, however, involve restrictions on the rights afforded the defendant, particularly the defendant's Sixth-Amendment right to confront the accusor and have a public trial, along with the public's First-Amendment right to access (through the press) the trial process. Efforts are needed to identify changes in court practices and procedures that can assist child victims without endangering the rights of defendants. Recently, the Supreme Court ruled in *Maryland v. Craig* (1990) that children should be allowed alternatives to face-to-face testimony in child abuse cases, if the courts can show that children will be overly traumatized by the experience (DeAngelis, 1990). Calling for a case-by-case determination of whether children are too vulnerable to testify reflects research showing that in many cases, children are traumatized by facing their abuser, whereas others can actually benefit from testifying (King, Hunter, & Runyan, 1988; Runyan, Everson, Edelsohn, Hunter, & Coulter, 1988).

Some have argued that the legal system's response to offenders perpetuates a message that the sexual abuse of children is not a serious crime. Several studies have documented that few sexual abuse perpetrators are convicted (e.g., Bradshaw & Marks, 1990; Rogers, 1982). Berliner (1985) has offered a number of reasons why so few sexual abuse cases result in criminal prosecution (e.g., like women, children are perceived as likely to make false reports; victims' families and criminal justice system personnel share concerns about whether or to what extent the law should be involved; the legal and medical and mental health professions have conflicting goals regarding punishment vs. rehabilitation). Rates of prosecution also reflect the degree to which society views CSA as morally and legally wrong. By failing to provide effective social controls, society is in essence condoning the sexual exploitation of children.

Some states have enacted legislation that provides for mandatory prison sentences for people convicted of certain sexual crimes against children (see Howell et al., 1989). Although enforcing mandatory prison sentences would certainly give a strong message to the public regarding the criminal nature of adult-child sexual activities and may possibly serve to deter potential perpetrators, it raises several issues that will need to be addressed. For example, in cases of intrafamilial sexual abuse, a child victim who learns that a parent faces an automatic prison sentence may be reluctant to report the crime or participate in investigation or court procedures, and family members may put pressure on the child to recant the accusation. Howell et al. (1989) suggest that mandatory imprisonment laws should include provisions that allow for a probated (no incarceration) or suspended sentence if certain conditions are met (e.g., if there is no continuing threat of harm to the child, if the defendant has been accepted for mental health treatment, and if it is in the victim's best interest that the perpetrator not be incarcerated). At this point, we do not know how recidivism rates and victims' reactions vary according to type of intervention used with the perpetrator (e.g., arrest, prosecution, incarceration vs. suspended sentence, probation, mandated treatment). What is needed is a systematic study of the outcomes of these types of interventions similar to what has been done in the area of domestic violence (see Sherman & Berk, 1984).

## COMMUNITY LEADERS

Community leaders, as policymakers, can impact the CSA prevention movement in a number of ways. They can assess what their communities are doing to enhance public and professional awareness about CSA; what resources exist in the community for victims, offenders, and families; and what their communities are doing to prevent CSA (see Ray-Keil, 1988). They can also sponsor multidisciplinary boards or interagency teams to provide and coordinate identification, prosecution, and treatment services among professionals from the law-enforcement, child protection, education, medical and mental health, and the criminal and juvenile justice systems (see Pettiford, 1981; Sgroi, 1982b; Wagner, 1987). As a result, the specific roles and responsibilities of each professional group will be clarified, the confusion among various professional groups (described in chapter 4 as a barrier to prevention involvement) will diminish, and children and their families will receive more coordinated community services.

Community leaders can also encourage the formation of a CSA prevention task force in their area to study the problem and take action against it. Such a task force might include representatives from schools, businesses, military groups, community mental health centers, hospitals, law enforcement, Child Protective Services, churches, service clubs (e.g., Junior League, Rotary, Kiwanis), and parents. Community leaders can press for public awareness programs to increase public sensitivity to CSA and inform the public about community efforts to prevent the problem.

For example, they can ensure that child-focused CSA prevention programs are advertised, which may serve as a deterrent by warning potential perpetrators that children are being taught not to keep such activities secret.

Community leaders can also play a role in making children's needs a social priority. They can do much to develop a "pro-child community" (Garbarino, 1980). For example, pro-child committees can push for increased availability, accessibility, and quality of child care, education, and health care for children, along with economic and social supports for families (e.g., housing and employment opportunities). Community leaders can also promote family-school and public-private partnerships aimed at improving the environment for children. Corporations within a community can be encouraged to help support families (e.g., by providing day care, employee assistance programs, flextime working schedules). We concur with Garbarino (1988) that a community should have a vested interest in and an obligation to insist upon high standards of care for all its children. Through such efforts, children might become more valued citizens and communities would be united in the front against CSA.

SCHOOL ADMINISTRATORS

As institutions serving children of every ethnic, race, creed, and socioeconomic group, schools serve as ideal settings in which to combat the widespread problem of CSA. In addition to offering comprehensive classroom-based prevention instruction, school administrators can do much to prevent CSA by supporting school-based approaches. School-based prevention involves efforts to modify the entire school environment to make it abuse free and safe for children, to improve the quality of response when abuse occurs, and to enhance the overall development of its students. As recommended by Hart, Brassard, and Germain (1987), schools can form task forces (composed of school psychologists, counselors, social workers, CPS workers, parents, and representatives of teaching and administrative staff) to: (a) ensure the healthy psychological development of their students, (b) follow appropriate investigation and reporting procedures for abuse cases, (c) work cooperatively with community resources to prevent maltreatment and provide supportive services to child victims and their families, and (d) actively solicit family and community involvement in schooling. In addition, schools could reduce the social isolation of families and serve as a family support system in which responsibility for the welfare of families is a central mission (Garbarino, 1979).

To enhance environmental modification, school administrators should encourage their personnel to continually reinforce the lessons children learn about relating to others in a nonexploitive way. This reinforcement should be offered throughout the day in a variety of situations to help children generalize the concepts they have learned. For example, school personnel should be encouraged to capitalize on "teachable moments," by modeling and reinforcing skills with students (e.g., by helping children assert their rights and make decisions for themselves). In order to be effective reinforcers of prevention concepts and skills, school employees should be themselves trained in prevention theory, concepts, and skills. School administrators play a key role in supporting, planning, and providing this type of in-service training.

By their comments and actions, male and female personnel can also enhance prevention efforts by reducing and eliminating sexist stereotypes and promoting egalitarian relationships and respect for all people (including children and adolescents). Teachers who demonstrate warmth, respect, and support for others provide children and adolescents with positive role models for interpersonal behavior. Modeling nonviolent methods of resolving conflicts are important ways teachers and school administrators can reduce the risk of maltreatment to children. In addition, school administrators can strive to eliminate the use of corporal punishment. As Holmes (1987) has stated, "Any school that encourages the use of corporal punishment with children in their care cannot hope to prevent or eliminate child abuse" (p.150). Abuse of any type must not be tolerated, and school administrators' actions will serve an important educational role by emphasizing this to children as well as the larger community.

The support of school administrators and school board members for classroom-based instruction in CSA is also of primary importance, particularly to diffuse community opposition and allay parents' and teachers' anxieties concerning such programming. (See Cosentino, 1989, for common concerns raised by parents and school personnel about these programs, and Meyers & Parsons, 1987, and Tennant, 1988, for ways to overcome resistance to prevention programs.) Administrators also play an important role in preparing and supporting teachers who teach these programs. Teachers need to be involved in all aspects of program development and may need in-service training and continuing consultative support to provide them with skills or knowledge needed to implement the programs. Having a clearly defined policy for reporting cases of suspected CSA, along with administrative support for identifying and reporting, can also make the schools more effective in combating CSA.

School administrators can become advocates not only for personal safety education but also for sexuality education. Sexuality education can serve as primary prevention when it is viewed from the perspective of discouraging the development of exploitive behaviors and encouraging nonexploitive behaviors and respect for others. As chapter 2 emphasizes, children and adolescents require instruction that promotes healthy sexuality, and they need this information at young ages. Parents should be an integral part of the planning process for sexuality education, consistent with an ecological perspective that views well-designed family-school partnerships as essential to the child's well-being (Pennekamp & Freeman, 1988). In addition, given the extent to which parents desire assistance from the schools in communicating about sex-related matters with their children (S. J. Alexander & Jorgensen, 1983), school administrators should strongly consider providing sexuality education for parents too, perhaps by providing workshops or free rental on books, films, and videos on the topic.

Schools can go far in helping reduce the social problem of CSA by integrating comprehensive sexuality and family life education (e.g., parenting classes, child development classes) into the standard curriculum for junior and senior high students (both males and females). Providing males and females with opportunities to gain experience in early child care and nurturance may reduce their risk of abuse. Finally, school administrators can advocate the kind of human relationship training described in chapter 2, which would be necessary given the educational system's reluctance to provide students with developmentally appropriate opportunities to learn these skills (Hart et al., 1987).

## Researchers

Researchers, as another group within the macrosystem, can continue to significantly impact the prevention movement. Through their systematic study of the problem, researchers generate knowledge about CSA: information of potential use to policymakers, professionals, and the general public. This information can also be used to guide prevention efforts. Indeed, good policy begins with good facts (U.S. Advisory Board on Child Abuse and Neglect, 1990). One way researchers can contribute to the prevention movement is by evaluating prevention programs directed at children, parents, and professionals both for their content and their effectiveness. Historically, the content for most programs came from anecdotal clinical experience (Conte et al., 1986). To be optimally effective, these programs need to be based on a solid foundation of knowledge. In-depth empirical studies of perpetrators and victims can help direct and refine the content of prevention programs.

### RESEARCH WITH VICTIMS

Research involving CSA victims can contribute to prevention efforts in a number of ways. For example, one untested assumption of classroom-based CSA prevention programs is that children who are deficient in CSA knowledge and personal safety skills are at risk for sexual exploitation. A few researchers have tested this assumption. For example, Gilgun (1986) interviewed 20 sexually abused girls (aged 10 to 15 years) about their knowledge of sexuality and sexual abuse. Results indicated that few victims were told about sexual abuse or had knowledge about sexual behavior in general. As a result, these victims were naïve regarding perpetrators' actions during the abuse. Prevention implications of this study are clear: children must be taught about sexuality and sexual abuse. The authors also noted, however, that three children who were quite knowledgeable about sexuality were still abused. They urge that prevention programmers convey to children that not all abuse is preventable and that when or if it does occur, children should tell someone immediately. More recently, B. N. Gordon, Schroeder, and Abrams (1990b) compared the sexual knowledge of a group of 22 children (aged 2 to 7 years) who had been sexually abused with that of nonabused children who were matched for age and social class. Sexually abused and nonabused children did not differ in their knowledge of sexual activities or body parts when social class and age were taken into account. Additional studies are needed to compare abused and nonabused children's knowledge about CSA specifically and their abilities to recognize, resist, and report sexual advances.

Another line of research has been to ask victims directly about their abuse experiences. Berliner and Conte (1990) interviewed 23 child victims (aged 10 to 18 years) about the process of their own sexual victimization and about potential prevention strategies. Three victimization processes were identified: (a) sexualization of the relationship (e.g., a gradual shift from normal affectionate contact or physical activities such as bathing, hugging, and tickling, to more sexual behaviors); (b) justification of the sexual contact (e.g., statements by offenders to rationalize or justify their behavior, such as "I need love and affection" or "I'm teaching you about sex"); and (c) maintenance of the victim's cooperation (e.g., threats, intimidation, persuasion). Few children felt that if they had said "no" to the perpetrator, the abuse would have stopped. Victims agreed, however, that children should be informed that offenders may try to trick them into thinking their sexual touching is acceptable and encouraged to tell someone immediately about the abuse.

In an indirect attempt to determine abuse experiences, Miller-Perrin et al. (1990) compared 25 sexually abused and 25 nonabused children's conceptions of CSA. Children were read a vignette depicting a body-safety violation and then asked a standard list of questions designed to probe their understanding of the incident. Abused children were more likely to describe the perpetrator as an older male relative and to say that the victim went along with the perpetrator out of fear and because the perpetrator used some type of threat or coercion. Thus, it is important to prepare children for the various tactics perpetrators employ to entice children into sexual activity. Although there were few differences between abused and nonabused children's conceptions of the victim, fewer nonabused children indicated they would like to have the victim as a friend, suggesting that nonabused children may be less likely to socialize with an abused peer. Emphasizing that sexual abuse of children is always the adult's responsibility should be an important component of prevention programs. In addition, nearly one-fourth of the abused children indicated that the victim in the story would not tell anyone about the incident, suggesting the need for prevention programs to stress the importance of children obtaining adult assistance.

Other studies have focused on the disclosure of victims. For example, Farrell (1988) explored how characteristics of sexual abuse victims and the abuse (i.e., victim age, duration of abuse, seriousness of abuse) related to the likelihood of their reporting the abuse experience. Results indicated that the likelihood of reporting increased as the age of the victim increased, with the largest percentage of disclosures occurring among 12–15 year olds. A victim's self-disclosure was also more likely if the duration of abuse was 24 or more months and when the abuse was less serious. Similarly, Sauzier (1989) reported that victimized children who told immediately had experienced more "minor" forms of abuse (e.g., exhibitionism) and were abused by an extrafamilial offender. These findings support the importance of encouraging children to disclose abuse immediately and of alerting parents and professionals to signs indicating that a child has been abused. Future studies should investigate other factors that might impede or promote disclosure in victims, such as fears that they will not be believed or that they will be blamed.

Children can be excellent sources of information and their perspectives can add to our CSA knowledge base. It appears that valuable information about what happens in abusive situations can be gained by asking victims either directly or indirectly about their experiences. Such information can then be incorporated into prevention materials (e.g., by alerting children about the grooming process of abuse and ways to avoid becoming involved in such situations). More research into the processes that children go through in order to repel or report abuse is needed. It would also be helpful if we knew more about how children and adolescents define CSA. In addition, we need to know more about predisposing factors for maltreatment so that we can target prevention efforts accordingly. Knowledge of how different risk factors create vulnerability at different developmental stages would also be important. Finally, studies of children who were successful in their attempts to prevent the occurrence of abuse need to be conducted. As Hazzard (1990) has suggested, we need to know if "abuse avoiders" are more knowledgeable about the inappropriateness of the activity, less fearful of the consequences of disclosure, or more assertive and confident overall.

RESEARCH WITH PERPETRATORS
Research with offenders also has the potential for contributing greatly to prevention efforts. Lang and Frenzel (1988) interviewed 52 incest offenders and 50 pedophiles from an in-patient treatment program about where and how they seduced children. Locations chosen for sexual assaults differed for incestuous and pedophilic men, with 100% of all sexual abuse occurring within the incest offender's home and 54% within the pedophile's home. Pedophiles either isolated the children in their own homes or gained entry to the child's home (e.g., via baby-sitting for a single mother). They also frequented places where children are often unsupervised (e.g., video arcades).

Ploys used to seduce children included beginning with seemingly accidental or affectionate touches and then proceeding to sexual touches, initiating the sex play as a game or sneaking into the bedroom while the child slept. Adult pornographic books or videos were also used by a few offenders to arouse the children's curiosity. Offenders often misrepresented moral standards (e.g., "It's OK, everybody does it") or misused their authority or adult sophistication to seduce children. Aggressive coercion was also common (e.g., frightening children, using physical force, or making threatening gestures). Significant force was used by one-third of the sexual offenders. Rewards or bribes (e.g., money, clothes, trips) were used about as often as physical force. To maintain further sexual contacts and ensure the child's silence, offenders often told children to "not tell about our special secret." Others used threats (e.g., of the family breaking up, of the offender being jailed, or of the child being spanked). Special privileges (e.g., to stay up late) were also offered as inducements for sexual favors. Many incest offenders used the "Daddy's Girl" approach, in which they maintained the sexual activity by saying "I love you" and taking advantage of the child's need for affection.

Conte et al. (1989) interviewed 20 adult sexual offenders from a treatment program about the ways they identified and recruited child victims and maintained their compliance. Offenders claimed to have a special ability to identify vulnerable children (e.g., living in a divorced home, young age, appearing depressed or needy), and they reported employing a range of coercive tactics to initiate and maintain the relationship (e.g., separating children from other protective adults, conditioning them through reward and punishment, forcing children to observe violence against their mothers). Like Lang and Frenzel (1988), they also reported that the offenders used sophisticated efforts to desensitize or groom children for the abuse, by progressing from nonsexual to sexual touch in the context of a developing relationship.

In Budin and Johnson (1989), 72 prison inmates incarcerated for CSA were surveyed about their modus operandi, perceptions of the ideal victim, and attitudes about various prevention strategies. Results indicated that the perpetrators gained victims' trust by "being a friend," playing children's games, and using bribery (e.g., giving money, toys, or candy). Threats (e.g., to hit the child or to hurt loved ones) were used by 22% of the subjects to gain the victims' cooperation and by 25% to ensure their silence. Perpetrators tended to prefer their own children and/or passive, quiet, troubled, lonely children from broken homes. To promote prevention, the majority of perpetrators agreed that children should learn about inappropriate touching of the genitals, to say "no" to assailants, and to disclose sexual abuse. In addition, they recommended that parents provide children with emotional fulfillment and good supervision, become more involved in their children's lives, and ask children periodically if they have experienced abuse.

Although these reports offer valuable insights into how offenders lure children, it must be noted that these studies were conducted with perpetrators who had been identified by some social system. Perpetrators who are not incarcerated or receiving treatment services may have a very different approach to victimization. In addition to broadening the subject pool, future studies need to determine if the victimization process differs depending on characteristics of the victim (e.g., age, relationship to the perpetrator) and perpetrator (e.g., socioeconomic status [SES], history of abuse, the "type" of perpetrator according to the classification systems described in chapter 1). It would also be interesting and potentially fruitful to determine what factors contribute to a perpetrator's discontinuing the molestation or deciding not to molest a particular child. Work with offenders also has great potential for the development of much-needed perpetrator-focused prevention efforts. The ultimate solution to the CSA problem is to prevent the development of offenders so that children are no longer at risk for sexual victimization.

### General Public

Combating CSA is ultimately the responsibility of every citizen. CSA is a pervasive, widespread problem affecting all kinds of children, families, and ultimately society as a whole. As Gentry (1978) notes, "denial, repugnance, feelings of guilt by association, anger, and uneasy fascination are frequent societal responses to incest" (p.355). Other responses include blaming victims for the abuse and denying the seriousness of the consequences of abuse (Broussard

& Wagner, 1988). To counteract such sentiments, we encourage citizens to become educated about the CSA problem and attend to characteristics of their communities that might be condoning the sexual exploitation of children. Indeed, as Hart (1988) has suggested, "Public awareness of the pervasive and powerfully destructive nature of maltreatment" (p.248) is the first step in generating public support for prevention efforts.

Media campaigns (through radio, television, newspapers, magazines, and billboards) are a central part of enhancing awareness of and informing the public about the CSA problem. The presentation on national television of films such as *Something About Amelia* or *Deadly Silence*, along with coverage on talk shows and programs such as *60 Minutes* and *20-20*, have most likely served to educate youth about the problem of sexual abuse and to teach them that adult-child sexual contact is inappropriate (primary prevention). In addition, such coverage can also serve a secondary prevention function, because viewers might be less reluctant to deny the widespread occurrence of CSA, less willing to blame the victims of abuse for their victimization, better prepared to identify suspected victims and / or respond more effectively to a victim's disclosure, and more knowledgeable about social and legal services for victims. Such programming may also facilitate victim disclosure (e.g., several victims in Seattle identified themselves after viewing a 30-second public-service announcement on television).

Media presentations also help to demystify and reduce the secrecy surrounding child sexual abuse. For example, stories of sexual abuse in the media prompted half of the parents surveyed by Finkelhor (1984) to discuss CSA with their children. Media presentations can also affect professionals. Recent highly visible prosecutions of a few educators for failing to report CSA cases likely serves to educate school professionals (and other professional groups) about their responsibilities to report. In addition, once produced, messages are low in cost per receiver. Finally, television and radio can influence people in the most private of homes and are watched and listened to by all socioeconomic and racial or ethnic classes (Comstock, 1983).

In the future, the media could be better used to disseminate information about the seriousness of the CSA problem. For example, a series of public-service announcements would be an efficient way of reaching victims, parents, and offenders. Concrete information could be provided to victims (e.g., that sexual abuse is not their fault, that it is important to seek help, and where to obtain assistance), and actors could model realistic refusal behaviors. It would be helpful to provide parents with information about how to recognize abuse and help their children (i.e., the early-warning signs, how to respond to a disclosure, and how to report instances of abuse) and to incorporate modeling of appropriate responses to disclosures.

For perpetrators, media presentations would be important to confront their rationalizations for offending, emphasize that such activities are illegal and harmful to children, outline possible consequences for their behavior, and provide information about obtaining assistance (Krivacska, 1990). Alone, mass-media strategies to deter or discourage offending behavior are unlikely to be successful (Sacco & Trotman, 1990), but as part of a comprehensive prevention effort within a community, they play an important role. Articles in local magazines and newspapers can also serve to educate the public about the topic and how their community has responded to the problem. Mass media could also be used to promote the values presented in programs for children and adolescents (see chapter 2)—values that emphasize self-worth, mutual respect, and sexual consent. Research will be needed to determine the potential efficacy of prevention initiatives that involve public education.

Conversely, the media has been criticized for potentially contributing to the CSA problem. With increasing frequency, the sexualization of children is depicted through advertising and films. Schetky (1988b) warns that through such adultification of children, adults receive mixed messages about childhood sexuality, potentially contributing to children's vulnerability to CSA. The media has also been criticized for attending to sex scandals and stories about CSA, focusing on the sensational aspects of such cases instead of ways to solve the problem. As a result, a victim's privacy is invaded and the public is at risk for becoming desensitized to child sexual abuse. There are additional costs of public information campaigns that need to be considered. For example, some writers have argued that campaigns intended to increase public awareness of CSA may heighten paranoia about touching and thus impair normal interaction between children and adults (Weinbach, 1987). In addition, successful dissemination of CSA publicity will likely increase reporting levels and thus must be accompanied by additional resources that allow agency personnel to meet the increased demand for services (Cohn, 1982). Once again, prevention efforts do not operate in a vacuum.

Citizens need to organize and use their collective vote to influence the media. Groups can be developed to carefully monitor the images portrayed in music, on television, and in advertising. In addition, children and adolescents need opportunities to discuss how the media uses sexuality and sexual stereotypes to try to influence them; they need help to become critical consumers of these forms of persuasion (see Peterson & Lewis, 1988).

Parents also need to press for federal, state, and local programs for children and families. In addition, parents play an important role as advocates for sex education and sex abuse prevention programs in the schools. Community centers and churches also need to be involved in discussing this type of abuse, providing sex education, and offering services to victims and victimizers. Community groups or service clubs can make the prevention of CSA a group project by informing members of the problem or raising funds for prevention or treatment services. Perhaps under the guidance of prevention organizations at the local level, every person can be encouraged to contribute to prevention efforts in their community (e.g., financial contribution, direct involvement in volunteer work).

## Summary

The primary prevention of CSA requires recognizing and transforming factors at the societal level that may foster or condone the sexual exploitation of children. These factors begin in the macrosystem and expand to influence groups in other systems and at other levels. An examination of societal factors revealed that there is much that policymakers (at the federal, state, and local levels) and the general public can do to prevent CSA and simultaneously improve the welfare of children. Researchers also play a vital role in these efforts by providing the facts to direct sound policies. A comprehensive approach to preventing CSA must study and modify the social context that fosters its occurrence.

*You're either part of the solution or part of the problem.*—ELDRIDGE
CLEAVER, 1968

Child sexual abuse is a complex, multiply determined social problem. As is true of physical child abuse, "to expect to eliminate it in
the foreseeable future is overly optimistic; not to try to eliminate
it is irresponsible and indefensibly callous" (Starr, 1979, p.877).
As we have seen, no single factor or condition explains the sexual
abuse of children. Thus, no single prevention strategy will be successful in preventing this widespread social problem. In this book,
our intention has been to encourage divergent thinking regarding
the appropriate scope and nature of prevention approaches, as we
advocate an expansion from a primary focus on child-victimization
prevention programs toward broader and more systemwide reforms. Child-centered approaches can only receive support and be
most effective when augmented by school-, family-, and community-based efforts, each of which should be viewed as contributing
to the prevention of CSA. In this final chapter, we will provide a
brief summary of our recommendations at each point on the prevention continuum.

## Programs for Children

Classroom-based programs were reviewed in chapter 2. We concluded that gains in distal outcomes (e.g., reducing incidence; increasing disclosures) have not been empirically demonstrated. We

concluded from published evaluations, however, that these programs do enhance children's knowledge and skill levels (i.e., proximal outcomes). Our analysis of the cost-benefit ratio of these programs indicated that they are relatively inexpensive to implement and result in no or minimal negative side effects to participants. In addition, some positive side effects have been noted (e.g., program participants feel safer and better able to protect themselves; increased discussion of CSA in the home). It appears that we have come a long way in a relatively short time toward educating children about body safety, even though we have yet to develop the ideal program. For the continued development of personal safety programs for children, we recommend the following:

- Refer to such programs as "body safety programs" or "personal safety programs" (instead of "sexual abuse prevention programs"), to avoid misleading the public and creating a false sense of security about what these programs can do.
- Evaluate programs regularly to determine their benefits and costs.
- Train children in the four Rs (i.e., Remember prevention concepts, Recognize abusive situations, Resist abuse through self-protective skills, Report past or ongoing abuse).
- Gear instruction to children's developmental levels and cognitive abilities.
- Examine the effects of different types of programs on children who vary in personal characteristics (e.g., age, sex, intelligence, self-concept, abuse or nonabuse status) and in family characteristics (e.g., socioeconomic level, cultural background, parental attitudes toward CSA prevention).
- Develop and evaluate programs targeting exceptional children (e.g., developmentally delayed; hearing impaired).
- Develop and evaluate programs targeting adolescents.
- Develop and evaluate programs targeting characteristics of children that may make them vulnerable to abuse (e.g., low self-esteem, limited decision-making and problem-solving skills, unassertiveness).
- Promote healthy sexuality through developmentally appropriate instruction for youths of all ages.

– Implement child-focused programs in the context of multilevel prevention efforts (i.e., in unison with other approaches directed at parents, professionals, policymakers, and the general public).

**Parents as Prevention Partners**

Parents are an additional prevention target group and should be included in efforts to combat CSA. In chapter 3 we reviewed the many advantages to involving parents in prevention efforts and also offered some reasons why parents may have been reluctant in the past to discuss CSA with their children. Encouragingly, recent surveys have indicated that parental attitudes toward CSA and its prevention are changing, with many parents supporting prevention programming and expressing a desire to be involved in the prevention movement. Thus, parents are a valuable resource waiting to be recognized as contributors to the CSA prevention movement. Future parent-focused approaches should:

– Inform parents about CSA to help them gain a deeper understanding of both the problem and their role in reducing risk factors and enhancing protective factors
– Help parents explore and clarify how their attitudes, values, and knowledge about sexuality (as well as their own abuse experiences) might influence their prevention attitudes and behaviors
– Familiarize parents with ways they can educate their children about CSA (e.g., teach specific body-safety skills; use role-play exercises, activities, and games with their children)
– Inform parents about the signs and symptoms associated with abuse, to enable them to accurately identify CSA cases and implement proper intervention to terminate the abuse
– Educate parents about normal, developmentally appropriate behavior (particularly sexual behavior) in order to place children's behavior in context
– Train parents to react supportively toward children who disclose abuse
– Inform parents about reporting issues, particularly about the consequences of both reporting and nonreporting

˙  ˙  ⌐ parents about the importance of therapeutic interven-
  ild victims and acquaint them with community ser-
  le to them and their children
    erested parents to become involved in the preven-
tion movement
- Evaluate the effectiveness of parent-focused programs and materials

## The Roles of Professionals

As chapter 4 emphasized, professionals are other target groups
with prevention potential. Various professional groups (e.g., teachers, day-care personnel, medical and mental health professionals,
law-enforcement personnel, and social-service employees) play
pivotal roles in furthering prevention efforts specific to their areas
of expertise. Unfortunately, their involvement in the prevention
movement has been limited because of their inadequate education
and training in CSA and its prevention, the emotional discomfort
that this topic engenders, the perceived lack of administrative support for prevention activities, their fears about the consequences
of reporting CSA cases (e.g., doubts that legal and social-service
agencies can effectively address the needs of the victim; conflicts
between mandated reporting and client confidentiality), and confusion among professional groups about their respective roles and
responsibilities. Professional-focused prevention efforts must address these issues in order to more fully involve professionals in
the battle against CSA. Future professional-focused efforts should
include:

- Information about the CSA problem including incidence and
  prevalence statistics, characteristics of victims and perpetrators,
  and the dynamics of abuse
- Training in educating children about sexual abuse
- Instruction in identifying victims of sexual abuse to facilitate
  termination of abuse and intervention for victims (including information about normal patterns of touching; physical, emotional, and behavioral indicators of sexual abuse; and child, family, and environmental risk factors associated with sexual abuse)

- Training in appropriate responses to victims' disclosures
- Information about reporting rights and responsibilities
- Outlining the respective roles and responsibilities of different professionals in managing CSA cases
- Emphasizing the importance of collaboration between professional groups in managing CSA cases
- Evaluating the effectiveness of professional-focused programs and materials

## Contributions of Researchers

Hopefully, researchers will continue to significantly impact the prevention movement through their systematic study of the CSA problem. Researchers generate knowledge about CSA—information of potential use to policymakers, professionals, and the general public. Such information not only adds to our understanding of the problem but also guides prevention efforts. Researchers can also contribute to the progress of the prevention movement by evaluating both the content and the effectiveness of prevention programs directed at children, parents, and professionals. To be optimally effective, such programs need to be based on a solid foundation of knowledge. Areas needing further research include:

- Scope of the CSA problem
- Causes of CSA
- Consequences of CSA (to children, families, society)
- Victims (e.g., risk factors, perceptions of the abuse, characteristics of disclosures)
- Nonabused youths (e.g., their definitions of CSA, successful attempts to prevent the occurrence of abuse)
- Perpetrators (e.g., how they identify, recruit, and maintain child victims; attitudes about prevention strategies)

## Policymakers as Prevention Proponents

In chapter 5 we suggested that changes within cultural and societal levels will be required to significantly impact the CSA problem.

Various groups within society could be targeted, including policy-makers such as legislators, community leaders, and school administrators.

### LEGISLATORS
Legislators (at the state and federal levels) are of key importance because of their ability to:

- Allocate funds for many of the prevention strategies suggested in this book. Although some monies have been allocated toward the problem of child abuse and neglect and the prevention of CSA, legislators must increase financial assistance to expand prevention research and programs
- Promote children's welfare. In order to both decrease risk factors and increase protective factors related to CSA, legislators need to affect change through the enhancement of child welfare
- Modify child abuse statutes, including those related to child pornography, reporting, mandatory training and prevention education, mandatory criminal history background checks for persons who apply to work with children, and the legal system's response to victims and perpetrators

### COMMUNITY LEADERS
Community leaders are an additional group of policymakers who can play pivotal roles in enhancing prevention efforts. Community leaders are in a key position to:

- Assess what their communities are doing to enhance public and professional awareness about CSA
- Assess what resources exist in their communities for victims, offenders, and families
- Assess what their communities are doing to prevent CSA
- Sponsor multidisciplinary boards to provide and coordinate identification, prosecution, and treatment services among professionals within their communities
- Sponsor a task force to examine what their communities are doing to prevent CSA

- Advocate for public awareness programs to increase public sensitivity to CSA
- Make children's needs a social priority

## SCHOOL ADMINISTRATORS

School administrators can do much in the way of prevention efforts, given their service to children of every ethnic group, race, creed, and socioeconomic group. School administrators can advance prevention efforts by:

- Modifying the school environment, by encouraging personnel to: (a) reinforce prevention lessons; (b) eliminate sexist stereotypes; (c) promote egalitarian relationships and respect for all people; (d) demonstrate warmth, respect, and support for youths; and (e) model nonviolent ways of resolving conflicts
- Creating multidisciplinary task forces to prevent maltreatment and provide supportive services to child victims and their families
- Promoting the concept of schools as a family support system
- Having clearly defined policies for reporting cases of suspected CSA, and supporting staff for identifying and reporting suspected cases
- Supporting classroom-based instruction in CSA to diffuse community opposition and allay parents' and teachers' anxieties regarding such programming
- Providing in-service training about CSA (and other types of child maltreatment) to school personnel
- Supporting sexuality education that can discourage the development of exploitive behaviors and encourage respect for others
- Assisting parents in communicating about sex-related matters with their children
- Integrating comprehensive sexuality and family life education into the standard curriculum for junior and senior high students (both males and females)
- Advocating for the kind of human relationship training described in chapter 2

## Public Responsibility

Combating CSA is ultimately the responsibility of every citizen. We encourage each citizen to become educated about the CSA problem and attend to characteristics of their communities that might be condoning the sexual exploitation of their children. Mass-media campaigns are a central part of enhancing awareness of, and informing the public about, the problem of CSA. The media can help reduce this social problem by targeting:

- Children (to help them recognize abuse; to inform victims where they can obtain help)
- Parents (to help them recognize abuse and assist victims)
- Professionals (to inform them about their reporting responsibilities)
- Perpetrators (to help them confront their rationalizations for offending, to inform them where they can obtain help)

Community groups should be developed to monitor the images portrayed in music, on television, and in advertising. In addition, parents and other concerned citizens need to:

- Press for federal, state, and local programs for children and families
- Advocate for sex education and personal safety programs in schools

## Final Conclusion

In conclusion, preventing CSA will require adopting multiple strategies, including:

- Classroom-based instruction in personal safety geared to children's developmental levels and cognitive abilities
- Education promoting healthy sexuality
- Parent-focused materials, workshops, and meetings to inform them about CSA and their role in preventing the sexual exploitation of children
- Education for professionals who work with children and coordination between professionals, policymakers, and researchers

- Community- and society-based efforts to support children and
  families and reduce aspects of the social system that condone or
  promote abusive behaviors
- Public awareness efforts emphasizing that the prevention of CSA
  is everyone's responsibility

   Targeting multiple groups with a variety of prevention strategies
is consistent with the notion that CSA is a complex problem that
requires the prevention efforts of all individuals and groups in our
society. To successfully combat CSA, we all must share the responsibility for this serious social problem and make a concerted effort
to put the sexual exploitation of children to an end. By sharing
responsibility for the CSA problem, each of us can contribute to
its solution. To do nothing is to tolerate the sexual abuse of children. As Eldridge Cleaver reminds us, if we are not part of the
solution, we are part of the problem.

# References

Abel, G. G., Becker, J. V., & Cunningham-Rathner, J. (1984). Complications, consent, and cognitions in sex between children and adults. *International Journal of Law and Psychiatry, 7*, 89–103.

Abel, G. G., Becker, J. V., Cunningham-Rathner, J., Mittelman, M., & Rouleau, J. L. (1988). Multiple paraphilic diagnoses among sex offenders. *Bulletin of the American Academy of Psychiatry and the Law, 16*, 153–168.

Abel, G. G., Becker, J. V., Cunningham-Rathner, J., Rouleau, J. L., Kaplan, M., & Reich, J. (1984). *The treatment of child molesters.* New York: Columbia University Press.

Abel, G. G., Becker, J. V., Mittelman, M., Cunningham-Rathner, J., Rouleau, J. L., & Murphy, W. D. (1987). Self-reported sex crimes of non-incarcerated paraphiliacs. *Journal of Interpersonal Violence, 2*, 3–25.

Abel, G. G., Gore, D. K., Holland, C. L., Camp, N., Becker, J. V., & Rathner, J. (1989). The measurement of the cognitive distortions of child molesters. *Annals of Sex Research, 2*, 135–153.

Abel, G. G., Mittelman, M. S., & Becker, J. V. (1985). Sexual offenders: Results of assessment and recommendations for treatment. In H. H. Ben-Aron, S. I. Hucker, & C. D. Webster (Eds.), *Clinical criminology: Current concepts* (pp. 191–205). Toronto: M & M Graphics.

Abel, G. G., & Rouleau, J. L. (1990). The nature and extent of sexual assault. In W. L. Marshall, D. R. Laws, & H. E. Barbaree (Eds.), *Handbook of sexual assault: Issues, theories, and treatment of the offender* (pp. 9–21). New York: Plenum Press.

Aber, J. L., & Zigler, E. (1981). Developmental considerations in the definition of child maltreatment. *New Directions for Child Development, 11*, 1–29.

Abrahams, N., Casey, K., & Daro, D. (1989). *Teachers confront child abuse: A national survey of teachers' knowledge, attitudes, and beliefs.* Chicago, IL: National Committee for the Prevention of Child Abuse.

Achenbach, T. M., & Edelbrock, C. (1983). *Manual for the child behavior checklist and revised child behavior profile.* Burlington, VT: University of Vermont Department of Psychiatry.

Adams, C., & Fay, J. (1981). *No more secrets: Protecting your child from sexual assault.* San Luis Obispo, CA: Impact Publishers.

Adams, C., & Fay, J. (1986). Parents as primary prevention educators. In M. Nelson & K. Clark (Eds.), *The educator's guide to preventing child sexual abuse* (pp.93–97). Santa Cruz, CA: Network Publications.

Adams, C., Fay, J., & Loreen-Martin, J. (1984). *No is not enough: Helping teenagers avoid sexual assault.* San Luis Obispo, CA: Impact Publishers.

Adams-Tucker, C. (1981). A socioclinical overview of 28 sex-abused children. *Child Abuse & Neglect, 5,* 361–367.

Adams-Tucker, C. (1982). Proximate effects of sexual abuse in childhood: A report on 28 children. *American Journal of Psychiatry, 139,* 1252–1256.

Ageton, S. (1983). *Sexual assault among adolescents.* Lexington, MA: Lexington Books.

Alexander, P. C. (1985). A systems theory conceptualization of incest. *Family Processes, 24,* 79–88.

Alexander, P. C., & Lupfer, S. L. (1987). Family characteristics and long-term consequences associated with sexual abuse. *Archives of Sexual Behavior, 16,* 235–245.

Alexander, P. C., Neimeyer, R. A., Follette, V. M., Moore, M. K., & Harter, S. (1989). A comparison of group treatments of women sexually abused as children. *Journal of Consulting and Clinical Psychology, 57,* 479–483.

Alexander, S. J., & Jorgensen, S. R. (1983). Sex education for early adolescents: A study of parents and students. *Journal of Early Adolescence, 3,* 315–325.

Allen, C. V. (1980). *Daddy's girl.* New York: Wyndham Books.

Allsopp, A., & Prosen, S. (1988). Teacher reactions to a child sexual abuse training program. *Elementary School Guidance and Counseling, 22,* 299–305.

Alter-Reid, K., Gibbs, M. S., Lachenmeyer, J. R., Sigal, J., & Massoth, N. A. (1986). Sexual abuse of children: A review of the empirical findings. *Clinical Psychology Review, 6,* 249–266.

American Academy of Pediatrics, Committee on Adolescence. (1983). Rape and the adolescent. *Pediatrics, 72,* 738–740.

American Association for Protecting Children. (1986). *Highlights of official child neglect and abuse reporting: 1984.* Denver, CO: American Humane Association.

American Association for Protecting Children. (1988). *Highlights of official child neglect and abuse reporting: 1986.* Denver, CO: American Humane Association.

American Psychiatric Association. (1987). *Diagnostic and Statistical Manual of Mental Disorders* (DSM-III-R) (3rd ed. rev.). Washington, DC: Author.

Anderson, C. (1979). *Child sexual abuse prevention project: An educational model for working with children.* Minneapolis, MN: Hennepin County Attorney's Office.

Anderson, S. C., Bach, C. M., & Griffith, S. (1981, April). *Psychosocial sequelae in intrafamilial victims of sexual assault and abuse.* Paper presented at the Third International Congress on Child Abuse and Neglect, Amsterdam, The Netherlands.

Anderson-Kent, C. (1982). *No easy answers.* Minneapolis: Illusion Theatre.

Armstrong, L. (1978). *Kiss daddy goodnight: A speakout on incest.* New York: Hawthorn Books.

Armstrong, L. (1983). *The home front.* New York: McGraw-Hill.

Asnes, R., Grebin, B., & Shore, W. B. (1972). Gonococcal infections in children. *Journal of Pediatrics, 81,* 192–193.

Atteberry-Bennett, J., & Reppucci, N. D. (1986, August). *What does child sexual abuse mean?* Paper presented at the annual convention of the American Psychological Association, Washington, DC.

Attias, R., & Goodwin, J. (1985). Knowledge and management strategies in incest cases: A survey of physicians, psychologists and family counselors. *Child Abuse & Neglect, 9,* 527–533.

Avery-Clark, C. A., & Laws, D. R. (1984). Differential erection response patterns of sexual child abusers to stimuli describing activities in children. *Behavior Therapy, 15,* 71–83.

Awad, G. A., & Saunders, E. B. (1989). Adolescent child molesters: Clinical observations. *Child Psychiatry and Human Development, 19,* 195–206.

Bagley, C. (1969). Incest behavior and incest taboo. *Social Problems, 16,* 505–519.

Bagley, C., & Ramsey, R. (1985). Sexual abuse in childhood: Psychosocial outcomes and implications for social work practice. *Journal of Social Work & Human Sexuality, 4,* 33–47.

Bagley, C., & Young, L. (1987). Juvenile prostitution and child sexual abuse: A controlled study. *Canadian Journal of Community Mental Health, 6,* 5–26.

Bailey, M. (1982). The failure of physicians to report child abuse. *University of Toronto Law Review, 49,* 49–66.

Baker, A. W., & Duncan, S. P. (1985). Child sexual abuse: A study of prevalence in Great Britain. *Child Abuse & Neglect, 9,* 457–467.

Bales, J. (1988, June). Child abuse prevention efficacy called in doubt. *APA Monitor,* p.27.

Banning, A. (1989). Mother-son incest: Confronting a prejudice. *Child Abuse & Neglect, 13,* 563–570.

Barbaree, H. E., & Marshall, W. L. (1989). Erectile responses among heterosexual child molesters, father-daughter incest offenders, and matched non-offenders: Five distinct age preference profiles. *Canadian Journal of Behavioural Science, 21,* 70–82.

Barber-Madden, R. (1983). Training day care program personnel in handling child abuse cases: Intervention and prevention outcomes. *Child Abuse & Neglect, 7,* 25–32.

Barnard, G. W., Fuller, A. K., Robbins, L., & Shaw, T. (1989). *The child molester: An integrated approach to evaluation and treatment.* New York: Brunner/Mazel.

Barnett, S. W. (1986). Methodological issues in economic evaluation of early intervention programs. *Early Childhood Research Quarterly, 1,* 249–268.

Barth, R. P., & Derezotes, D. S. (1990). *Preventing adolescent abuse: Effective intervention strategies and techniques.* Lexington, MA: Lexington Books.

Becker, J. V., & Coleman, E. M. (1988). Incest. In V. B. Van Hasselt, R. L. Morrison, A. S. Bellack, & M. Hersen (Eds.), *Handbook of family violence* (pp.187–205). New York: Plenum Press.

Becker, J. V., Cunningham-Rathner, J., & Kaplan, M. S. (1986). Adolescent sexual offenders: Demographics, criminal and sexual histories, and recommendations for reducing future offenses. *Journal of Interpersonal Violence, 1,* 431–445.

Becker, J. V., Kaplan, M. S., Cunningham-Rathner, J., & Kavoussi, R. (1986). Characteristics of adolescent sexual perpetrators: Preliminary findings. *Journal of Family Violence, 1,* 85–97.

Bell, A. P., Weinberg, M. S., & Hammersmith, S. K. (1981). *Sexual preference: Its development in men and women.* Bloomington, IN: University Press.

Belsky, J. (1980). Child maltreatment: An ecological integration. *American Psychologist, 35,* 320–335.

Bem, S. L. (1989). Genital knowledge and gender constancy in preschool children. *Child Development, 60, 649–662.*

Bender, L., & Blau, A. (1937). The reactions of children to sexual relationships with adults. *American Journal of Orthopsychiatry, 7,* 500–518.

Benjamin, H., & Masters, R. E. L. (1964). *Prostitution and morality.* New York: Julian Press.

Berliner, L. (1985). The child and the criminal justice system. In A. W. Burgess (Ed.), *Rape and sexual assault* (pp. 199–208). New York: Garland Publications.

Berliner, L., & Conte, J. R. (1990). The process of victimization: The victims' perspective. *Child Abuse & Neglect, 14,* 29–40.

Berliner, L., & Stevens, D. (1982). Clinical issues in child sexual abuse. *Journal of Social Work & Human Sexuality, 1,* 93–108.

Berrick, J. D. (1988). Parental involvement in child abuse prevention training: What do they learn? *Child Abuse & Neglect, 12,* 543–553.

Besharov, D. J. (1985). "Doing something" about child abuse: The need to narrow the grounds for state intervention. *Harvard Journal of Law and Public Policy, 8,* 539–589.

Besharov, D. J. (1986). Unfounded allegations—a new child abuse problem. *The Public Interest, 83,* 18–33.

Besharov, D. J. (1988). Child abuse and neglect reporting and investigation: Policy guidelines for decision-making. *Family Law Quarterly, 22,* 1–15.

Bianchi, S. M. (1990). America's children: Mixed prospects. *Population Bulletin, 45,* 3–41.

Binder, R. L., & McNiel, D. E. (1987). Evaluation of a school-based sexual abuse prevention program: Cognitive and emotional effects. *Child Abuse & Neglect, 11,* 497–506.

Bliss, E. L. (1984). A symptom profile of patients with multiple personality, including MMPI results. *Journal of Nervous and Mental Disorders, 172,* 197–202.

Bloom, B. L. (1979). Prevention of mental disorders: Recent advances in theory and practice. *Community Mental Health Journal, 15,* 179–191.

Bloom, B. L. (1981). The logic and urgency of primary prevention. *Hospital & Community Psychiatry, 32,* 839–843.

Bloom, B. L. (1984). Basic concepts in prevention. In B. L. Bloom, *Community mental health: A general introduction* (pp.191–243). Monterey, CA: Brooks/Cole.

Blumberg, E. J., Chadwick, M. W., Fogarty, L. A., Speth, T. W., & Chadwick, D. L. (1991). The touch discrimination component of sexual abuse prevention training: Unanticipated positive consequences. *Journal of Interpersonal Violence, 6,* 12–28.

Borkin, J., & Frank, L. (1986). Sexual abuse prevention for preschoolers: A pilot program. *Child Welfare, 65,* 75–82.

Botvin, G. J. (1983). *Life Skills training: Teachers manual.* New York: Smithfield Press.

Bradshaw, T. L., & Marks, A. E. (1990). Beyond a reasonable doubt: Factors that influence the legal disposition of child sexual abuse cases. *Crime & Delinquency, 36,* 276–285.

Brant, R. S. T., & Tisza, V. B. (1977). The sexually misused child. *American Journal of Orthopsychiatry, 47,* 80–90.

Brassard, M. R., Tyler, A. H., & Kehle, T. J. (1983). School programs to prevent intrafamilial child sexual abuse. *Child Abuse & Neglect, 7,* 241–245.

Braun, D. (1988). *Responding to child abuse: Action and planning for teachers and other professionals.* London: Bedford Square Press.

Breines, W., & Gordon, L. (1983). The new scholarship on family violence. *Signs: Journal of Women and Culture and Society, 8,* 490–531.

Bresee, P., Stearns, G. B., Bess, B. H., & Packer, L. S. (1986). Allegations of child sexual abuse in child custody disputes: A therapeutic assessment model. *American Journal of Orthopsychiatry, 56,* 560–569.

Briere, J. (1989). *Therapy for adults molested as children: Beyond survival.* New York: Springer.

Briere, J., & Runtz, M. (1989). University males' sexual interest in children: Predicting potential indices of "pedophilia" in a nonforensic sample. *Child Abuse & Neglect, 13,* 65–75.

Briere, J., & Zaidi, L. Y. (1989). Sexual abuse histories in female psychiatric emergency room patients. *American Journal of Psychiatry, 146,* 1602–1606.

Broderick, C. B. (1969). Normal sociosexual development. In C. B. Broderick & J. Bernard (Eds.), *The individual, sex and society* (pp.23–29). Baltimore, MD: Johns Hopkins University Press.

Bronfenbrenner, U. (1977). Toward an experimental ecology of human development. *American Psychologist, 32,* 513–531.

Bronfenbrenner, U. (1979). *The ecology of human development: Experiments by nature and design.* Cambridge, MA: Harvard University Press.

Brookhouser, P. E., Sullivan, P., Scanlan, J. M., & Garbarino, J. (1986). Identifying the sexually abused deaf child: The otolaryngologist's role. *Laryngoscope, 96,* 152–158.

Brooks, B. (1982). Familial influences in father-daughter incest. *Journal of Psychiatric Treatment and Evaluation, 4,* 117–124.

Broussard, S. D., & Wagner, W. G. (1988). Child sexual abuse: Who is to blame? *Child Abuse & Neglect, 12,* 563–569.

Brown, R. H., & Truitt, R. B. (1978). Civil liability in child abuse cases. *Chi-Kent Law Review, 54,* 753–772.

Browne, A., & Finkelhor, D. (1986). Impact of child sexual abuse: A review of the research. *Psychological Bulletin, 99,* 66–77.

Browning, D. H. & Boatman, B. (1977). Incest: Children at risk. *American Journal of Psychiatry, 134,* 69–72.

Bryer, J. B., Nelson, B. A., Miller, J. B., & Krol, P. A. (1987). Childhood sexual and physical abuse as factors in adult psychiatric illness. *American Journal of Psychiatry, 144,* 1426–1430.

Budin, L. E., & Johnson, C. F. (1989). Sex abuse prevention programs: Offenders' attitudes about their efficacy. *Child Abuse & Neglect, 13,* 77–87.

Burgess, A. W. (1985). *The sexual victimization of adolescents* (PHIS Publication No. ADM 85-1382). Washington, DC: U.S. Government Printing Office.

Burgess, A. W., Groth, A. N., & McCausland, M. P. (1981). Child sex initiation rings. *American Journal of Orthopsychiatry, 51*, 110–119.

Burgess, A. W., & Hartman, C. R. (1987). Child abuse aspects of child pornography. *Psychiatric Annals, 17*, 248–253.

Burgess, A. W., Hartman, C. R., Kelley, S. J., Grant, C. A., & Gray, E. B. (1990). Parental response to child sexual abuse trials involving day care settings. *Journal of Traumatic Stress, 3*, 395–405.

Burnam, M. A., Stein, J. A., Golding, J. M., Siegel, J. M., Sorenson, S. B., Forsythe, A. B., & Telles, C. A. (1988). Sexual assault and mental disorders in a community population. *Journal of Consulting and Clinical Psychology, 56*, 843–850.

Burt, M. R. (1980). Cultural myths and supports for rape. *Journal of Personality and Social Psychology, 38*, 217–230.

Butler, S. (1978). *Conspiracy of silence: The trauma of incest.* San Francisco: New Guild Publications.

Calderone, M. S. (1983). *Childhood sexuality: Approaching the prevention of sexual disease.* In G. W. Albee, S. Gordon, & H. Leitenberg (Eds.), *Promoting sexual responsibility and preventing sexual problems* (pp. 333–344). Hanover, NH: University Press of New England.

Camp, B. W., & Bash, M. A. (1981). *Think aloud: Increasing social and cognitive skills—A problem solving program for children, Primary level.* Champaign, IL: Research Press.

Caplan, G. (1964). *Principles of preventive psychiatry.* New York: Basic Books.

Carmen, E. H., & Rieker, P. P. (1989). A psychosocial model of the victim-to-patient process. *Psychiatric Clinics of North America, 12*, 431–443.

Carnes, P. (1983). *Sexual addiction.* Minneapolis: CompCare Publications.

Carson, D. K., Gertz, L. M., Donaldson, M. A., & Wonderlich, S. A. (1990). Family-of-origin characteristics and current family relationships of female adult incest victims. *Journal of Family Violence, 5*, 153–171.

Carter, D. L., Prentky, R. A., Knight, R. A., Vanderveer, P. L., & Boucher, R. J. (1987). Use of pornography in the criminal and developmental histories of sexual offenders. *Journal of Interpersonal Violence, 2,* 196-211.

Carver County Program for Victims of Sexual Assault. (1980). *Children need protection: A guide to talking to children about sexual assault.* (Available from Carver County Program for Victims of Sexual Assault, 401 East 4th Street, Chaska, MN 55318.)

Castelle, K. (1990). *In the child's best interest: A primer on the UN Convention on the Rights of the Child* (3rd ed.). New York: Foster Parents Plan International & Defense for Children International.

Cavaiola, A. A., & Schiff, M. (1988). Behavioral sequelae of physical and/or sexual abuse in adolescents. *Child Abuse & Neglect, 12,* 181-188.

Child Assault Prevention Project. (1983). *Strategies for free children.* (Available from CAPP, P.O. Box 02084, Columbus, OH 43202).

Children's Self-Help Project. (1981). (Available from Children's Self-Help Project, 170 Fell Street, Room 34, San Francisco, CA 94102.)

Children's Self-Help Project. (1988). *Middle school and high school sexual abuse prevention programs.* (Available from Children's Self-Help Project, 170 Fell Street, Room 34, San Francisco, CA 94102.)

Christian, R., Dwyer, S., Schumm, W. R., & Coulson, L. A. (1988). Prevention of sexual abuse for preschoolers: Evaluation of a pilot program. *Psychological Reports, 62,* 387-396.

Clabby, J. F., & Elias, M. J. (1987). *Teach your child decision-making.* Garden City, NY: Doubleday.

Cohen, A. J. (1988). Sexual abuse in childcare: A special case in regulation and legislation. In A. Maney & S. Wells (Eds.), *Professional responsibilities in protecting children: A public health approach to child sexual abuse* (pp. 166-188). New York: Praeger.

Cohen, C. P., & Naimark, H. (1991). United Nations Convention on the Rights of the Child: Individual rights concepts and their significance for social scientists. *American Psychologist, 46,* 60-65.

Cohen, J. A., & Mannarino, A. P. (1988). Psychological symptoms in sexually abused girls. *Child Abuse & Neglect, 12,* 571-577.

Cohn, A. H. (1982). The role of media campaigns in preventing child abuse. In K. Oates (Ed.), *Child abuse: A community concern* (pp. 215-230). New York: Brunner/Marzel.

Cohn, A. H. (1986). Preventing adults from becoming sexual molesters. *Child Abuse & Neglect, 10,* 559–562.

Cohn, A. H., Finkelhor, D., & Holmes, C. (1985). *Preventing adults from becoming child molesters.* Chicago, IL: National Committee for Prevention of Child Abuse.

Colao, F., & Hosansky, T. (1987). *Your children should know: Personal-safety strategies for parents to teach their children.* New York: Harper & Row.

Cole, P. M., & Woolger, C. (1989). Incest survivors: The relation of their perceptions of their parents and their own parenting attitudes. *Child Abuse & Neglect, 13,* 409–416.

Cole, S. S. (1984–1986). Facing the challenges of sexual abuse in persons with disabilities. *Sexuality and Disability, 7,* 71–87.

Collier, S. A. (1983). Reporting child abuse: When moral obligations fail. *Pacific Law Journal, 15,* 189–215.

Comment. (1984). Vanishing exception to the psychotherapist-patient privilege: The child abuse reporting act. *Pacific Law Journal, 16,* 335–352.

Committee for Children. (1983). *Talking about touching: A personal safety curriculum.* (Available from Committee for Children, 172 20th Avenue, Seattle, WA 98122.)

Committee for Children. (1987). *Talking about touching II: Personal safety for preschoolers.* (Available from Committee for Children, 172 20th Avenue, Seattle, WA 98122.)

Committee for Children. (1989). *Second step: A violence prevention curriculum.* (Available from Committee for Children, 172 20th Avenue, Seattle, WA 98122).

Comstock, G. (1983). The mass media and social change. In E. Seidman (Ed.), *Handbook of social intervention* (pp.268–287). Beverly Hills, CA: Sage.

Constantine, L. L., & Martinson, F. M. (1981). Child sexuality: Here there be dragons. In L. L. Constantine & F. M. Martinson (Eds.), *Children and sex: New findings, new perspectives* (pp.3–8). Boston: Little, Brown.

Conte, J. R. (1985). The effects of sexual abuse on children: A critique and suggestions for further research. *Victimology: An International Journal, 10,* 110–130.

Conte, J. R. (1987). Ethical issues in evaluation of prevention programs. *Child Abuse & Neglect, 11,* 171–172.

Conte, J. R. (1988). Structural reconciliation of therapeutic and criminal justice cultures. In A. Maney & S. Wells (Eds.), *Professional responsibilities in protecting children: A public health approach to child sexual abuse* (pp.139–149). New York: Praeger.

Conte, J. R., & Berliner, L. (1981). Sexual abuse of children: Implications for practice. *Social Casework: The Journal of Contemporary Social Work, 12,* 601–606.

Conte, J. R., & Fogarty, L. A. (1989). *Attitudes on sexual abuse prevention programs: A national survey of parents.* Manuscript submitted for publication.

Conte, J. R., Rosen, C., & Saperstein, L. (1986). An analysis of programs to prevent the sexual victimization of children. *Journal of Primary Prevention, 6,* 141–155.

Conte, J. R., Rosen, C., Saperstein, L., & Shermack, R. (1985). An evaluation of a program to prevent the sexual victimization of young children. *Child Abuse & Neglect, 9,* 319–328.

Conte, J. R., & Schuerman, J. R. (1987). Factors associated with an increased impact of child sexual abuse. *Child Abuse & Neglect, 11,* 201–211.

Conte, J. R., Wolf, S., & Smith, T. (1989). What sexual offenders tell us about prevention strategies. *Child Abuse & Neglect, 13,* 293–301.

Coons, P. M., Bowman, E. S., Pellow, T. A., & Schneider, P. (1989). Posttraumatic aspects of the treatment of victims of sexual abuse and incest. *Psychiatric Clinics of North America, 12,* 325–335.

Coons, P. M., & Milstein, V. (1986). Psychosexual disturbances in multiple personality: Characteristics, etiology, and treatment. *Journal of Clinical Psychiatry, 47,* 106–110.

Cooper, S., Lutter, Y., & Phelps, C. (1983). *Strategies for free children.* Columbus, OH: The Child Assault Prevention Project.

Cosentino, C. E. (1989). Child sexual abuse prevention: Guidelines for the school psychologist. *School Psychology Review, 18,* 371–385.

Council on Child Abuse. (1982). *Would you know if your child were being molested?* (Available from Council on Child Abuse, P.O. Box 1357, Tacoma, WA 98401.)

Courtois, C. A. (1988). *Healing the incest wound: Adult survivors in therapy.* New York: W. W. Norton.

Crewdson, J. (1988). *By silence betrayed: Sexual abuse of children in America.* Boston: Little, Brown.

Cruz, V. K., Price-Williams, D., & Andron, L. (1988). Developmentally disabled women who were molested as children. *Social Casework: The Journal of Contemporary Social Work, 69,* 411–419.

Cupoli, J. M., & Sewell, P. M. (1988). One thousand fifty-nine children with a chief complaint of sexual abuse. *Child Abuse & Neglect, 12,* 151–162.

Daro, D., Abrahams, N., & Robson, K. (1988). *Reducing child abuse 20% by 1990: 1985–1986 Baseline data.* NCPCA paper #843. (Available from National Committee for the Prevention of Child Abuse, 332 South Michigan Avenue, Suite 1250, Chicago, IL 60604-4357.)

Davidson, H. (1988). Failure to report child abuse: Legal penalties and emerging issues. In A. Maney & S. Wells (Eds.), *Professional responsibilities in protecting children: A public health approach to child sexual abuse* (pp.93–102). New York: Praeger.

Davis, G. E., & Leitenberg, H. (1987). Adolescent sex offenders. *Psychological Bulletin, 101,* 417–427.

Davis, L. L. (1986). The role of the teacher in preventing child sexual abuse. In M. Nelson & K. Clark (Eds.), *The educator's guide to preventing child sexual abuse* (pp.87–92). Santa Cruz, CA: Network Publications.

Dayee, F. S. (1982). *Private zone: A book teaching children sexual assault prevention tools.* Edmonds, WA: The Chas. Franklin Press.

DeAngelis, T. (1990, September). Ruling tracks brief by APA. *The APA Monitor, 1,* 16.

DeBeauvoir, S. (1953). *The second sex.* New York: Bantam.

DeFrancis, V. (1969). *Protecting the child victim of sex crimes committed by adults.* Denver, CO: American Humane Association.

Deisher, R. W., Robinson, G., & Boyer, D. (1982). The adolescent female and male prostitute. *Pediatric Annals, 11,* 819–825.

Deisher, R. W., Wenet, G. A., Paperny, D. M., Clark, T. F., & Fehrenbach, P. A. (1982). Adolescent sexual offense behavior: The role of the physician. *Journal of Adolescent Health Care, 2,* 279–286.

DeJong, A. R. (1988). Maternal responses to the sexual abuse of their children. *Pediatrics*, *81*, 14–21.

DeJong, A. R., Emmett, G. A., & Hervada, A. R. (1982). Sexual abuse of children: Sex-, race-, and age-dependent variations. *American Journal of Diseases of Children*, *136*, 129–134.

DeJong, A. R., Hervada, A. R., & Emmett, G. A. (1983). Epidemiologic variations in childhood sexual abuse. *Child Abuse & Neglect*, *7*, 155–162.

Dell, P. F., & Eisenhower, J. W. (1990). Adolescent Multiple Personality Disorder: A preliminary study of eleven cases. *Journal of the American Academy of Child and Adolescent Psychiatry*, *29*, 359–366.

DeMause, L. (1974). *The history of childhood*. New York: Psychotherapy Press.

Department of Health & Human Services. (1981). *Study findings: National study of the incidence and severity of child abuse and neglect* (DHHS Publication No. OHDS 81-30325). Washington, DC: U.S. Government Printing Office.

Department of Health & Human Services. (1984). *Child sexual abuse prevention: Tips to parents* (DHHS Publication No. 0-454-460: QL3). Washington, DC: U.S. Government Printing Office.

Department of Health & Human Services. (1988). *Study findings: Study of national incidence and prevalence of child abuse and neglect* (DHHS Publication No. ADM 20-01099). Washington, DC: U.S. Government Printing Office.

de Young, M. (1981). Siblings of Oedipus: Brothers and sisters of incest victims. *Child Welfare*, *60*, 561–568.

de Young, M. (1982). *The sexual victimization of children*. Jefferson, NC: McFarland.

de Young, M. (1987). Toward a theory of child sexual abuse. *Journal of Sex Education and Therapy*, *13*, 17–21.

de Young, M. (1988). The indignant page: Techniques of neutralization in the publications of pedophile organizations. *Child Abuse & Neglect*, *12*, 583–591.

Dimock, P. T. (1988). Adult males sexually abused as children. *Journal of Interpersonal Violence*, *3*, 203–221.

Donnerstein, E. (1984). Pornography: Its effect on violence against women. In N. M. Malamuth & E. Donnerstein (Eds.), *Pornography and sexual aggression* (pp. 143–172). Orlando, FL: Academic Press.

Doughty, D. L., & Schneider, H. G. (1987). Attribution of blame in incest among mental health professionals. *Psychological Reports, 60,* 1159–1165.

Downer, A. (1985). *Prevention of child sexual abuse: A trainer's manual.* Seattle, WA: Committee for Children.

Downer, A. (1986). Training teachers to be partners in prevention. In M. Nelson & K. Clark (Eds.), *The educator's guide to preventing child sexual abuse* (pp.80–86). Santa Cruz, CA: Network Publications.

Downer, A., & Beland, K. (1985). *Personal safety and decision-making.* Seattle, WA: Committee for Children.

Dreyer, L. B., & Haseltine, B. A. (1986). *The Woodrow Project: A sexual abuse prevention curriculum for the developmentally disabled.* Fargo, ND: Rape and Abuse Crisis Center.

Drossman, D. A., Leserman, J., Nachman, G., Li, Z., Gluck, H., Toomey, T. C., & Mitchell, C. M. (1990). Sexual and physical abuse in women with functional or organic gastrointestinal disorders. *Annals of Internal Medicine, 113,* 828–833.

Duquette, D. N. (1988). Legal interventions. In K. C. Faller, *Child sexual abuse: An interdisciplinary manual for diagnosis, case management, and treatment* (pp.392–404). New York: Columbia University Press.

Duthie, B., & McIvor, D. L. (1990). A new system for cluster-coding child molester MMPI profile types. *Criminal Justice and Behavior, 17,* 199–214.

Earls, C. M., & Quinsey, V. L. (1985). What is to be done? Future research on the assessment and behavioral treatment of sex offenders. *Behavioral Sciences & the Law, 3,* 377–390.

Eckenrode, J., Munsch, J., Powers, J., & Doris, J. (1988). The nature and substantiation of official sexual abuse reports. *Child Abuse & Neglect, 12,* 311–319.

Egeland, B., Jacobvitz, D., & Papatola, K. (1987). Intergenerational continuity of abuse. In R. Gelles & J. Lancaster (Eds.), *Child abuse and neglect: Biosocial dimensions* (pp.255–276). New York: Aldine de Gruyter.

Egeland, B., Jacobvitz, D., & Sroufe, L. A. (1988). Breaking the cycle of abuse. *Child Development, 59,* 1080–1088.

Einbender, A. J., & Friedrich, W. N. (1989). Psychological functioning and behavior of sexually abused girls. *Journal of Consulting and Clinical Psychology, 57,* 155–157.

Eisenberg, N., Owens, R. G., & Dewey, M. E. (1987). Attitudes of health professionals to child sexual abuse and incest. *Child Abuse & Neglect, 11*, 109–116.

Elias, M. J., & Clabby, J. F. (1988). *Social skills and social decision-making skills for the elementary grades: A curriculum guide for educators.* Rockville, MD: Aspen.

Ellerstein, N. S., & Canavan, W. (1980). Sexual abuse of boys. *American Journal of Diseases of Children, 134*, 255–257.

Ellis, H. (1933). *Psychology of sex.* London: Pan Books.

Elwell, M. E., & Ephros, P. H. (1987). Initial reactions of sexually abused children. *Social Casework: The Journal of Contemporary Social Work, 68*, 109–116.

Erickson, M. F., Egeland, B., & Pianta, R. (1989). The effects of maltreatment on the development of young children. In D. Cicchetti & V. Carlson (Eds.), *Child maltreatment: Theory and research on the causes and consequences of child abuse and neglect* (pp.647–684). New York: Cambridge University Press.

Esquilin, S. C. (1987). Family responses to the identification of extrafamilial child sexual abuse. *Psychotherapy in Private Practice, 5*, 105–113.

Everson, M. D., & Boat, B. W. (1989). False allegations of sexual abuse by children and adolescents. *Journal of the American Academy of Child and Adolescent Psychiatry, 28*, 230–235.

Everson, M. D., Hunter, W. M., Runyon, D. K., Edelsohn, G. A., & Coulter, M. L. (1989). Maternal support following disclosure of incest. *American Journal of Orthopsychiatry, 59*, 197–207.

Faller, K. C. (1985). Unanticipated problems in the United States child protection system. *Child Abuse & Neglect, 9*, 63–69.

Faller, K. C. (1988). *Child sexual abuse: An interdisciplinary manual for diagnosis, case management, and treatment.* New York: Columbia University Press.

Faller, K. C. (1989a). Characteristics of a clinical sample of sexually abused children: How boy and girl victims differ. *Child Abuse & Neglect, 13*, 281–291.

Faller, K. C. (1989b). Why sexual abuse? An exploration of the intergenerational hypothesis. *Child Abuse & Neglect, 13*, 543–548.

Faller, K. C. (1990). *Understanding child sexual maltreatment.* Newbury Park, CA: Sage.

Farrell, L. T. (1988). Factors that affect a victim's self-disclosure in father-daughter incest. *Child Welfare, 67,* 462–468.

Fay, J. (1986). Guidelines for selecting prevention education resources. In M. Nelson & K. Clark (Eds.), *The educator's guide to preventing child sexual abuse* (pp.98–192). Santa Cruz, CA: Network Publications.

Fay, J., & Flerchinger, B. J. (1982). *Top Secret: Sexual assault for teenagers only.* Denver, CO: C. Henry Kempe National Center.

Fehrenbach, P. A., Smith, W., Monastersky, C., & Deisher, R. W. (1986). Adolescent sexual offenders: Offender and offense characteristics. *American Journal of Orthopsychiatry, 56,* 225–233.

Feis, C. L., & Simons, C. (1985). Training preschool children in interpersonal cognitive problem-solving skills: A replication. *Prevention in Human Services, 4,* 59–70.

Felner, R. D., Jason, L., Moritsugu, J., & Farber, S. S. (Eds.). (1983). *Preventive psychology: Theory, research and practice in community intervention.* New York: Pergamon Press.

Film Fair Communications. (1979). *Better safe than sorry II* [Film]. (Available from Author, 900 Ventura Blvd., Box 1728, Studio, CA 91604.)

Finkelhor, D. (1979). *Sexually victimized children.* New York: The Free Press.

Finkelhor, D. (1980). Risk factors in the sexual victimization of children. *Child Abuse & Neglect, 4,* 265–273.

Finkelhor, D. (1984). *Child sexual abuse: New theory and research.* New York: The Free Press.

Finkelhor, D., & Araji, S. (1983). *The prevention of child sexual abuse: A review of current approaches.* (Available from Family Violence Research Program, University of New Hampshire, Durham, NH 03824.)

Finkelhor, D., & Baron, L. (1986). Risk factors for sexual abuse. *Journal of Interpersonal Violence, 1,* 43–71.

Finkelhor, D., Gomes-Schwartz, B., & Horowitz, J. (1984). Professionals' responses. In D. Finkelhor, *Child sexual abuse: New theory and research* (pp.200–220). New York: The Free Press.

Finkelhor, D., Hotaling, G., Lewis, I. A., & Smith, C. (1990). Sexual abuse in a national survey of adult men and women: Prevalence, characteristics, and risk factors. *Child Abuse & Neglect, 14,* 19–28.

Finkelhor, D., & Lewis, I. A. (1988). An epidemiologic approach to the study of child molestation. *Annals of the New York Academy of Sciences, 528,* 64–78.

Finkelhor, D., & Redfield, D. (1984). How the public defines sexual abuse. In D. Finkelhor, *Child sexual abuse: New theory and research* (pp.107–133). New York: The Free Press.

Finkelhor, D., & Strapko, N. (1992). Sexual abuse prevention education: A review of evaluation studies. In D. J. Willis, E. W. Holden, & M. Rosenberg (Eds.), *Child Abuse Prevention* (pp. 150–167). New York: Wiley.

Finkelhor, D., Williams, L. M., & Burns, N. (1988). *Nursery crimes: Sexual abuse in day care.* Newbury Park, CA: Sage.

Fortune, M. M. (1984). *Sexual abuse prevention: A study for teenagers.* New York: United Church Press.

Forward, S., & Buck, C. (1978). *Betrayal of innocence: Incest and its devastation.* New York: Penguin.

Fox, P. E. (1977). How do we get started? In M. A. Thomas (Ed.), *Children alone: What can be done about abuse and neglect?* (pp.79–89). Reston, VA: Council for Exceptional Children.

Fox, R. (1980). *The red lamp of incest.* New York: Dutton.

Friedrich, W. N. (1990). *Psychotherapy of sexually abused children and their families.* New York: W. W. Norton.

Friedrich, W. N., Grambsch, P., Broughton, D., Kuiper, J., & Beilke, R. L. (1991). Normative sexual behavior in children. *Pediatrics, 88,* 456–464.

Friedrich, W. N., Urquiza, A. J., & Beilke, R. L. (1986). Behavior problems in sexually abused young children. *Journal of Pediatric Psychology, 11,* 47–57.

Fritz, G. S., Stoll, K., & Wagner, N. W. (1981). A comparison of males and females who were sexually molested as children. *Journal of Sex and Marital Therapy, 7,* 54–59.

Fromuth, M. E. (1986). The relationship of childhood sexual abuse with later psychological and sexual adjustment in a sample of college women. *Child Abuse & Neglect, 10,* 5–15.

Fryer, G. E., Kraizer, S. K., & Miyoshi, T. (1987a). Measuring actual reduction of risk to child abuse: A new approach. *Child Abuse & Neglect, 11*, 173–179.

Fryer, G. E., Kraizer, S. K., & Miyoshi, T. (1987b). Measuring children's retention of skills to resist stranger abduction: Use of the simulation technique. *Child Abuse & Neglect, 11*, 181–185.

Gagnon, J. (1965). Female child victims of sex offenses. *Social Problems, 13*, 176–192.

Galdston, R. (1978). Sexual survey #12: Current thinking on sexual abuse of children. *Medical Aspects of Human Sexuality, 12*, 44–47.

Gale, J., Thompson, R. J., Moran, T., Sack, W. H. (1988). Sexual abuse in young children: Its clinical presentation and characteristic patterns. *Child Abuse & Neglect, 12*, 163–170.

Garbarino, J. (1977). The human ecology of child maltreatment: A conceptual model for research. *Journal of Marriage and the Family, 39*, 721–735.

Garbarino, J. (1979). The role of the school in the human ecology of child maltreatment. *School Review, 87*, 190–213.

Garbarino, J. (1980). Preventing child maltreatment. In R. H. Price, R. F. Ketterer, B. C. Bader, & J. Monahan (Eds.), *Prevention in mental health: Research, policy, and practice* (pp.63–79). Beverly Hills, CA: Sage.

Garbarino, J. (1987). Children's response to a sexual abuse prevention program: A study of the Spiderman comic. *Child Abuse & Neglect, 11*, 143–148.

Garbarino, J. (1988). But are we really preventing child abuse? *Division of Child, Youth and Family Services Newsletter, 11*, 3, 12.

Gazda, G., & Pistole, M. C. (1986). Life skills training: A model. *Counseling and Human Development, 19*, (whole issue).

Gebhard, P. (1977). The acquisition of basic sex information. *Journal of Sex Research, 13*, 148–169.

Gelfand, D. M., & Peterson, L. (1985). *Child development and psychopathology.* Beverly Hills, CA: Sage.

Gelinas, D. J. (1983). The persisting negative effects of incest. *Psychiatry, 46*, 312–332.

Gelles, R. (1974). *The Violent Home.* Beverly Hills, CA: Sage.

Gentry, C. E. (1978). Incestuous abuse of children: The need for an objective view. *Child Welfare, 57,* 355–364.

Gilbert, N. (1988). Teaching children to prevent sexual abuse. *The Public Interest, 93,* 3–15.

Gilbert, N., Berrick, J. D., Le Prohn, N., & Nyman, N. (1989). *Protecting young children from sexual abuse: Does preschool training work?* Lexington, MA: Lexington.

Gilgun, J. F. (1986). Sexually abused girls' knowledge about sexual abuse and sexuality. *Journal of Interpersonal Violence, 1,* 309–325.

Gilgun, J. F. (1988). Self-centeredness and the adult male perpetrator of child sexual abuse. *Contemporary Family Therapy, 10,* 216–242.

Gilgun, J. F., & Connor, T. M. (1989). How perpetrators view child sexual abuse. *Social Work, 34,* 249–251.

Ginsburg, H., Wright, L. S., Harrell, P. M., & Hill, D. W. (1989). Childhood victimization: Desensitization effects in the later lifespan. *Child Psychiatry and Human Development, 20,* 59–71.

Goldman, R. J., & Goldman, J. D. G. (1988). The prevalence and nature of child sexual abuse in Australia. *Australian Journal of Sex, Marriage and Family, 9,* 94–106.

Goldman, R. J., & Goldman, J. D. G. (1989). *Show me yours! Understanding children's sexuality.* Victoria, Australia: Penguin Books.

Gomes-Schwartz, B., Horowitz, J. M., & Cardarelli, A. P. (1990). *Child sexual abuse: The initial effects.* Newbury Park, CA: Sage.

Gomes-Schwartz, B., Horowitz, J. M., & Sauzier, M. (1985). Severity of emotional distress among sexually abused preschool, school-age and adolescent children. *Hospital and Community Psychiatry, 36,* 503–508.

Goodwin, J. (1981). Suicide attempts in sexual abuse victims and their mothers. *Child Abuse & Neglect, 3,* 217–221.

Goodwin, J., McCarthy, T., & DiVasto, P. (1981). Prior incest in mothers of abused children. *Child Abuse & Neglect, 5,* 87–95.

Goodwin, J., Sahd, D., & Rada, R. T. (1982). False accusations and false denials of incest: Clinical myths and clinical realities. In J. Goodwin (Ed.), *Sexual abuse: Incest victims and their families* (pp.17–26). Boston: John Wright.

Gordon, B. N., Schroeder, C. S., & Abrams, J. M. (1990a). Age and social-class differences in children's knowledge of sexuality. *Journal of Clinical Child Psychology, 19,* 33–43.

Gordon, B. N., Schroeder, C. S., & Abrams, J. M. (1990b). Children's knowledge of sexuality: A comparison of sexually abused and non-abused children. *American Journal of Orthopsychiatry, 60,* 250–257.

Gordon, L. (1990). The politics of sexual abuse: Notes from American history. In O. Pocs (Ed.), *Human Sexuality 90/91* (pp.12–16). Guildford, CT: Dushkin Publishing Group.

Gordon, M. (1989). The family environment of sexual abuse: A comparison of natal and stepfather abuse. *Child Abuse & Neglect, 13,* 121–130.

Gordon, M., & Creighton, S. J. (1988). Natal and non-natal fathers as sexual abusers in the United Kingdom: A comparative analysis. *Journal of Marriage and the Family, 50,* 99–105.

Gordon, S., & Gordon, J. (1984). *A better safe than sorry book.* Fayetteville, NY: Ed-U Press.

Green, F. C. (1975). Child abuse and neglect. *Pediatric Clinics of North America, 22,* 329–339.

Gross, A. (1978). The male role and heterosexual behavior. *Journal of Social Issues, 34,* 87–107.

Groth, A. N. (1977). The adolescent sexual offender and his prey. *International Journal of Offender Therapy and Comparative Criminology, 21,* 249–254.

Groth, A. N. (1979a). *Men who rape: The psychology of the offender.* New York: Plenum.

Groth, A. N. (1979b). Sexual trauma in the life histories of rapists and child molesters. *Victimology, 4,* 10–16.

Groth, A. N. (1982). The incest offender. In S. M. Sgroi, *Handbook of clinical intervention in child sexual abuse* (pp.215–239). Lexington, MA: Lexington Books.

Groth, A. N., & Birnbaum, H. J. (1978). Adult sexual orientation and attraction to underage persons. *Archives of Sexual Behavior, 7,* 175–181.

Groth, A. N., Burgess, A. W., Birnbaum, H. J., & Gary, T. S. (1978). A study of the child molester: Myths and realities. *Journal of the American Criminal Justice Association, 41,* 17–22.

Groth, A. N., Hobson, W. F., & Gary, T. S. (1982). The child molester: Clinical observations. In J. Conte & D. A. Shore (Eds.), *Social Work and Child Sexual Abuse* (pp.129–144). New York: Haworth.

Groth, A. N., & Loredo, C. M. (1981). Juvenile sexual offenders: Guidelines for assessment. *International Journal of Offender Therapy and Comparative Criminology, 25*, 31–39.

Grubb, W. N., & Lazerson, M. (1988). *Broken promises: How Americans fail their children.* Chicago: University of Chicago Press.

Gruber, K. J., & Jones, R. J. (1983). Identifying determinants of risk of sexual victimization of youth: A multivariate approach. *Child Abuse & Neglect, 7,* 17–24.

Guerney, B., Jr. (1977). *Relationship enhancement: Skill training programs for therapy, problem prevention, and enrichment.* San Francisco: Jossey-Bass.

Gundersen, B. H., Melas, P. S., & Skar, J. E. (1981). Sexual behavior of preschool children: Teachers' observations. In L. L. Constantine & F. M. Martinson (Eds.), *Children and sex: New findings, new perspectives* (pp.45–61). Boston: Little, Brown.

Guyon, R. (1941). *Ethics of sexual acts.* New York: Blue Ribbon.

Hagans, K. B., & Case, J. (1988). *When your child has been molested: A parent's guide to healing and recovery.* Lexington, M A: Lexington Books.

Hall, E. R., & Flannery, P. J. (1984). Prevalence and correlates of sexual assault experiences in adolescents. *Victimology: An International Journal, 9,* 398–406.

Hall, R. C. W., Tice, L., Beresford, T. P., Wooley, B., & Hall, A. K. (1989). Sexual abuse in patients with anorexia nervosa and bulimia. *Psychosomatics, 40,* 73–79.

Hallingby, L., & Brick, P. (1984). Child sexual abuse education and prevention: A selected bibliography of materials for sale. *SIECUS Reports, 13,* 13–16.

Hanson, R. K. (1990). The psychological impact of sexual assault on women and children: A review. *Annals of Sex Research, 3,* 187–232.

Hanson, R. K., & Slater, S. (1988). Sexual victimization in the history of child sexual abusers: A review. *Annals of Sex Research, 1,* 485–499.

Haroian, L. M. (1983). Sexual problems of children. In C. E. Walker & M. C. Roberts (Eds.), *Handbook of clinical child psychology* (pp.573–592). New York: Wiley.

Harrison, P. A., Hoffmann, N. G., & Edwall, G. E. (1989). Sexual abuse correlates: Similarities between male and female adolescents in chemical dependency treatment. *Journal of Adolescent Research, 4,* 385–399.

Hart, S. N. (1988). Psychological maltreatment: Emphasis on prevention. *School Psychology International, 9,* 243–255.

Hart, S. N., Brassard, M. R., & Germain, R. B. (1987). Psychological maltreatment in education and schooling. In M. R. Brassard, R. Germain, & S. N. Hart (Eds.), *Psychological maltreatment of children and youth* (pp.217–242). New York: Pergamon.

Hartman, C. R., & Burgess, A. W. (1988). Information processing of trauma. *Journal of Interpersonal Violence, 3,* 443–457.

Hart-Rossi, J. (1984). *Protect your child from sexual abuse: A parent's guide.* Seattle, WA: Parenting Press.

Harvey, P., Forehand, R., Brown, C., & Holmes, T. (1988). The prevention of sexual abuse: Examination of the effectiveness of a program with kindergarten-age children. *Behavior Therapy, 19,* 429–435.

Haseltine, B., & Miltenberger, R. G. (1990). Teaching self-protection skills to persons with mental retardation. *American Journal of Mental Retardation, 95,* 188–197.

Haugaard, J. J., & Emery, R. E. (1989). Methodological issues in child sexual abuse research. *Child Abuse & Neglect, 13,* 89–100.

Haugaard, J. J., & Reppucci, N. D. (1988). *The sexual abuse of children.* San Francisco: Jossey-Bass.

Haugaard, J. J., & Tilly, C. (1988). Characteristics predicting children's responses to sexual encounters with other children. *Child Abuse & Neglect, 12,* 209–218.

Hazzard, A. (1984). Training teachers to identify and intervene with abused children. *Journal of Clinical Child Psychology, 13,* 288–293.

Hazzard, A. (1990). Prevention of child sexual abuse. In R. T. Ammerman & M. Hersen (Eds.), *Treatment of family violence: A sourcebook* (pp.354–384). New York: Wiley.

Hazzard, A., Kleemeier, C. P., & Webb, C. (1990). Teacher versus expert presentations of sexual abuse prevention programs. *Journal of Interpersonal Violence, 5,* 23–36.

Hazzard, A., & Rupp, G. (1986). A note on the knowledge of professional groups toward child abuse. *Journal of Community Psychology, 14,* 219–223.

Hazzard, A., Webb, C., Kleemeier, C., Angert, L., & Pohl, L. (1991). Child sexual abuse prevention: Evaluation and one-year follow-up. *Child Abuse & Neglect, 15,* 123–138.

Hechler, D. (1988). *The battle and the backlash: The child sexual abuse war.* Lexington, MA: Lexington Books.

Helfer, R. E. (1975). Why most physicians don't get involved in child abuse cases and what to do about it. *Children Today, 4,* 28–32.

Henderson, D. (1972). Incest: A synthesis of data. *Canadian Psychiatric Association Journal, 17,* 299–313.

Henderson, J. (1983). Is incest harmful? *Canadian Journal of Psychiatry, 28,* 34–40.

Herman, J. L. (1981). *Father-daughter incest.* Cambridge, MA: Harvard University Press.

Herman, J. L., & Hirschman, L. (1977). Father-daughter incest. *Signs: Journal of Women in Culture and Society, 2,* 735–756.

Herman, J. L., & Hirschman, L. (1981). Families at risk for father-daughter incest. *American Journal of Psychiatry, 138,* 967–970.

Herman, J. L., Perry, J. C., & van der Kolk, B. A. (1989). Childhood trauma in borderline personality disorder. *American Journal of Psychiatry, 146,* 490–495.

Herman, J. L., Russell, D., & Trocki, K. (1986). Long-term effects of incestuous abuse in childhood. *American Journal of Psychiatry, 143,* 1293–1296.

Herzberger, S. D. (1988). Cultural obstacles to the labeling of abuse by professionals. In A. Maney & S. Wells (Eds.), *Professional responsibilities in protecting children: A public health approach to child sexual abuse* (pp. 33–44). New York: Praeger.

Hibbard, R. A., Serwint, J., & Connolly, M. (1987). Educational program on evaluation of alleged sexual abuse victims. *Child Abuse & Neglect, 11,* 513–519.

Hibbard, R. A., & Zollinger, T. W. (1990). Patterns of child sexual abuse knowledge among professionals. *Child Abuse & Neglect, 14,* 347–355.

Hill, J. L., & Jason, L. A. (1987). An evaluation of a school-based child sexual abuse primary prevention program. *Psychotherapy Bulletin, 22,* 36–38.

Hillman, D., & Solek-Tefft, J. (1988). *Spiders and flies: Help for parents and teachers of sexually abused children*. Lexington, MA: Lexington Books.

Hite, S. (1981). *The Hite report on male sexuality*. New York: Knopf.

Hoagwood, K., & Stewart, J. M. (1989). Sexually abused children's perceptions of family functioning. *Child and Adolescent Social Work*, *6*, 139–149.

Hofferth, S. L., & Phillips, D. H. (1987). Child care in the United States, 1970–1995. *Journal of Marriage and the Family*, *49*, 559–571.

Holmes, C. P. (1987). Prevention of child abuse: Possibilities for educational systems. *Special Services in the Schools*, *8*, 139–154.

Howell, J. C., Lloyd, D. W., Schretter, J. D., & Stevens, P. L. (1989). *Selected state legislation: A guide for effective state laws to protect children* (2nd ed.). Washington, DC: National Center for Missing and Exploited Children.

Howells, K. (1981). Adult sexual interest in children: Considerations relevant to theories of aetiology. In M. Cook & K. Howells (Eds.), *Adult sexual interest in children* (pp. 55–94). New York: Academic Press.

Hubbard, G. B. (1989). Perceived life changes for children and adolescents following disclosure of father-daughter incest. *Journal of Child and Adolescent Psychiatry and Mental Health Nursing*, *2*, 78–82.

Hughes, J., & Sandler, B. (1987). *Friends raping friends: Could it happen to you?* Washington, DC: Project on the Status and Education of Women, Association of American Colleges.

Hunt, P., & Baird, M. (1990). Children of sex rings. *Child Welfare*, *69*, 195–207.

Hyde, M. O. (1984). *Sexual abuse: Let's talk about it*. Philadelphia, PA: Westminster Press.

Illusion Theater Company & Media Ventures (Coproducers). (1984). *Touch* [Film]. Deerfield, IL: MTI Teleprograms.

Jacobson, A., & Herald, C. (1990). The relevance of childhood sexual abuse to adult psychiatric inpatient care. *Hospital and Community Psychiatry*, *41*, 154–158.

James, J., & Meyerding, J. (1977). Early sexual experience as factor in prostitution. *Archives of Sexual Behavior*, *7*, 31–42.

James, J., Womack, W. M., & Strauss, F. (1978). Physician reporting of sexual abuse of children. *Journal of the American Medical Association, 240,* 1145–1146.

Janus, M. D., Burgess, A. W., & McCormack, A. (1987). Histories of sexual abuse in adolescent male runaways. *Adolescence, 12,* 405–417.

Janus, S. S., & Bess, B. E. (1981). Latency: Fact or fiction? In L. L. Constantine & F. M. Martinson (Eds.), *Children and sex: New findings, new perspectives* (pp.75–82). Boston: Little, Brown.

Jaudes, P. K., & Morris, M. (1990). Child sexual abuse: Who goes home? *Child Abuse & Neglect, 14,* 61–68.

Jehu, D. (1989a). *Beyond sexual abuse: Therapy with women who were childhood victims.* Chichester, UK: John Wiley.

Jehu, D. (1989b). Mood disturbances among women clients sexually abused in childhood: Prevalence, etiology, treatment. *Journal of Interpersonal Violence, 4,* 164–184.

Jenny, C., Sutherland, S. E., & Sandahl, B. B. (1986). Developmental approach to preventing the sexual abuse of children. *Pediatrics, 78,* 1034–1038.

Johnson, R. L., & Shrier, D. K. (1985). Sexual victimization of boys. *Journal of Adolescent Health Care, 6,* 372–376.

Johnson, T. C. (1988). Child perpetrators: Children who molest other children: Preliminary findings. *Child Abuse & Neglect, 12,* 219–229.

Johnson, T. C. (1989). Female child perpetrators: Children who molest other children. *Child Abuse & Neglect, 13,* 571–585.

Jones, D. P. H., & McGraw, J. M. (1987). Reliable and fictitious accounts of sexual abuse to children. *Journal of Interpersonal Violence, 2,* 27–45.

Jones, J. G., Rickert, C. P., Balentine, J., Lawson, L., Rickert, V. I., & Holder, J. (1990). Residents' attitudes toward the legal system and court testimony in child abuse. *Child Abuse & Neglect, 14,* 79–85.

Jones, R. E. (1984). *Human reproduction and sexual behavior.* Englewood Cliffs, NJ: Prentice-Hall.

Justice, B., & Justice, R. (1979). *The broken taboo.* New York: Human Sciences Press.

Kagan, J. (1979). Family experience and the child's development. *American Psychologist, 34,* 886–891.

Kagan, S. L., Powell, D. R., Weissbourd, B., & Zigler, E. F. (1987). *America's family support programs*. New Haven, CT: Yale University Press.

Kahn, A. J., & Kamerman, S. B. (1988). *Child support: From debt collection to social policy*. Beverly Hills, CA: Sage.

Kahn, T. J., & Lafond, M. A. (1988). Treatment of the adolescent sexual offender. *Child and Adolescent Social Work, 5*, 135–148.

Kalichman, S. C., & Craig, M. E. (1990). Victims of incestuous abuse: Mental health professionals' attitudes and the tendency to report. In E. Viano (Ed.), *The victimology handbook* (pp. 51–60). New York: Garland.

Kalichman, S. C., & Craig, M. E. (1991). Professional psychologists' decisions to report suspected child abuse: Clinician and situation influences. *Professional Psychology, 1*, 84–89.

Kalichman, S. C., Craig, M. E., & Follingstad, D. R. (1988). Mental health professionals and suspected cases of child abuse: An investigation of factors influencing reporting. *Community Mental Health Journal, 24*, 43–51.

Kalichman, S. C., Craig, M. E., & Follingstad, D. R. (1989). Factors influencing the reporting of father-child sexual abuse: Study of licensed practicing psychologists. *Professional Psychology: Research and Practice, 20*, 84–89.

Kalichman, S. C., Craig, M. E., & Follingstad, D. R. (1990). Professionals' adherence to mandatory child abuse reporting laws: Effects of responsibility attribution, confidence ratings, and situational factors. *Child Abuse & Neglect, 14*, 69–77.

Kaplan, M. S. (1989). A description of self reports of convicted child molesters following incarceration. *International Journal of Offender Therapy and Comparative Criminology, 33*, 69–75.

Karpman, B. (1954). *The sexual offender and his offenses*. New York: Julian.

Kassees, J., & Hall, R. (1987). *Adolescent sexual abuse project*. Wilmington, DE: Parents Anonymous of Delaware.

Katz, R. C. (1990). Psychosocial adjustment in adolescent child molesters. *Child Abuse & Neglect, 14*, 567–575.

Kaufman, I., Peck, A., & Tagiuri, C. K. (1954). The family constellation and overt incestuous relations between father and daughter. *American Journal of Orthopsychiatry, 24*, 266–279.

Kaufman, J., & Zigler, E. (1987). Do abused children become abusive parents? *American Journal of Orthopsychiatry, 57,* 186–192.

Kean, T. H. (1989). The life you save may be your own: New Jersey addresses prevention of adolescent problems. *American Psychologist, 44,* 828–830.

Kelley, S. J. (1990). Responsibility and management strategies in child sexual abuse: A comparison of child protective workers, nurses, and police officers. *Child Welfare, 69,* 43–51.

Kelly, R. J. (1982). Behavioral reorientation of pedophiliacs: Can it be done? *Clinical Psychology Review, 2,* 387–408.

Kempe, R. S., & Kempe, C. H. (1978). *Child abuse.* Cambridge, MA: Harvard University Press.

Kempe, R. S., & Kempe, C. H. (1984). *The common secret: Sexual abuse of children and adolescents.* New York: W. S. Freeman.

Kendall, P. C., & Braswell, L. (1985). *Cognitive-behavioral therapy for impulsive children.* New York: Guilford.

Kercher, G. A., & McShane, M. (1984a). Characterizing child sexual abuse on the basis of a multi-agency sample. *Victimology: An International Journal, 9,* 364–382.

Kercher, G. A., & McShane, M. (1984b). The prevalence of child sexual abuse victimization in an adult sample of Texas residents. *Child Abuse & Neglect, 8,* 495–501.

Khan, M., & Sexton, M. (1983). Sexual abuse of young children. *Clinical Pediatrics, 22,* 369–372.

Kile, M. J. (1986). *What would you do if . . . ? A guide to preventing sexual abuse of your children.* Circle Pines, MN: American Guidance Service.

Kilpatrick, D. G., Best, C. L., Veronen, L. J., Amick, A. E., Villeponteaux, L. A., & Ruff, G. A. (1985). Mental health correlates of criminal victimization: A random community survey. *Journal of Consulting and Clinical Psychology, 53,* 866–873.

King, M. P., Hunter, W. M., & Runyan, D. K. (1988). Going to court: The experience of child victims of intrafamilial sexual abuse. *Journal of Health Politics, Policy and Law, 13,* 705–721.

Kinsey, A., Pomeroy, W., & Martin, C. (1948). *Sexual behavior in the human male.* Philadelphia, PA: W. B. Saunders.

Kinsey, A., Pomeroy, W., Martin, C., & Gebhardt, P. (1953). *Sexual behavior in the human female*. Philadelphia, PA: W. B. Saunders.

Kleemeier, C., Webb, C., Hazzard, A., & Pohl, J. (1988). Child sexual abuse prevention: Evaluation of a teacher training model. *Child Abuse & Neglect, 12*, 555–561.

Knight, R. A., Carter, D. L., & Prentky, R. A. (1989). A system for the classification of child molesters: Reliability and application. *Journal of Interpersonal Violence, 4*, 3–23.

Knight, R. A., Rosenberg, R., & Schneider, B. A. (1985). Classification of sexual offenders; perspectives, methods, and validation. In A. W. Burgess (Ed.), *Rape and sexual assault* (pp.222–293). New York: Garland Publications.

Knopp, F. H. (1982). *Remedial intervention in adolescent sex offenses: Nine program descriptions*. Syracuse, NY: Safer Society Press.

Knudsen, D. D. (1988). Child sexual abuse and pornography: Is there a relationship? *Journal of Family Violence, 3*, 253–267.

Kohan, M. J., Pothier, P., & Norbeck, J. S. (1987). Hospitalized children with history of sexual abuse: Incidence of care issues. *American Journal of Orthopsychiatry, 57*, 258–264.

Kolko, D. J. (1987). Treatment of child sexual abuse: Programs, progress, and prospects. *Journal of Family Violence, 2*, 303–318.

Kolko, D. J., Moser, J. T., & Hughes, J. (1989). Classroom training in sexual victimization awareness and prevention skills: An extension of the Red Flag / Green Flag people program. *Journal of Family Violence, 4*, 25–45.

Kolko, D. J., Moser, J. T., Litz, J., & Hughes, J. (1987). Promoting awareness and prevention of child sexual victimization using the Red Flag / Green Flag program: An evaluation with follow-up. *Journal of Family Violence, 2*, 11–35.

Kolko, D. J., Moser, J. T., & Weldy, S. R. (1988). Behavioral/emotional indicators of sexual abuse in child psychiatric inpatients: A controlled comparison with physical abuse. *Child Abuse & Neglect, 12*, 529–541.

Koss, M. P., & Dinero, T. E. (1988). Predictors of sexual aggression among a national sample of male college students. *Annals of the New York Academy of Sciences, 528*, 133–146.

Koss, M. P., & Dinero, T. E. (1989). A discriminant analysis of risk factors for rape among a national sample of college women. *Journal of Consulting and Clinical Psychology, 57,* 242–250.

Kraizer, S. (1985). *The safe child book.* New York: Dell Publishing.

Kraizer, S. (1988). *The safe child program.* Palisades, NY: Health Education Systems.

Kraizer, S., Witte, S. S., & Fryer, G. E., Jr. (1989). Child sexual abuse prevention programs: What makes them effective in protecting children? *Children Today, 18,* 23–27.

Krenk, C. J. (1984). Training residence staff for child abuse treatment. *Child Welfare, 63,* 167–173.

Krents, E., & Atkins, D. (1985). *No-Go-Tell! A child protection curriculum for very young disabled children.* New York: Lexington Center.

Krents, E., Schulman, V., & Brenner, S. (1987). Child abuse and the disabled child: Perspectives for parents. *The Volta Review, 89,* 78–95.

Krivacska, J. J. (1989). Child sexual abuse prevention programs and accusations of child sexual abuse: An analysis. *Issues in Child Abuse Accusations, 1,* 8–13.

Krivacska, J. J. (1990). *Designing child sexual abuse prevention programs: Current approaches and a proposal for the prevention, reduction, and identification of sexual misuse.* Springfield, IL: Charles C. Thomas.

Krugman, R. D. (1986). Recognition of sexual abuse in children. *Pediatrics in Review, 8,* 25–39.

Krugman, R. D. (1990). Future role of the pediatrician in child abuse and neglect. *Pediatric Clinics of North America, 37,* 1003–1011.

LaBarre, A., Hinkley, K. R., & Nelson, M. F. (1986). *Sexual abuse! What is it? An informational book for the hearing impaired.* St. Paul, MN: St. Paul-Ramsey Foundation.

Ladson, S., Johnson, C. F., & Doty, R. E. (1987). Do physicians recognize sexual abuse? *American Journal of Diseases of Children, 141,* 411–415.

Landis, J. (1956). Experiences of 500 children with adult sexual deviants. *Psychiatric Quarterly Supplement, 30,* 91–109.

Lang, R. A., & Frenzel, R. R. (1988). How sex offenders lure children. *Annals of Sex Research, 1,* 303–317.

Lang, R. A., Rouget, A. C., & van Santen, V. (1988). The role of victim age and sexual maturity in child sexual abuse. *Annals of Sex Research*, *1*, 467–484.

Langevin, R. (1983). *Sexual strands: Understanding and treating sexual anomalies in men*. Hillsdale, NJ: Erlbaum.

Langevin, R., Lang, R. A., Wright, P., Handy, L., Frenzel, R. R., & Black, E. L. (1988). Pornography and sexual offenses. *Annals of Sex Research*, *1*, 335–362.

Langevin, R., Wortzman, G., Wright, P., & Handy, L. (1989). Studies of brain damage and dysfunction in sex offenders. *Annals of Sex Research*, *2*, 163–179.

Lanning, K. V., & Burgess, A. W. (1984, January). Child pornography and sex rings. *FBI Law Enforcement Bulletin*, 10–16.

Lawren Productions. (1980). *Not in my family* [videocassette]. (Available from Lawren Productions, P.O. Box 666, Mendocino, CA 95460.)

Laws, D. R., & Marshall, W. L. (1990). A conditioning theory of the etiology and maintenance of deviant sexual preferences and behavior. In W. L. Marshall, D. R. Laws, & H. E. Barbaree (Eds.), *Handbook of sexual assault: Issues, theories, and treatment of the offender* (pp.209–229). New York: Plenum Press.

Legrand, R., Wakefield, H., & Underwager, R. (1989). Alleged behavioral indicators of sexual abuse. *Issues in Child Abuse Accusations*, *1*, 1–5.

Levang, C. A. (1989). Father-daughter incest families: A theoretical perspective from balance theory and GST. *Contemporary Family Therapy*, *11*, 28–44.

Levin, P. (1983). Teachers' perceptions, attitudes, and reporting of child abuse/neglect. *Child Welfare*, *62*, 14–20.

Lewis, M., & Sarrel, P. M. (1969). Some psychological aspects of seduction, incest, and rape in childhood. *Journal of the American Academy of Child Psychiatry*, *8*, 606–619.

Lieff, S., & Parker, S. (1981). *Sexual abuse: A guide for your child's safety*. (Available from Children and Youth Services, 601 Rosenwald Street, Burlington, NC 27215.)

Liem, R., & Liem, J. (1978). Social class and mental illness reconsidered: The role of economic stress and social support. *Journal of Health and Social Behavior*, *19*, 136–156.

Liem, R., & Ramsay, P. (1982). Health and social costs of unemployment: Research and policy considerations. *American Psychologist, 37,* 1116–1123.

Lindberg, F. H., & Distad, L. J. (1985). Survival responses to incest: Adolescents in crisis. *Child Abuse & Neglect, 9,* 521–526.

Livingston, R. (1987). Sexually and physically abused children. *Journal of the American Academy of Child and Adolescent Psychiatry, 26,* 413–415.

Lusk, R., & Waterman, J. (1986). Effects of sexual abuse on children. In K. MacFarlane, J. Waterman, S. Conerly, L. Damon, M. Durfee, & S. Long (Eds.), *Sexual abuse of young children* (pp.101–118). New York: Guilford Press.

Lustig, N., Dresser, J. W., Spellman, S. W., & Murray, T. B. (1966). Incest: A family group survival pattern. *Archives of General Psychiatry, 14,* 31–40.

Luther, S. L., & Price, J. H. (1980). Child sexual abuse: A review. *The Journal of School Health, 50,* 161–165.

Lutheran Social Services. (1983). *Training tape for educators* [videocassette]. (Available from Lutheran Social Services, N. 1226 Howard Street, Spokane, WA 99201.)

Lynch, A. (1975). Child abuse in the school-age population. *Journal of School Health, 45,* 141–148.

MacFarlane, K. (1986). Helping parents cope with extrafamilial molestation. In K. MacFarlane, J. Waterman, S. Conerly, L. Damon, M. Durfee, & S. Long (Eds.), *Sexual abuse of young children* (pp.299–311). New York: Guilford Press.

MacFarlane, K., Waterman, J., Conerly, S., Damon, L., Durfee, M., & Long, S. (Eds.). (1986). *Sexual abuse of young children.* New York: Guilford Press.

MacVicar, K. (1979). Psychotherapeutic issues in the treatment of sexually abused girls. *Journal of the American Academy of Child Psychiatry, 18,* 342–353.

Maholick, M. (1986). Special procedures urged for child sex abuse testimony. *Journal of Child and Adolescent Psychotherapy, 3,* 226.

Maisch, H. (1972). *Incest.* New York: Stein and Day.

Malamuth, N. M., & Briere, J. (1986). Sexual violence in the media: Indirect effects on aggression against women. *Journal of Social Issues, 42,* 75–92.

Maney, A., & Wells, S. (1988). *Professional responsibilities in protecting children: A public health approach to child sexual abuse.* New York: Praeger.

Mannarino, A. P., & Cohen, J. A. (1986). A clinical-demographic study of sexually abused children. *Child Abuse & Neglect, 10,* 17–23.

Margolin, L., & Craft, J. L. (1989). Child sexual abuse by caretakers. *Family Relations, 38,* 450–455.

Margolin, L., & Craft, J. L. (1990). Child abuse by adolescent caregivers. *Child Abuse & Neglect, 14,* 365–373.

Marshall, W. L. (1989). Intimacy, loneliness and sexual offenders. *Behavior Research & Therapy, 27,* 491–503.

Marshall, W. L., & Barbaree, H. E. (1988). The long-term evaluation of a behavioral treatment program for child molesters. *Behavior Research & Therapy, 26,* 499–511.

Marshall, W. L., Barbaree, H. E., & Butt, J. (1988). Sexual offenders against male children: Sexual preferences. *Behavior Research & Therapy, 26,* 383–391.

Marshall, W. L., & Christie, M. M. (1981). Pedophilia and aggression. *Criminal Justice and Behavior, 8,* 145–158.

Martinson, F. M. (1981). Eroticism in infancy and childhood. In L. L. Constantine & F. M. Martinson (Eds.), *Children and sex: New findings, new perspectives* (pp.23–35). Boston: Little, Brown.

Massie, M. E., & Johnson, S. M. (1989). The importance of recognizing a history of sexual abuse in female adolescents. *Journal of Adolescent Health Care, 10,* 184–191.

Masson, J. M. (1984). *The assault on truth: Freud's suppression of the seduction theory.* New York: Farrar, Straus, & Giroux.

Mazur, S., & Pekor, C. (1985). Can teachers touch children anymore? *Young Children, 40,* 10–12.

Mazura, A. C. (1977). Negligence-malpractice-physicians' liability for failure to diagnose and report child abuse. *Wayne Law Review, 23,* 1187–1201.

McCaffrey, M., & Tewey, S. (1978). Preparing educators to participate in the community response to child abuse and neglect. *Exceptional Children, 44/45,* 114–122.

McCarty, L. M. (1986). Mother-child incest: Characteristics of the offender. *Child Welfare, 65,* 447–458.

McCormack, A., & Selvaggio, M. (1989). Screening for pedophiles in youth-oriented community agencies. *Social Casework: The Journal of Contemporary Social Work, 70*, 37–42.

McDonald, A. E., & Reece, R. M. (1979). Child abuse: Problems of reporting. *Pediatric Clinics of North America, 26*, 785–879.

McGrath, P., Cappelli, M., Wiseman, D., Khalil, N., & Allan, B. (1987). Teacher awareness program on child abuse: A randomized controlled trial. *Child Abuse & Neglect, 11*, 125–132.

McIntyre, K. (1981). Role of mothers in father-daughter incest: A feminist analysis. *Social Work, 26*, 462–466.

McIntyre, T. C. (1987). Teacher awareness of child abuse and neglect. *Child Abuse & Neglect, 11*, 133–135.

McLoyd, V. C. (1989). Socialization and development in a changing economy: The effects of paternal job and income loss on children. *American Psychologist, 44*, 293–302.

Meddin, B. J., & Rosen, A. L. (1986). Child abuse and neglect: Prevention and reporting. *Young Children, 41*, 26–30.

Meiselman, K. C. (1978). *Incest: A psychological study of causes and effects with treatment recommendations.* San Francisco: Jossey-Bass Publications.

Meiselman, K. C. (1990). *Resolving the trauma of incest: Reintegration therapy with survivors.* San Francisco: Jossey-Bass Publications.

Melton, G. B. (1985). Sexually abused children and the legal system: Some policy recommendations. *The American Journal of Family Therapy, 13*, 61–67.

Melton, G. B. (1991). Socialization in the global community: Respect for the dignity of children. *American Psychologist, 46*, 66–71.

Melton, G. B. (1992). The improbability of prevention of sexual abuse. In D. J. Willis, E. W. Holden, & M. Rosenberg (Eds.), *Child abuse prevention* (pp. 168–189). New York: Wiley.

Meriwether, M. H. (1986). Child abuse reporting laws: Time for a change. *Family Law Quarterly, 20*, 141–171.

Meyers, J., & Parsons, R. D. (1987). Prevention planning in the school system. In J. Hermalin & J. A. Morell (Eds.), *Prevention planning in mental health* (pp. 111–150). Newbury Park, CA: Sage.

Mian, M., Wehrspann, W., Klajner-Diamond, H., LeBaron, D., & Winder, C. (1986). Review of 125 children 6 years of age and under who were sexually abused. *Child Abuse & Neglect, 10*, 223–229.

Miller, R. D., & Weinstock, R. (1987). Conflict of interest between therapist-patient confidentiality and the duty to report sexual abuse of children. _Behavioral Sciences & the Law, 5_, 161–174.

Miller-Perrin, C. L., & Wurtele, S. K. (1988). The child sexual abuse prevention movement: A critical analysis of primary and secondary approaches. _Clinical Psychology Review, 8_, 313–329.

Miller-Perrin, C. L., & Wurtele, S. K. (1990). Reactions to childhood sexual abuse: Implications for post-traumatic stress disorder. In C. Meek (Ed.), _Post-traumatic stress disorder: Assessment, differential diagnosis, forensic evaluation_ (pp.91–135). Sarasota, FL: Professional Resource Exchange.

Miller-Perrin, C. L., Wurtele, S. K., & Kondrick, P. A. (1990). Sexually abused and nonabused children's conceptions of personal body safety. _Child Abuse & Neglect, 14_, 99–112.

Miltenberger, R. G., & Thiesse-Duffy, E. (1988). Evaluation of home-based programs for teaching personal safety skills to children. _Journal of Applied Behavior Analysis, 21_, 81–87.

Miltenberger, R. G., Thiesse-Duffy, E., Suda, K., Kozak, C., & Bruellman, J. (1990). Teaching prevention skills to children: The use of multiple measures to evaluate parent versus expert instruction. _Child & Family Behavior Therapy, 12_, 65–87.

Mitchell, R. E., Billings, A. G., & Moos, R. H. (1982). Social support and well-being: Implications for prevention programs. _Journal of Primary Prevention, 3_, 77–98.

Moglia, R. (1986). Sexual abuse and disability. _SIECUS Reports, 14_, 9–10.

Mohr, J. W. (1981). Age structures in pedophilia. In M. Cook & K. Howells (Eds.), _Adult sexual interest in children_ (pp.41–54). New York: Academic Press.

Molnar, B., & Cameron, P. (1975). Incest syndromes: Observations in a general hospital psychiatric unit. _Canadian Psychiatric Association Journal, 20_, 1–24.

Morrison, J. L. (1988). Perpetrator suicide following incest report: Two case studies. _Child Abuse & Neglect, 12_, 115–117.

Mrazek, P. B. (1981a). Definition and recognition of sexual child abuse: Historical and cultural perspectives. In P. B. Mrazek & C. H. Kempe

(Eds.), *Sexually abused children and their families* (pp.5-16). New York: Pergamon Press.

Mrazek, P. B. (1981b). The nature of incest: A review of contributing factors. In P. B. Mrazek & C. H. Kempe (Eds.), *Sexually abused children and their families* (pp.97-107). New York: Pergamon Press.

Mrazek, P. J., Lynch, M. A., & Bentovim, A. (1983). Sexual abuse of children in the United Kingdom. *Child Abuse & Neglect, 7,* 147-153.

Muehleman, T., & Kimmons, C. (1981). Psychologists' views on child abuse reporting, confidentiality, life, and the law: An exploratory study. *Professional Psychology, 12,* 631-637.

Mulhern, S. (1990). Incest: A laughing matter. *Child Abuse & Neglect, 14,* 265-271.

Murrin, M. R., & Laws, D. R. (1990). The influence of pornography on sexual crimes. In W. L. Marshall, D. R. Laws, & H. E. Barbaree (Eds.), *Handbook of sexual assault: Issues, theories, and treatment of the offender* (pp.73-91). New York: Plenum Press.

Nasjleti, M. (1980). Suffering in silence: The male incest victim. *Child Welfare, 59,* 269-275.

National Center on Child Abuse and Neglect. (1978). *Child sexual abuse: Incest, assault, and sexual exploitation, a special report.* Washington, DC: Author.

National Center on Child Abuse and Neglect. (1989). *State statutes related to child abuse and neglect: 1988.* Washington, DC: Author.

National Committee for the Prevention of Child Abuse. (1990). *Current trends in child abuse reporting and fatalities: The results of the 1989 Annual Fifty State Survey.* (Available from NCPCA, 332 South Michigan Ave., Suite 1250, Chicago, IL 60604-4357.)

National Film Board of Canada (1985). *Feeling yes, feeling no* [video]. Evanston, IL: Perennial Education.

Neinstein, L. S., Goldenring, J., & Carpenter, S. (1984). Nonsexual transmission of sexually transmitted diseases: An infrequent occurrence. *Pediatrics, 74,* 64-75.

Network Against Teenage Violence. (1987). *When love really hurts: Dating violence curriculum.* Williston, ND: Family Crisis Shelter.

Newberger, C. M., & Newberger, E. (1982). Prevention of child abuse: Theory, myth, and practice. *Journal of Preventive Psychiatry, 1,* 443-451.

Newberger, E. H. (1983). The helping hand strikes again: Unintended consequences of child abuse reporting. *Journal of Clinical and Child Psychology, 12,* 307–311.

Nibert, D., Cooper, S., & Ford, J. (1989). Parents' observations of the effect of a sexual-abuse prevention program on preschool children. *Child Welfare, 68,* 539–546.

Nibert, D., Cooper, S., Ford, J., Fitch, L. K., & Robinson, J. (1989). The ability of young children to learn abuse prevention. *Response, 12,* 14–20.

Note. (1982). Unequal and inadequate protection under the law: State child abuse statutes. *George Washington Law Review, 50,* 243–274.

O'Day, B. (1983). *Preventing sexual abuse of persons with disabilities: A curriculum for hearing impaired, physically disabled, blind and mentally retarded students.* St. Paul, MN: Program for Victims of Sexual Assault, Department of Corrections.

ODN Productions. (1985). *Talking helps* [videocassette]. New York: ODN Productions.

Ogata, S. N., Silk, K. R., Goodrich, S., Lohr, N. E., Westen, D., & Hill, E. M. (1990). Childhood sexual and physical abuse in adult patients with borderline personality disorder. *American Journal of Psychiatry, 147,* 1008–1013.

Otey, E. M., & Ryan, G. D. (1985). *Adolescent sex offenders: Issues in research and treatment.* Rockville, MD: U.S. Department of Health and Human Services.

Otto, R. K., & Melton, G. B. (1990). Trends in legislation and case law on child abuse and neglect. In R. T. Ammerman & M. Hersen (Eds.), *Children at risk: An evaluation of factors contributing to child abuse and neglect* (pp.55–83). New York: Plenum Press.

Overholser, J. C., & Beck, S. (1986). Multimethod assessment of rapists, child molesters, and three control groups on behavioral and psychological measures. *Journal of Consulting and Clinical Psychology, 54,* 682–687.

Overholser, J. C., & Beck, S. J. (1989). The classification of rapists and child molesters. *Journal of Offender Counseling, Services & Rehabilitation, 13,* 15–25.

Ozer, E. M., & Bandura, A. (1990). Mechanisms governing empowerment effects: A self-efficacy analysis. *Journal of Personality and Social Psychology, 58,* 472–486.

Paddison, P. L., Gise, L. H., Lebovits, A., Strain, J. J., Cirasole, D. M., & Levine, J. P. (1990). Sexual abuse and premenstrual syndrome: Comparison between a lower and higher socioeconomic group. *Psychosomatics, 31*, 265–272.

Paperny, D. M., & Deisher, R. W. (1983). Maltreatment of adolescents: The relationship to a predisposition toward violent behavior and delinquency. *Adolescence, 18*, 499–506.

Paradise, J. E. (1990). The medical evaluation of the sexually abused child. *Pediatric Clinics of North America, 37*, 839–862.

Parent Education Center of Yakima. (1984). *Childproof for sexual abuse: A guide for parents of young children.* (Available from Parent Education Center of Yakima, 408 North 39th Avenue, Yakima, WA 98902.)

Parker, H., & Parker, S. (1986). Father-daughter sexual abuse: An emerging perspective. *American Journal of Orthopsychiatry, 56*, 531–549.

Pascoe, D. J., & Duterte, B. O. (1981). Medical diagnosis of sexual abuse in the premenarcheal child. *Pediatric Annals, 10*, 187–190.

Paulson, M. J. (1978). Incest and sexual molestation: Clinical and legal issues. *Journal of Clinical Child Psychology, 7*, 177–180.

Paveza, G. J. (1988). Risk factors in father-daughter child sexual abuse: A case-control study. *Journal of Interpersonal Violence, 3*, 290–306.

Peake, A. (1989). Issue of under-reporting: The sexual abuse of boys. *Educational and Child Psychology, 6*, 42–50.

Pelcovitz, D. (1978). Child abuse as viewed by suburban elementary teachers. *Dissertation Abstracts International, 38*, (8-A), 4694. (University Microfilms No. 7730239)

Pelletier, G., & Handy, L. C. (1986). Family dysfunction and the psychological impact of child sexual abuse. *Canadian Journal of Psychiatry, 31*, 407–412.

Pennekamp, M., & Freeman, E. M. (1988). Toward a partnership perspective: Schools, families, and school social workers. *Social Work in Education, 10*, 246–259.

Peters, J. J. (1976). Children who are victims of sexual assault and the psychology of offenders. *American Journal of Psychotherapy, 30*, 398–421.

Peterson, L., & Lewis, K. E. (1988). Preventive intervention to improve children's discrimination of the persuasive tactics in televised advertising. *Journal of Pediatric Psychology, 13*, 163–170.

Peterson, L., Mori, L., Selby, V., & Rosen, B. N. (1988). Community interventions in children's injury prevention: Differing costs and differing benefits. *Journal of Community Psychology, 16,* 188–204.

Pettiford, E. K. (1981). *Improving child protecting services through the use of multidisciplinary teams.* Washington, DC: National Center on Child Abuse and Neglect.

Pierce, R., & Pierce, L. H. (1985). The sexually abused child: A comparison of male and female victims. *Child Abuse & Neglect, 9,* 191–199.

Pithers, W. D., Kashima, K. M., Cumming, G. F., & Beal, L. S. (1988). Relapse prevention: A method of enhancing maintenance of change in sex offenders. In A. C. Salter, *Treating child sex offenders and victims: A practical guide* (pp.131–170). Beverly Hills, CA: Sage.

Plummer, C. A. (1986). Prevention education in perspective. In M. Nelson & K. Clark (Eds.), *The educator's guide to preventing child sexual abuse* (pp.1–14). Santa Cruz, CA: Network Publications.

Poche, C., Brouwer, R., & Swearingen, M. (1981). Teaching self-protection to young children. *Journal of Applied Behavior Analysis, 14,* 169–176.

Poche, C., Yoder, P., & Miltenberger, R. (1988). Teaching self-protection to children using television techniques. *Journal of Applied Behavioral Analysis, 21,* 253–261.

Pogrebin, L. C. (1983). *Family politics: Love and power on an intimate frontier.* New York: McGraw-Hill.

Pope, A. W., McHale, S. M., & Craighead, W. E. (1988). *Self-esteem enhancement with children and adolescents.* Elmsford, NY: Pergamon Press.

Pope, K., Tabachnick, B., & Keith-Spiegel, P. (1987). Ethics of practice: The beliefs and behaviors of psychologists as therapists. *American Psychologist, 42,* 993–1006.

Porch, T. L., & Petretic-Jackson, P. A. (1986, August). *Child sexual assault prevention: Evaluating parent education workshops.* Paper presented at the convention of the American Psychological Association, Washington, DC.

Powers, J. L., Eckenrode, J., & Jaklitsch, B. (1990). Maltreatment among runaway and homeless youth. *Child Abuse & Neglect, 14,* 87–98.

Project SAAFE. (1984). (Available from Jackson Mental Health Center, 969 Lakeland Drive, Jackson, MS 39216-4699.)

Putnam, F. W., Guroff, J. J., Silberman, E. K., Barban, L., & Post, R. M. (1986). The clinical phenomenology of multiple personality disorder: Review of 100 cases. *Journal of Clinical Psychiatry, 47,* 285–293.

Racusin, R. J., & Felsman, J. K. (1986). Reporting child abuse: The ethical obligation to inform parents. *Journal of the American Academy of Child Psychiatry, 25,* 485–489.

Rada, R. T. (1976). Alcoholism and the child molester. *Annals of the New York Academy of Sciences, 273,* 492–496.

Ratto, R., & Bogat, G. A. (1990). An evaluation of a preschool curriculum to educate children in the prevention of sexual abuse. *Journal of Community Psychology, 18,* 289–297.

Ray, J. (1984). *Evaluation of the child sex abuse prevention project.* (Available from Rape Crisis Network, N. 1226 Howard, Spokane, WA 98201.)

Ray-Keil, A. (1988). *Intersect of social theory and management practice in preventing child exploitation.* Seattle: Committee for Children.

Regehr, C. (1990). Parental responses to extrafamilial child sexual assault. *Child Abuse & Neglect, 14,* 113–120.

Reich, J. W., & Gutierres, S. E. (1979). Escape/aggression incidence in sexually abused juvenile delinquents. *Criminal Justice & Behavior, 6,* 239–243.

Rencken, R. H. (1989). *Intervention strategies for sexual abuse.* Alexandria, VA: American Association for Counseling and Development.

*Report to the President from the President's Commission on Mental Health.* (1978). Washington, DC: U.S. Government Printing Office.

Reppucci, N. D., & Haugaard, J. J. (1989). Prevention of child sexual abuse: Myth or reality. *American Psychologist, 44,* 1266–1275.

Rew, L., & Esparza, D. (1990). Barriers to disclosure among sexually abused male children. *Journal of Child and Adolescent Psychiatric and Mental Health Nursing, 3,* 120–127.

Rich, D. (1988). *MegaSkills: How families can help children succeed in school and beyond.* Boston: Houghton Mifflin.

Riggs, R. S. (1982). Incest: The school's role. *The Journal of School Health, 52,* 365–370.

Rimsza, M. E., Berg, R. A., & Locke, C. (1988). Sexual abuse: Somatic and emotional reactions. *Child Abuse & Neglect, 12,* 201–208.

Rimsza, M. E., & Niggemann, E. H. (1982). Medical evaluation of sexually abused children: A review of 311 cases. *Pediatrics, 69,* 8–14.

Ringwalt, C., & Earp, J. (1988). Attributing responsibility in cases of father-daughter sexual abuse. *Child Abuse & Neglect, 12,* 273–281.

Risin, L. I., & Koss, M. P. (1987). The sexual abuse of boys: Prevalence and descriptive characteristics of childhood victimizations. *Journal of Interpersonal Violence, 2,* 309–323.

Rist, K. (1979). Incest: Theoretical and clinical views. *American Journal of Orthopsychiatry, 49,* 680–691.

Roberts, M. C., Alexander, K., & Fanurik, D. (1990). Evaluation of commercially available materials to prevent child sexual abuse and abduction. *American Psychologist, 45,* 782–783.

Roberts, M. C., & Peterson, L. (1984). *Prevention of problems in childhood: Psychological research and implications.* New York: Wiley-Interscience.

Rogers, C. M. (1982). Child sexual abuse and the courts: Preliminary findings. *Journal of Social Work and Human Sexuality, 1,* 145–153.

Rogers, C. M., & Thomas, J. N. (1984). Sexual victimization of children in the USA: Patterns and trends. *Clinical Proceedings, Children's Hospital National Medical Center, 40,* 211–221.

Rohner, R. P. (1975). *They love me, they love me not: A worldwide study of the effects of parental acceptance and rejection.* New Haven, CT: HRAF Press.

Rohsenow, D. J., Corbett, R., & Devine, D. (1988). Molested as children: A hidden contribution to substance abuse? *Journal of Substance Abuse Treatment, 5,* 13–18.

Roiphe, H., & Galenson, E. (1981). *Infantile origins of sexual identity.* New York: International Universities Press.

Rosenfeld, A. A., Bailey, R., Siegel, B., & Bailey, G. (1986). Determining incestuous contact between parent and child: Frequency of children touching parents' genitals in a nonclinical population. *Journal of the American Academy of Child Psychiatry, 25,* 481–484.

Rosenfeld, A. A., Nadelson, C., & Krieger, M. (1979). Fantasy and reality in patients' reports of incest. *Journal of Clinical Psychiatry, 40,* 159–164.

Rosenfeld, A. A., Nadelson, C., Krieger, M., & Backman, J. (1979). Incest and sexual abuse of children. *Journal of the American Academy of Child Psychiatry, 16*, 327–339.

Rosenfeld, A. A., Siegel, B., & Bailey, R. (1987). Familial bathing patterns: Implications for cases of alleged molestation and for pediatric practice. *Pediatrics, 79*, 224–229.

Ross, C. A., Anderson, G., Heber, S., & Norton, G. R. (1990). Dissociation and abuse among multiple-personality patients, prostitutes, and exotic dancers. *Hospital and Community Psychiatry, 41*, 328–330.

Ross, C. A., Miller, S. D., Reagor, P., Bjornson, L., Fraser, G. A., & Anderson, G. (1990). Structured interview data on 102 cases of multiple personality disorder from four centers. *American Journal of Psychiatry, 147*, 596–601.

Rothblum, E. D., Solomon, L. J., & Albee, G. W. (1986). A sociopolitical perspective of DSM-III. In T. Millon & G. L. Klerman (Eds.), *Contemporary directions in psychopathology: Toward the DSM-IV* (pp.167–189). New York: Guilford Press.

Rotheram-Borus, M. J. (1988). Assertiveness training with children. In R. H. Price, E. L. Cowen, R. P. Lorion, & J. Ramos-McKay (Eds.), *Fourteen ounces of prevention: A casebook for practitioners* (pp.83–97). Washington, DC: American Psychological Association.

Runyan, D. K., Everson, M. D., Edelsohn, G. A., Hunter, W. M., & Coulter, M. L. (1988). Impact of legal intervention on sexually abused children. *The Journal of Pediatrics, 113*, 647–653.

Rush, F. (1980). *The best kept secret: Sexual abuse of children.* Englewood Cliffs, NJ: Prentice-Hall.

Russell, A. B., & Trainor, C. M. (1984). *Trends in child abuse and neglect: A national perspective.* Denver, CO: American Humane Association.

Russell, D. E. H. (1983). The incidence and prevalence of intrafamilial and extrafamilial sexual abuse of female children. *Child Abuse & Neglect, 7*, 133–146.

Russell, D. E. H. (1984a). *Sexual exploitation: Rape, child sexual abuse, and work place harassment.* Beverly Hills, CA: Sage.

Russell, D. E. H. (1984b). The prevalence and seriousness of incestuous abuse: Stepfathers vs. biological fathers. *Child Abuse & Neglect, 8*, 15–22.

Russell, D. E. H. (1986). *The secret trauma: Incest in the lives of girls and women.* New York: Basic Books.

Russell, D. E. H. (1988). Pornography and rape: A causal model. *Political Psychology, 9,* 41–73.

Rutter, M. (1985). Resilience in the face of adversity: Protective factors and resistance to psychiatric disorder. *British Journal of Psychiatry, 147,* 598–611.

Ryan, G. (1989). Victim to victimizer: Rethinking victim treatment. *Journal of Interpersonal Violence, 4,* 325–341.

Ryerson, E. (1984). Sexual abuse and self-protection education for developmentally disabled youth: A priority need. *SIECUS Reports, 13,* 6–7.

Sacco, V. F., & Trotman, M. (1990). Public information programming and family violence: Lessons from the mass media crime prevention experience. *Canadian Journal of Criminology, 32,* 91–105.

Salter, A. C. (1988). *Treating child sex offenders and victims: A practical guide.* Beverly Hills, CA: Sage.

Saltzman, A. (1985). Protection for the child or the parent? The conflict between the federal drug and alcohol abuse confidentiality requirements and the state child abuse and neglect reporting laws. *Southern Illinois University Law Journal, 1985,* 181–241.

Sanford, L. T. (1980). *The silent children: A parent's guide to the prevention of child sexual abuse.* New York: Doubleday.

Sanford, L. T. (1982). *Come tell me right away: A positive approach to warning children about sexual abuse.* Fayetteville, NY: Ed-U Press.

Saslawsky, D. A., & Wurtele, S. K. (1986). Educating children about sexual abuse: Implications for pediatric intervention and possible prevention. *Journal of Pediatric Psychology, 11,* 235–245.

Saulsbury, T., & Campbell, R. E. (1985). Evaluation of child abuse reporting by physicians. *American Journal of Diseases of Children, 139,* 393–395.

Saunders, E. J. (1988). A comparative study of attitudes toward child sexual abuse among social work and judicial system professionals. *Child Abuse & Neglect, 12,* 83–90.

Sauzier, M. (1989). Disclosure of child sexual abuse: For better or worse. *Psychiatric Clinics of North America, 12,* 455–469.

Schaefer, C. E. (1984). *How to talk to children about really important things.* New York: Harper & Row.

Schetky, D. H. (1988a). Child sexual abuse in mythology, religion and history. In D. H. Schetky & A. H. Green, *Child sexual abuse: A handbook for health care and legal professionals* (pp.19–29). New York: Brunner/Mazel.

Schetky, D. H. (1988b). Prevention of child sexual abuse. In D. H. Schetky & A. H. Green, *Child sexual abuse: A handbook for health care and legal professionals* (pp.209–216). New York: Brunner/Mazel.

Schetky, D. H., & Green, A. H. (1988). *Child sexual abuse: A handbook for health care and legal professionals.* New York: Brunner/Mazel.

Schor, D. P., & Sivan, A. B. (1989). Interpreting children's labels for sex-related body parts of anatomically explicit dolls. *Child Abuse & Neglect, 13,* 523–531.

Schorr, L. B. (1988). *Within our reach: Breaking the cycle of disadvantage.* New York: Doubleday.

Schroeder, C. S., Gordon, B. N., & McConnell, P. (1986). Books for parents and children on sexual abuse prevention. *Journal of Clinical Child Psychology, 15,* 178–185.

Schultz, L. G. (1982). Child sexual abuse in historical perspective. *Journal of Social Work & Human Sexuality, 1,* 21–35.

Schultz, L. G., & Jones, P. (1983). Sexual abuse of children: Issues for social service and health professionals. *Child Welfare, 62,* 99–108.

Schultz, R., Braun, B. G., & Kluft, R. P. (1989). Multiple personality disorder: Phenomenology of selected variables in comparison to major depression. *Dissociation, 2,* 45–51.

Schwab, J. & Schwab, M. (1978). *Sociocultural roots of mental illness: An epidemiological study.* New York: Plenum Press.

Scott, R. L., & Flowers, J. V. (1988). Betrayal by the mother as a factor contributing to psychological disturbance in victims of father-daughter incest: An MMPI analysis. *Journal of Social and Clinical Psychology, 6,* 147–154.

Scott, R. L., & Stone, D. A. (1986). MMPI profile constellations in incest families. *Journal of Consulting and Clinical Psychology, 54,* 364–368.

Seattle Rape Relief. (1980). *Sexual assault of handicapped students.* (Available from Seattle Rape Relief, 1825 South Jackson, Suite 102, Seattle, WA 98144.)

Sedlak, A. J. (1990). *Technical amendment to the study findings—National Incidence and Prevalence of Child Abuse and Neglect: 1988.* Rockville, MD: Westat.

Sedney, M. A., & Brooks, B. (1984). Factors associated with a history of childhood sexual experience in a nonclinical female population. *Journal of the American Academy of Child Psychiatry, 23,* 215–218.

Segal, Z. V., & Marshall, W. L. (1985). Heterosexual social skills in a population of rapists and child molesters. *Journal of Consulting and Clinical Psychology, 53,* 55–63.

Segal, Z. V., & Stermac, L. E. (1990). The role of cognition in sexual assault. In W. L. Marshall, D. R. Laws, & H. E. Barbaree (Eds.), *Handbook of sexual assault: Issues, theories, and treatment of the offender* (pp.161–174). New York: Plenum Press.

Sgroi, S. M. (1977). Kids with clap: Gonorrhea as an indication of child sexual assault. *Victimology, 2,* 251–267.

Sgroi, S. M. (1982a). Family treatment of child sexual abuse. *Journal of Social Work & Human Sexuality, 1,* 109–128.

Sgroi, S. M. (1982b). Multidisciplinary team review of child-sexual-abuse cases. In S. M. Sgroi (Ed.), *Handbook of clinical intervention in child sexual abuse* (pp.335–343). Lexington, MA: D.C. Heath.

Sgroi, S. M., Blick, L. C., & Porter, F. S. (1982). A conceptual framework for child sexual abuse. In S. M. Sgroi, *Handbook of clinical intervention in child sexual abuse* (pp.9–37). Lexington, MA: D. C. Heath.

Sgroi, S. M., Bunk, B. S., & Wabrek, C. J. (1988). Children's sexual behaviors and their relationship to sexual abuse. In S. M. Sgroi (Ed.), *Vulnerable populations: Evaluation and treatment of sexually abused children and adult survivors* (pp.1–24). Lexington, MA: Lexington Books.

Shah, C. P., Holloway, C. P., & Valkill, D. V. (1982). Sexual abuse of children. *Annals of Emergency Medicine, 11,* 41–46.

Sherman, L. W., & Berk, R. A. (1984). The specific deterrent effects of arrest for domestic violence. *American Sociological Review, 49,* 261–272.

Shore, W. B., & Winkelstein, J. A. (1971). Nonvenereal transmission of gonococcal infections to children. *Journal of Pediatrics, 79,* 661–663.

Shure, M. B., & Spivack, G. (1988). Interpersonal cognitive problem solving. In R. H. Price, E. L. Cowen, R. P. Lorion, & J. Ramos-McKay (Eds.), *Fourteen ounces of prevention: A casebook for practitioners* (pp.69–82). Washington, DC: American Psychological Association.

Siegel, J. M., Sorenson, S. B., Golding, J. M., Burnam, M. A., & Stein, J. A. (1987). The prevalence of childhood sexual assault: The Los Angeles epidemiologic catchment area project. *American Journal of Epidemiology, 126,* 1141–1153.

Sigurdson, E., Strang, M., & Doig, T. (1987). What do children know about preventing sexual assault? How can their awareness be increased? *Canadian Journal of Psychiatry, 32,* 551–557.

Silbert, M. H., & Pines, A. M. (1981). Sexual child abuse as an antecedent to prostitution. *Child Abuse & Neglect, 5,* 407–411.

Silbert, M. H., & Pines, A. M. (1983). Early sexual exploitation as an influence in prostitution. *Social Work, 28,* 285–289.

Sirles, E. A., & Franke, P. J. (1989). Factors influencing mothers' reactions to intrafamily sexual abuse. *Child Abuse & Neglect, 13,* 131–139.

Sirles, E. A., Smith, J. A., & Kusama, H. (1989). Psychiatric status of intrafamilial child sexual abuse victims. *Journal of the American Academy of Child and Adolescent Psychiatry, 28,* 225–229.

Siskind, A. B. (1986). Issues in institutional child sexual abuse: The abused, the abuser, and the system. *Residential Treatment for Children & Youth, 4,* 9–30.

Smith, T. A. (1987). *You don't have to molest that child.* Chicago, IL: National Committee for Prevention of Child Abuse.

Smith, W. (1988). Delinquency and abuse among juvenile sexual offenders. *Journal of Interpersonal Violence, 3,* 400–413.

Sonnerstein, F. L., Pleck, J. H., & Ku, L. C. (1989). Sexual activity, condom rise, and AIDS awareness among adolescent males. *Family Planning Perspectives, 21,* 152–158.

Sparks, C. H., & Bar On, B. (1985). A social change approach to the prevention of sexual violence toward women. *Stone Center for Developmental Services and Studies, 6,* 1–8.

Starr, R. H., Jr. (1979) Child abuse. *American Psychologist, 34,* 872–878.

State Documents Center. (1982). *Are children with disabilities vulnerable to sexual abuse?* (Available from State Documents Center, 117 University Avenue, St. Paul, MN 55155.)

Stermac, L. E., & Segal, Z. V. (1989). Adult sexual contact with children: An examination of cognitive factors. *Behavior Therapy, 20,* 573–584.

Stilwell, S. L., Lutzker, J. R., & Greene, B. F. (1988). Evaluation of a sexual abuse prevention program for preschoolers. *Journal of Family Violence, 3,* 269–281.

Stowell, J., & Dietzel, M. (1982). *My very own book about me.* (Available from Lutheran Social Services of Washington, N. 1226 Howard, Spokane, WA 99201.)

Strasser, E., & Bailey, E. (1984, April 9). A sordid preschool "game." *Newsweek,* p.38.

Straus, M., Gelles, R., & Steinmetz, S. (1980). *Behind closed doors: Violence in the American family.* New York: Doubleday.

Stringer, G. M. (1986). An overview of reporting. In M. Nelson & K. Clark (Eds.), *The educator's guide to preventing child sexual abuse* (pp.175–177). Santa Cruz, CA: Network Publications.

Strong, K., Tate, J., Wehman, B., & Wyss, A. (1986). *Project Safe: A sexual assault perpetrator prevention curriculum for junior high school students.* Cumberland, WI: Human Growth and Development Program.

Summit, R. (1983). The child sexual abuse accommodation syndrome. *Child Abuse & Neglect, 7,* 177–193.

Summit, R. (1988). Hidden victims, hidden pain: Societal avoidance of child sexual abuse. In G. E. Wyatt & G. J. Powell (Eds.), *Lasting effects of child sexual abuse* (pp.39–60). Newbury Park, CA: Sage.

Summit, R. & Kryso, J. (1978). Sexual abuse of children: A clinical spectrum. *American Journal of Orthopsychiatry, 48,* 237–251.

Swan, H. L., Press, A. N., & Briggs, S. L. (1985). Child sexual abuse prevention: Does it work? *Child Welfare, 64,* 395–405.

Swift, C. (1979). The prevention of sexual child abuse: Focus on the perpetrator. *Journal of Clinical Child Psychology, 8,* 133–136.

Swift, C. (1982). *Consultation in the area of child sexual abuse: Final report* (Report No. NIMH 83-213). Rockville, MD: National Institute of Mental Health.

Swift, C., & Levin, G. (1987). Empowerment: An emerging mental health technology. *Journal of Primary Prevention, 8,* 71-93.

Swoboda, J. S., Elwork, A., Sales, B. D., & Levine, D. (1978). Knowledge of and compliance with privileged communication and child-abuse-reporting laws. *Professional Psychology, 9,* 448-458.

Tennant, C. G. (1988). Preventive sexual abuse programs: Problems and possibilities. *Elementary School Guidance and Counseling, 23,* 48-53.

Tharinger, D. J., Horton, C. B., & Millea, S. (1990). Sexual abuse and exploitation of children and adults with mental retardation and other handicaps. *Child Abuse & Neglect, 14,* 301-312.

Tharinger, D. J., Krivacska, J. J., Laye-McDonough, M., Jamison, L., Vincent, G. G., & Hedlund, A. D. (1988). Prevention of child sexual abuse: An analysis of issues, educational programs, and research findings. *School Psychology Review, 17,* 614-634.

Tharinger, D. J., Russian, T., & Robinson, P. (1989). School psychologists' involvement in the response to child sexual abuse: A national sample of NASP members. *School Psychology Review, 18,* 386-399.

Tharinger, D. J., & Vevier, E. (1987). Child sexual abuse: A review and intervention framework for the teacher. *Journal of Research and Development in Education, 20,* 12-24.

Thompson, S. K. (1975). Gender labels and early sex-role development. *Child Development, 46,* 339-347.

Tierney, K. J., & Corwin, D. L. (1983). Exploring intrafamilial child sexual abuse: A systems approach. In D. Finkelhor, R. J. Gelles, G. T. Hotaling, & M. A. Straus (Eds.), *The dark side of families: Current family violence research* (pp. 102-116). Beverly Hills, CA: Sage.

Tilelli, J. A., Turek, D., & Jaffe, A. C. (1980). Sexual abuse of children: Clinical findings and implications for management. *New England Journal of Medicine, 320,* 319-323.

Tong, L., Oates, K., & McDowell, M. (1987). Personality development following sexual abuse. *Child Abuse & Neglect, 11,* 371-383.

Tormes, Y. M. (1972). *Child victims of incest.* Denver, CO: The American Human Association, Children's Division.

Tower, C. C. (1984). *Child abuse and neglect: A teacher's handbook for detection, reporting, and classroom management.* Washington, DC: National Education Association.

Tower, C. C. (1987). *How schools can help combat child abuse and neglect* (2nd. ed.). Washington, DC: National Education Association.

Trudell, B., & Whatley, M. H. (1988). School sexual abuse prevention: Unintended consequences and dilemmas. *Child Abuse & Neglect, 12,* 103–113.

Truesdell, D. L., McNeil, J. S., & Deschner, J. P. (1986). Incidence of wife abuse in incestuous families. *Social Work, 31,* 138–140.

United Nations. (1989). *Adoption of a Convention on the Rights of the Child* (U.N. Doc. No. A/44/736). New York: Author.

U.S. Advisory Board on Child Abuse and Neglect. (1990). *Child abuse and neglect: Critical first steps in response to a national emergency.* (DHHS Publication No. 017-092-00104-5). Washington, DC: U.S. Government Printing Office.

U.S. Bureau of the Census (1988). Money income and poverty status in the United States: 1988. *Current population reports* (Series P-60, No. 166, Table 19). Washington, DC: U.S. Government Printing Office.

Vernon, A. (1989a). *Thinking, feeling, behaving: An emotional educational curriculum for children, Grades 1–6.* Champaign, IL: Research Press.

Vernon, A. (1989b). *Thinking, feeling, behaving: An emotional educational curriculum for children, Grades 7–12.* Champaign, IL: Research Press.

Viinikka, S. (1989). Child sexual abuse and the law. In E. Driver & A. Droisen (Eds.), *Child sexual abuse: A feminist reader* (pp.132–157). New York: Washington Square.

von Krafft-Ebing, R. (1935). *Psychopathia sexualis.* New York: Physicians and Surgeons Book Co.

Wagner, W. G. (1987). Child sexual abuse: A multidisciplinary approach to case management. *Journal of Counseling and Development, 65,* 435–439.

Wakefield, H., & Underwager, R. (1988). *Accusations of child sexual abuse.* Springfield, IL: Charles C. Thomas.

Walker, C. E., Bonner, B. L., & Kaufman, K. L. (1988). *The physically and sexually abused child: Evaluation and treatment.* New York: Pergamon Press.

Walters, D. R. (1975). *Physical and sexual abuse of children: Causes and treatment*. Bloomington, IN: Indiana University Press.

Washington State Department of Social & Health Services. (1988). *Operational definitions of child abuse and neglect: Guidelines for CPS investigations* (Publication Number 22-614 x). Olympia, WA: Department of Social & Health Services.

Waterman, J. (1986). Developmental considerations. In K. MacFarlane, J. Waterman, S. Conerly, L. Damon, M. Durfee, & S. Long, *Sexual abuse of young children* (pp.15–29). New York: Guilford.

Watson, H., & Levine, M. (1989). Psychotherapy and mandated reporting of child abuse. *American Journal of Orthopsychiatry, 59*, 246–256.

Wattenberg, E. (1985). In a different light: A feminist perspective on the role of mothers in father-daughter incest. *Child Welfare, 64*, 203–211.

Weinbach, R. W. (1987). Public awareness of sexual abuse: Costs and victims. *Social Work, 32*, 532–533.

Weinberg, S. K. (1955). *Incest behavior*. New York: Citadel.

Weiner, I. B. (1962). Father-daughter incest: A clinical report. *Psychiatric Quarterly, 36*, 607–632.

Weisberg, R., & Wald, M. (1984). Confidentiality laws and state efforts to protect abused or neglected children: The need for statutory reform. *Family Law Quarterly, 18*, 143–212.

Weiss, E. H., & Berg, R. F. (1982). Child victims of sexual assault: Impact of court procedures. *Journal of the American Academy of Child Psychiatry, 21*, 513–518.

Weiss, H. B. (1989). State family support and education programs: Lessons from the pioneers. *American Journal of Orthopsychiatry, 59*, 32–48.

Weiss, H. B., & Jacobs, F. H. (Eds.). (1988). *Evaluating family programs*. New York: Aldine de Gruyter.

Weiss, J., Rogers, E., Darwin, M., & Dutton, C. (1955). A study of girl sex victims. *Psychiatric Quarterly, 29*, 1–27.

Westen, D., Ludolph, P., Misle, B., Ruffins, S., & Block, J. (1990). Physical and sexual abuse in adolescent girls with borderline personality disorder. *American Journal of Orthopsychiatry, 60*, 55–66.

Westermeyer, J. (1978). Incest in psychiatric practice: A description of patients and incestuous relationships. *Journal of Clinical Psychology, 39*, 643–648.

Wheeler, H. (1985). Pornography and rape: A feminist perspective. In A. W. Burgess (Ed.), *Rape and sexual assault* (pp.374-391). New York: Garland Publications.

Whitcomb, D. (1986). Prosecuting child sexual abuse—new approaches. *National Institute of Justice Reports, 197,* 1-5.

White, K. R. (1988). Cost analyses in family support programs. In H. B. Weiss & F. H. Jacobs (Eds.), *Evaluating family programs* (pp.429-443). New York: Aldine de Gruyter.

White, S., Halpin, B. M., Strom, G. A., & Santilli, G. (1988). Behavioral comparisons of young sexually abused, neglected and nonreferred children. *Journal of Clinical Child Psychology, 17,* 53-61.

Whittaker, J. K. (1987). The role of residential institutions. In J. Garbarino, P. E. Brookhouser, & K. J. Authier (Eds.), *Special children, special risks: The maltreatment of children with disabilities* (pp.83-100). New York: Aldine de Gruyter.

Wild, N. J. (1989). Prevalence of child sex rings. *Pediatrics, 83,* 553-558.

Wilk, R. J., & McCarthy, C. R. (1986). Intervention in child sexual abuse: A survey of attitudes. *Social Casework: The Journal of Contemporary Social Work, 67,* 20-26.

Williams, J. (1980). *Red flag, green flag people.* Fargo, ND: Rape and Abuse Crisis Center.

Williams, L. M., & Finkelhor, D. (1990). The characteristics of incestuous fathers: A review of recent studies. In W. L. Marshall, D. R. Laws, & H. E. Barbaree (Eds.), *Handbook of sexual assault: Issues, theories, and treatment of the offender* (pp.231-255). New York: Plenum Press.

Winton, M. A. (1990). An evaluation of a support group for parents who have a sexually abused child. *Child Abuse & Neglect, 14,* 397-405.

Wolfe, D. A., MacPherson, T., Blount, R., & Wolfe, V. V. (1986). Evaluation of a brief intervention for educating school children in awareness of physical and sexual abuse. *Child Abuse & Neglect, 10,* 85-92.

Wolfe, V. V., Sas, L., & Wilson, S. K. (1987). Some issues in preparing sexually abused children for courtroom testimony. *The Behavior Therapist, 10,* 107-113.

Wolfe, V. V., & Wolfe, D. A. (1988). The sexually abused child. In E. J. Mash & L. G. Terdal (Eds.), *Behavioral assessment of childhood disorders* (pp.670-714). New York: Guilford Press.

Woods, S. C., & Dean, K. S. (1986). Sexual abuse prevention: Evaluating educational strategies. *SIECUS Reports, 15*, 8-9.

Wurtele, S. K. (1986). *Teaching young children personal body safety: The Behavioral Skills Training program.* Colorado Springs, CO: Author.

Wurtele, S. K. (1988, August). *Harmful effects of sexual abuse prevention programs? Results and implications.* Paper presented at the annual convention of the American Psychological Association, Atlanta, GA.

Wurtele, S. K. (1990a, September). *Evaluating programs designed to prevent child sexual abuse: Measuring the six Rs.* Paper presented at the 8th International Congress on Child Abuse and Neglect, Hamburg, Germany.

Wurtele, S. K. (1990b). Teaching personal safety skills to four-year-old children: A behavioral approach. *Behavior Therapy, 21*, 25-32.

Wurtele, S. K., Currier, L. L., Gillispie, E. I., & Franklin, C. F. (1991). The efficacy of a parent-implemented program for teaching preschoolers personal safety skills. *Behavior Therapy, 22*, 69-83.

Wurtele, S. K., Gillispie, E. I., Currier, L. L., & Franklin, C. F. (1992). A comparison of teachers vs. parents as instructors of a personal safety program for preschoolers. *Child Abuse & Neglect, 16*, 127-137.

Wurtele, S. K., Kaplan, G. M., & Keairnes, M. (1990). Childhood sexual abuse among chronic pain patients. *The Clinical Journal of Pain, 6*, 110-113.

Wurtele, S. K., Kast, L. C., & Melzer, A. M. (in press). Sexual abuse prevention education for young children: A comparison of teachers and parents as instructors. *Child Abuse & Neglect.*

Wurtele, S. K., Kast, L. C., Miller-Perrin, C. L., & Kondrick, P. A. (1989). A comparison of programs for teaching personal safety skills to preschoolers. *Journal of Consulting and Clinical Psychology, 57*, 505-511.

Wurtele, S. K., Kvaternick, M., & Franklin, C. F. (in press). Sexual abuse prevention for preschoolers: A survey of parents' behaviors, attitudes, and beliefs. *Journal of Child Sexual Abuse.*

Wurtele, S. K., Marrs, S. R., & Miller-Perrin, C. L. (1987). Practice makes perfect? The role of participant modeling in sexual abuse prevention programs. *Journal of Consulting and Clinical Psychology, 55*, 599–602.

Wurtele, S. K., & Miller-Perrin, C. L. (1987). An evaluation of side effects associated with participation in a child sexual abuse prevention program. *Journal of School Health, 57*, 228–231.

Wurtele, S. K., Saslawsky, D. A., Miller, C. L., Marrs, S. R., & Britcher, J. C. (1986). Teaching personal safety skills for potential prevention of sexual abuse: A comparison of treatments. *Journal of Consulting and Clinical Psychology, 54*, 688–692.

Wurtele, S. K., & Schmitt, A. (in press). Child care workers' knowledge about reporting suspected child sexual abuse. *Child Abuse & Neglect.*

Wyatt, G. E. (1985). The sexual abuse of Afro-American and white-American women in childhood. *Child Abuse & Neglect, 9*, 507–519.

Wyatt, G. E., & Mickey, M. R. (1987). Ameliorating the effects of child sexual abuse: An exploratory study of support by parents and others. *Journal of Interpersonal Violence, 2*, 403–414.

Wyatt, G. E., & Powell, G. J. (Eds.) (1988). *Lasting effects of child sexual abuse.* Newbury Park, CA: Sage.

Yates, A. (1978). *Sex without shame: Encouraging the child's healthy sexual development.* New York: William Morrow.

Yorukoglu, A., & Kemph, J. P. (1966). Children not severely damaged by incest with a parent. *Journal of American Academy of Child Psychiatry, 5*, 111–124.

Zambrana, R. E., & Aguirre-Molina, M. (1987). Alcohol abuse prevention among Latino adolescents: A strategy for intervention. *Journal of Youth and Adolescence, 16*, 97–113.

Zellman, G. L. (1990a). Child abuse reporting and failure to report among mandated reporters: Prevalence, incidence, and reasons. *Journal of Interpersonal Violence, 5*, 3–22.

Zellman, G. L. (1990b). Linking schools and social services: The case of child abuse reporting. *Educational Evaluation and Policy Analysis, 12*, 41–55.

Zellman, G. L. (1990c). Report decision-making patterns among mandated child abuse reporters. *Child Abuse & Neglect, 14*, 325–336.

Zelnick, M., & Kantner, J. F. (1980). Sexual activity, contraceptive use, and pregnancy among metropolitan-area teenagers: 1971-1979. *Family Planning Perspectives, 12,* 231.

Zigler, E., & Black, K. B. (1989). America's family support movement: Strengths and limitations. *American Journal of Orthopsychiatry, 59,* 6-19.

Zins, J. E., Conyne, R. K., & Ponti, C. R. (1988). Primary prevention: Expanding the impact of psychological services in schools. *School Psychology Review, 17,* 542-549.

Zuelzer, N., & Reposa, R. (1983). Mothers in incestuous families. *International Journal of Family Therapy, 5,* 98-109.

# Author Index

## DATE DUE

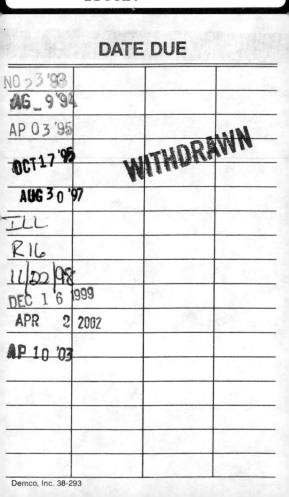

| | | | |
|---|---|---|---|
| NO 23 '93 | | | |
| AG _ 9 '94 | | | |
| AP 03 '95 | | | |
| OCT 17 '95 | | WITHDRAWN | |
| AUG 3 0 '97 | | | |
| ILL | | | |
| R16 | | | |
| 11/00/98 | | | |
| DEC 1 6 1999 | | | |
| APR 2 2002 | | | |
| AP 10 '03 | | | |
| | | | |
| | | | |
| | | | |
| | | | |